THE LYTTELTON HART-DAVIS LETTERS

Correspondence of George Lyttelton
and Rupert Hart-Davis
Volume Two 1956–57

Edited and introduced by
RUPERT HART-DAVIS

All letters, methinks, should be free
and easy as one's discourse,
not studied as an oration,
nor made up of hard words
like a charm.
DOROTHY OSBORNE
1653

Academy
Chicago
Publishers

Published in 1985 by

Academy Chicago Publishers
425 N. Michigan Ave.
Chicago, IL 60611

Lyttelton letters and appendix copyright © 1979
by Humphrey Lyttelton

Hart-Davis letter and notes copyright © 1979
by Sir Rupert Hart-Davis

Printed and bound in the USA

Library of Congress Cataloging in Publication Data

(Revised for Volume II)

Lyttelton, George, 1883–1962.
    The Lyttelton Hart-Davis letters.

    Reprint.   Originally published: London: J. Murray, ©1978.
    Includes indexes.
    Contents: v. 1. 1955–56 —v. 2. 1956–57.
    1. Lyttelton, George, 1883–1962.   2. Teachers—
England —Correspondence.   3. Hart-Davis, Rupert,
1907–   —Correspondence.   4. Authors, English —20th
century —Correspondence.   I. Hart-Davis, Rupert, Sir.
    II. Title.
PR55.L9A4   1984   809.2'4   [B]   84-2771
ISBN 0-89733-105-2 (v. 1)

CONTENTS

INTRODUCTION

Here is slightly more than another year's worth of this correspondence, starting where the last volume ended. Happily it attracted enough enthusiasm to persuade my intrepid publisher to venture on a sequel. The possibility of further volumes depends on the response to this one.

As before, I have silently removed from both sides of the correspondence libellous or hurtful passages; most references to the weather and to contemporary politics; a good deal of the mutual admiration which some readers found cloying; almost all George's gratitude for the books I continued to send him; and an increasing amount of repetition, for it is difficult to remember exactly what one wrote or quoted in a letter a year or two ago. Eton and cricket have also been pruned a little.

Once again, in the first letters I have retained the opening and signature, which are afterwards omitted, since they are almost always the same: any variation is printed. Similarly I have given our full home addresses in the first two letters and then abbreviated them. From Monday to Friday I lived in a flat above my publishing office at 36 Soho Square.

To avoid an excess of footnotes identifying minor characters, most of such names and nicknames will now be found briefly identified in the index.

For beginners I should perhaps add that in 1926 I had been taught by George at Eton, where he was an outstanding teacher and housemaster. He taught mostly classics but in my last year he had started an English course, and it was then that I fell under the spell of his infectious enthusiasm for literature. After I left Eton our ways parted. George taught for a further twenty years before retiring to Suffolk. We met again in 1949 and thereafter saw and wrote to each other occasionally, but the origin of this correspondence was a dinner party in 1955 during which George complained that no one wrote to him in

Suffolk and I accepted his challenge. At the beginning of this volume George was seventy-three and I was forty-nine.

Marske-in-Swaledale   RUPERT HART-DAVIS
July 1979

24 October 1956

My dear Rupert

It is very odd how completely unable so many men are to put themselves in the place of their own audience—so very unlike the old Duke of Devonshire, who yawned during his own maiden speech because, as he told somebody, 'it was so damned dull'. It isn't a matter of brains at all. Dr Sheppard, once Provost of King's, is bursting with brains, but the blend of gush and childishness in his speeches is one of the most embarrassing things I know.

You *must* try a spell in bed; it is tremendously restful, and you could, like Winston (and many others), get through a lot of dictating to secretaries etc. And if your bed is well organised *qua* bed-rest, 'donkey' (i.e. bolster tied across bed just below the b-tt-cks), *and* the service of meals is cheerful, punctual, and lavish, life soon takes on a paradisal, Nepenthean, lotus-eating atmosphere which is deliciously demoralising.

Your family doings fill me with joy—so exactly like mine when home was still their H.Q.—keys, clothes (especially father's), trains, money—all are lost with the utmost regularity and unconcern. O Youth! . . . (here a little eloquent apostrophe from Conrad's Marlow. What a good story! Do you remember the death of the ship 'Judea, London. Do or Die'?) I look forward to meeting them all some day. And Dec or Jan will certainly see us at Bromsden Farm; one should be able to see one's best correspondents' surroundings as well as their face and form.

I entirely agree with you about all that Crawfie literature. But, human nature being what it is, how are those who run the Press ever going to forgo what is profitable and legal? If they knew their classics, they would only answer as Vespasian did when his prim son protested against his (somehow, I forget the details) taxing sewage. The old

I

vulgarian laughed coarsely and retorted '*Pecunia non olet.*'[1] What have ninety years of popular education done to weaken commercial criteria? Less than nothing.

You refer, *en passant*, to your 'student-days' at the Old Vic. Why have I heard nothing about them? They must have been full of rich experience. You are full of surprises, and I shouldn't be the least surprised some day to hear you referring unconcernedly to the time when you ran a hummum in Belgrade.

I am for the moment in London for a meeting, and writing this in my club—the Royal Empire Society. Its name is the only thing un-drab about it. I am surrounded by coal-black clergymen—some conference, I believe. Christianity is marking time in Dahomey, where it is apparently impossible to persuade the natives that to eat a missionary is not the shortest cut to heaven. The policy shortly to be adopted is to send only young parsons from Balliol Ox and Christ's Cam, as practically all cannibal chiefs hail from one or the other. The fact that they are all to be lank, stringy, sallow young men rather shows that the Church is not wholly relying on the old college tie.

Yours ever
G.W.L.

Bromsden Farm
Henley-on-Thames
Oxon

27 October 1956

My dear George

My delivery of Guy Chapman's lecture on 'The French Army and Politics' at King's College, London last Monday was, I think, a decided success.[2] I prefaced it with a bit of dialogue about what Silas Wegg should read to the Golden Dustman:

> 'Was you thinking at all of poetry?' Mr Wegg inquired, musing.
> 'Would it come dearer?' Mr Boffin asked.
> 'It would come dearer,' Mr Wegg returned. 'For when a person

---

[1] 'Money doesn't smell.'
[2] Guy was recovering from an operation.

comes to grind off poetry night after night, it is but right he should expect to be paid for its weakening effect on his mind.'

Then I launched into the lecture with as much *élan*, punch, and *brio* as my lack of acquaintance with the script allowed. Knowing nothing of the subject, I probably read it better than Guy himself would have done, and he knows *all* about it! The audience (some fifty bodies 'of repellent aspect, remotely connected with education', old and young, black and white, male and female) sat motionless—whether riveted or stunned I couldn't be sure. The many French names (particularly those whose spelling seemed peculiar) I enunciated with such confidence and in so French an accent that they added to the wretches' stupefaction—enough of that.

My son's leave ends on Wednesday, and we shall miss him, despite the cyclone which he creates around him. My children have one tiresome trait in common: directly they get home, they put several long-playing records of American musicals on the radiogram in the nursery, turn it up as loud as it will go, open every door and then leave the house. I hesitate to turn the machine off lest I break it. Just now, in preparation for long winter evenings in Düsseldorf, the boy is trying to teach himself to play the recorder from a book: this produces a sound at once dismal and alarming. However, he has also picked all the apples, and after wrapping up and putting away enough for us, he peddled the rest from door to door in the car (a station waggon) and succeeded in selling 350 lbs at fourpence a lb! Youth—*youth*—yes, that is my favourite of all Conrad's stories, and I plan to include it in a volume of C's sea-stories for publication on his centenary in November 1957. I have a Mariners Library into which it will fit neatly.

My student days at the Old Vic were indeed full of rich experience, and one day you shall hear more of it. Which reminds me—on Friday evening my wife and I, the boy and a friend drove over to Oxford to see my previous wife (Peggy Ashcroft) in a play called *The Good Woman of Setzuan* by Bertolt Brecht, which opens in London next week.

I thought both her and the play enchanting, and remembered that it was in that very theatre in 1929 (when we were both acting in Nigel Playfair's tour of *She Stoops to Conquer*) that P.A. and I plighted our troth.

3

Afterwards, to please the boy, I took them all round to P's dressing-room—an agreeable but disturbing occasion. One thing has not changed: the first time I saw her act (in the same halcyon year) I knew she was the greatest actress I had ever seen (she was quite unknown then), and now I am more than ever certain of it.

Meanwhile, in the intervals of Oscar Wilde, I am still tidying up George Moore, and tomorrow I am to be received in audience by Sir Thomas Beecham, Bart. Since he supplanted G.M. as Lady Cunard's lover, he could clearly spill a bibful—but will he? I doubt it. Full report next week. I'm thinking of calling the book:

DEAR LADY OF MY THOUGHTS

Letters from George Moore
to Lady Cunard
(1894–1933)

It's a bit cumbersome, but utterly apt. What is your frankest opinion? The quotation[1] is from the dedication of one of his books, which runs:

> Dear Lady of my thoughts, dear Lady Cunard,
> Time turns all things into analogues and symbols,
> and in the course of the years I have come to
> think of you as an evening fountain under embosoming
> trees. The fountain murmurs, sings, exults; it
> welcomes every coming minute; and when the dusk
> deepens in the garden and the gallants enfold their
> ladies in scarves and veils and the rout disperses,
> the fountain sings alone the sorrows of the water-
> lilies to the moon.   G.M.

Isn't that beautiful? I shall of course quote it in full. *The Evening Fountain* won't do as a title, since it implies twilight, whereas the letters start when she is a girl. I shall greatly value your judgment.

I have just listened to the News and learned of the death of my beloved friend of thirty years, Viola Meynell. In some ways it is a mercy, for she was suffering from progressive muscular atrophy, and had just reached the point where she could no longer walk or write,

[1] By kind permission of Mr Christopher Medley.

4

but I shall miss her a lot. I last saw her in August, when I drove over to see her in Sussex. Oh dear, I do hate people dying, don't you? V.M. wrote some lovely poems: here is one called Dusting:[1]

> The dust comes secretly day after day,
> Lies on my ledge and dulls my shining things.
> But O this dust that I shall drive away
>   Is flowers and kings,
> Is Solomon's temple, poets, Nineveh.

She was a lovely person—and so I go sadly to bed.

Yours ever
Rupert

Barbon Manor
Westmorland

1 November 1956

Your letter found me here yesterday—the home of Roger Fulford, all among the moors, and altogether very pleasant and comfortable. Roger was delighted when I told him you had said—roughly—that you would prefer almost any form of death to being driven by him over the Brenner Pass—and he sends you his love. He really seems to me a very serene and skilful driver, and these moorland roads must be good practice for the Brenner. The roads are blind and narrow and gradients of 1 in 5 are quite common. Today we had lunch by the roadside in a spot empty of all life except an obviously short-tempered and resentful bull in the field over the wall. We thought Roger's duffle coat—dyed reddish, which he says was the local Liberal colour—was annoying it, though I read somewhere lately that bulls are in fact colour-blind (another mare's tale gone west). So he took it off and in a 'monstrous little voice' tried to placate the bull with endearments—'Bullie, bullie, poor old bullie,' which so increased its rage and hatred that it bayed like the trombones in *Tannhäuser*, and pawed a great hole in the ground; so we retreated—a little too fast for dignity, but, we hoped, not fast enough to indicate fear.

The countryside is endlessly lovely—mile after mile of what Hous-

[1] By kind permission of Mr Jacob Dallyn.

man calls 'solitude of shepherds High in the folded hill,' and the sky produces different effects with extraordinary rapidity. I am sure you would love it, and R. would love to get you here. Of course it *is* far away—275 miles from Grundisburgh in one day. P. says she finds that less tiring than taking two bites, and I rather agree. Roger has a large and very readable library. The Squeers country was very near us today, and we passed the abode of the famous old geologist Adam Sedgwick, a Cambridge eccentric. His bedmaker once sent his favourite chair to be re-seated. This was done in cane, and he was furious. He was always expecting sudden death and apostrophised her 'Woman, do you expect me to go into the presence of my Maker with my backside imprinted with small hexagons?'

I was not at all surprised to hear that your reading of G. Chapman's lecture went down well. Really good reading will carry off anything, and if the stuff is good—*a fortiori*. Silas Wegg was a happy thought. Hindenburg in 1916 said 'No, I read no poetry now; it might soften me'. Curious parallel. N.B. The *quietness* of an audience—except in church—indicates attention not somnolence. Somnolence is *always* preceded by fidgeting. As to your boy learning the recorder from a book, would it encourage him to know that that is exactly the way Humphrey learnt the trumpet? He never had a lesson.

George Moore's dedication is *delicious*. I discussed (I hope you don't mind; he is a discreet man) the title with Roger. As you say, it is a *little* cumbersome, and hasn't it just a soupçon of preciousness? I don't object—after all there are many such, and R. thinks that for that section of the public who want to read about George M. it doesn't matter, but that the Philistine would blush to ask his bookseller: 'Have you the Lady of my Thoughts?' But he thinks it is as good a title as the circs permit. You know, however, much more about these things than either of us, and also how much a title matters.[1]

I am sorry about Viola Meynell; such spirits are ill-spared from the world of today. Why have I never seen 'Dusting' before? It is exquisite and is on the way into my book next to the last entry which is Austin Dobson's

All passes. Art alone
Enduring stays to us;

[1] The book eventually appeared as *George Moore: Letters to Lady Cunard.*

6

> The Bust outlasts the throne—
> The Coin, Tiberius.

They won't resent their company.

We go back on Sunday, and next week I go to tell the boys of Bromsgrove that education is not a mere passing of examinations; they must read for themselves and ruminate. The headmaster says he is going to insist on his masters being present, as they are the real Philistines of the community. I expect I shall tread on a good many toes, but that is what toes are for—academic toes anyway.

When I get to the Judgment Seat, I will see to it that all is in 'the Book where good deeds are entered'. But of course I may be knocking at a different door and seeing—rather ecstatically—through its bars Byron and Helen of Troy, and John Wilkes, and Oscar Wilde and other terribly attractive company. Do you remember that delightful passage of Samuel Butler's which pictures Heaven as immensely tedious— Jupiter with Ganymede sitting on his everlasting knee, while in the other place Prometheus was having his liver agreeably stimulated by the vulture, and the shades all gather 'about stone-time' to bet on the distance to which the stone of Sisyphus will roll. Though I don't really like Butler and his sneers and his rather dreadful young woman— Miss Savage was it? How few satirical folk keep their contempt for the contemptible and don't let it sour all or nearly all their judgments. I like that remark of T.S.E.'s that the critical attitude ends by preventing one *enjoying any book*—and that is the ultimate damnation of him who shall be nameless, whom you will soon call my King Charles's head.[1] Housman was at Bromsgrove and I shall put that in their pipes. If the science master is there I shall ask him if *his* backbone tingles and the flesh of his cheeks creeps if he thinks of a verse from the psalms as A.E.H.'s did.

I end with a little *trouvaille* from Roger's shelves—the last stanza of a hymn 'in use in a church near Cambridge' seventy years ago:

> Milk of the breast that cannot cloy
> He, like a nurse, will bring;
> And when we see His promise nigh,
> Oh how we'll suck and sing!

[1] F.R. Leavis.

7

Don't tell Jonah[1] that because I want to next week.

P.S. Silly of me to enthuse about the moors; of course you know them well. But they can take it.

Your raptures about the moors struck straight to my heart, especially since you had clearly forgotten my passion for the neighbouring ones just across the Yorkshire border. That Housman line is splendid —'solitude of shepherds'—I must look it up.

I love to think of you and dear Roger discussing my G.M. title. I agree with all your gentle strictures, but it looks like an occasion for *faute de mieux*. I have made the great (but not wholly avoidable) mistake of getting immersed in Oscar Wilde before old G.M. was finally tucked up in bed with his dear lady. So this week-end, distracted by the garden and the ghastly state of the world, I have been making a fierce effort to catch up. Extra footnotes have been peppered into the text, the last five stubbornly undateable letters inserted with arbitrary haste, and now it only remains for me to revise the introduction, have it and the footnotes re-typed, and submit the whole caboodle to Sachie Sitwell (the owner of the letters) and C.D. Medley (G.M.'s literary executor). How long, oh Lord, how long? Meanwhile the notes to, and dating of, Oscar's letters provide the greatest fun. Unlike G.M., Oscar has occasioned an enormous literature of comment, biography, criticism, bibliography etc—much of it written by chronic liars like Frank Harris and Lord Alfred Douglas. Last week, following a clue in another letter, I ran to earth an unknown letter which O.W. contributed anonymously to the *Daily Telegraph* of 2 Feb 91—on modern dress—a great find, though I must confess the clue wasn't all that difficult to follow.

Yes, I knew those fine lines by Austin Dobson. They are 'imitated' from a poem by Théophile Gautier: does that mean translated or cribbed? I haven't got G's poems here—one can *never* have enough

[1] L.E. (Sir Laurence) Jones.

8

books. That hymn-stanza is superb. Jonah will love it, and I promise not to tell him first.

Oh yes—my interview with Beecham was most civilised and agreeable, but produced little of value. He was courteously hospitable, giving me sherry and a good cigar. His flat in Weymouth Street is very grand, white-coated manservant and all. Lady B., a good thirty-five years younger than he and good-looking, was present all the time, so I could see there was no chance of any indiscretions about Lady Cunard. I fenced round the subject with incessant questions and found his memory excellent. He rolls well-chosen words off his tongue with relish and precision. He told me all he could remember of G.M., but since they never spoke to each other after 1911, it wasn't much. I was there just over an hour.

He told me that George V went to the opera once a year—always to *La Bohème*. Once Beecham asked him if it was his favourite. 'Yes', said the King. 'That's most interesting, Sir. I'd be most interested to know why.' 'Because it's much the shortest', said His Majesty. An excellent reason indeed!

On Friday I went down to Sussex for Viola Meynell's funeral, travelling with Shane Leslie, who was grotesquely and most unsuitably dressed in a saffron-coloured kilt, with a bright green scarf round his shoulders. A bald head and thick tufts of hair on his cheek-bones (like Gow only more so) completed a figure from comic opera. However he gossiped entertainingly, and when we were met at Pulborough by a sorrowing brother-in-law, Shane said: 'I was here at the opening of the First World War, and I look like being here for the opening of the Third.' Twenty or thirty of the family were gathered sadly in the house I have known and loved so long. The service was a harsh Catholic one (not, thank heaven, a full mass) mostly in gabbled Latin. It was all very damp and chilly and sad, and I felt it had little to do with my dear Viola.

8 November 1956   *Hagley*

Of course I knew that your spiritual home is the moors, but—what is it the Doctor says in his preface to the Dictionary? 'What is known is not always present' then some rolling polysyllables about casual inadvertence seducing attention. No great man ever admitted error with more serene humility—unlike so many modern scientists who think that to know all about the atom establishes their right to dogmatise about man and his destiny. The Housman phrase comes from his 'The Merry Guide' which is my favourite, and if any Connolly says it is not first-rate, I shall tell him to have his ears syringed and his brain washed, after which he can begin to learn the elements of his job. The other pictures in the poem struck home as we journeyed southward—the hanging woods and hamlets, and blowing realms of woodland with sunstruck vanes afield, and cloud-led shadows, and valley-guarded granges and silver waters wide. Yes, yes, I know I needn't have quoted them all, but the writing of them gives me physical and mental pleasure (and of course you know that perfectly well, and will forgive).

I like your blunt label 'chronic liars' for Frank H. and Lord A.D. The former must have been immensely repellent always, but A.D. wrote some good poetry, and one must say that, even if put considerably off by his bland declaration that no one ever wrote better. A tragic life—and the physical alterations in him between the ages of twenty and sixty-five are simply those of Dorian Gray. I suppose one cannot have so loathsome a father without paying for it. I like the little interchange between old Agate and Douglas. J.A. wrote 'Milton's poetry flames in the forehead of the morning sky. Housman's twinkles in the Shropshire gloaming; yours, my dear A., glitters like Cartier's window at lunch-time.' To which A.D. replied 'Are you not aware that seventeen of my best sonnets were written in Wormwood Scrubbs?'

Jonah was in good form—he still has the figure he had at Oxford, and that was as good as any Greek's. He spoke of you with great affection, and the rest of his discourse was equally on the spot.

Roger and I teaed at Dotheboys Hall last Friday (at Bowes). They told us there was no doubt it *is* the building where Squeers's prototype Shaw had his school. Dickens of course said S wasn't founded on S but nobody believed him and Shaw was ruined. What an odd artist Dickens was (if one at all). Squeers was first a sadist, then a figure of comedy ('Natur' she's a rum 'un' etc), then a criminal. And D did much the same with Pecksniff. The truth no doubt is that—like Shakespeare—he didn't bother about probability or consistency, but just let his fancy fly—and, by gum, what wings each one's fancy had!

I must finish this to-morrow. I am not at Hagley yet but go there in a few minutes. To talk to the boys and masters of Bromsgrove. I shall quote that inimitable page of W. Cory's on the object of education, containing *inter alia* that you go to learn 'the art of indicating assent or dissent in graduated terms', and I shall not be able to resist pointing out how few of our newspapers and politicians do that.

I am once again writing in my club—and rather slowly, as I *must* hear why a stoutish man is urging a still stouter one to have a local and not general anaesthetic. I itch to tell the speaker to be more lucid and set my mind at rest on the precise nature and geography of the contemplated operation. I only think, and cannot be absolutely certain, that the trouble calling for the knife is a boil on the gluteus maximus, but it *may* be that distressing and almost universal complaint. ('Poor Alfred, he's got 'em again,' as Tennyson's doctor said when he read *Maud*.)

A beautiful smooth motor-drive in the dark landed my nephew and me here at 10 p.m. and I am now about to warm up my Bromsgrove discourse and try to persuade myself that it is less dull than I suspect it is. What a lot depends on the audience, and how they vary—from the nadir of the Ipswich Old Boys to the zenith of the Greenwich cadets.

11 November 1956   *Bromsden Farm*

Prepare for a short and scrappy letter. Long Leave has broken into my week-end brutally, and there are piles of proofs urgently awaiting correction. Before I forget it, have you seen the current number of the *New Statesman*? In it Priestley trounces Leavis splendidly. If you haven't got the paper, send me a postcard to Soho Square and I'll get you another copy. Pass hurriedly over the pernicious b-lls at the beginning of the paper if you have any regard for your blood-pressure.

I completely agree about Alfred Douglas's poetry—and with what you say of Dickens. Perhaps part of the inconsistency of many of his characters was due to the extraordinary way he wrote the novels—a monthly instalment at a time, and sometimes two going at once! Where does that sentence of Cory's come from? I couldn't, as my children say, agree with it more. Long Leave began with a bumper day, on which huge meals were fitted into visits to an Agatha Christie play and the film of *Moby Dick*, which is first-rate. Do see it if you have an opportunity: I'm sure you'd like it. Eric Linklater's boy is here too (he's at Marsden's), and yesterday E.L. himself came down to lunch. He's a sterling fellow and I loved seeing him, but he was here for five hours, and you, dear George, are the loser.

Little else to report from last week. George Moore has almost given way to Oscar. My enjoyment of literary detective work is unbounded: how happily would I settle down to six solid months of it! As it is, goodness knows how long this job will take me, done at odd moments.

15 November 1956   *Grundisburgh*

This too is a scraplet, as I am just back from Hagley and find a mass of little jobs that, I grant you, do not materially affect the progress of civilisation, but do take up time—and a meeting or two of course. November is the month for them. When I write to R.H-D I like to contemplate a gracious reach of time like smooth-sliding Mincius before me, unruffled by any little duties irrupting like tributaries. How *you* with no such quiet times ever manage to send me more than a p.c. is one of the world's mysteries.

Yes, I saw the Priestley article and greatly liked it. There seems to be a good deal of 'gunning' for Leavis, and the more the merrier. That contempt for practically all the stuff that has ever been praised and liked borders, to my mind, on the insane, like other forms of conceit.

There is no reason, my dear Rupert, why you should fetch us from Eton; give fool-proof directions and over we nip in our motor. We go to Eton on the 22nd, Saturday, and we can and will with pleasure lunch on whichever day after that suits you. I look forward to meeting your family—though under no illusion about what adolescents think of their father's old friends.

When I get a moment I will copy and send that page of William Cory's. It is one of the supreme utterances.

Once again you're out of luck, for it's eleven p.m. and I am too sleepy for a decent letter. To make up a little, here is a delicious letter from Sydney Smith:[1] I only hope you don't know it already. It was copied out for me by William Plomer, and before transferring it to my book, I thought you might like to put it in yours. Send it back some-time—no hurry. You speak of 'a gracious reach of time', a conception which I am rapidly coming to equate with Paradise, so crammed is every unforgiving minute—but one gets used to most things in time.

So glad you saw and enjoyed the Priestley article. I heard last week that Helen Gardner (a very intelligent English don at Oxford) was recently viva-ing a pupil or ex-pupil of Leavis's and asked her: 'Do you *enjoy* Jane Austen (or whoever)?' To which the girl answered: 'It isn't a question of enjoyment: it's a question of evaluation.' Ugh!

Cuthbert Headlam shirked last week's Lit. Soc. (praise be), as well as his brother's funeral. It was a good evening. I sat between Roger (to whom I talked most of the time) and Bruce Lockhart, who is an

---

[1] Dear Lady Georgiana [Morpeth]

. . . Nobody has suffered more from low spirits than I have done—so I feel for you. 1st. Live as well as you dare. 2nd. Go into the shower-bath with a small quantity of water at a temperature low enough to give you a slight sensation of cold, 75° or 80°. 3rd. Amusing books. 4th. Short views of human life—not further than dinner or tea. 5th. Be as busy as you can. 6th. See as much as you can of those friends who respect and like you. 7th. And of those acquaintances who amuse you. 8th. Make no secret of low spirits to your friends, but talk of them freely—they are always worse for dignified concealment. 9th. Attend to the effects tea and coffee produce upon you. 10th. Compare your lot with that of other people. 11th. Don't expect too much from human life—a sorry business at the best. 12th. Avoid poetry, dramatic representations (except comedy), music, serious novels, melancholy sentimental people, and everything likely to excite feeling or emotion not ending in active benevolence. 13th. *Do good*, and endeavour to please every-body of every degree. 14th. Be much as you can in the open air without fatigue. 15th. Make the room where you commonly sit, gay and pleasant. 16th. Struggle by little and little against idleness. 17th. Don't be too severe upon yourself, or underrate yourself, but do yourself justice. 18th. Keep good blazing fires. 19th. Be firm and constant in the exercise of rational religion. 20th. Believe me, dear Lady Georgiana, very truly yours, SYDNEY SMITH

egotistical bore. Martin Charteris told me that the script of my five minutes on commercial T.V. had been shown to the Queen!

On Thursday I dined with the Hamish Hamiltons. Earlier that evening I attended another meeting of the A.P. Herbert Committee on the reform of the law concerning obscene books. Yesterday my wife and I drove over to the Gollanczes near Newbury and took 9/– off them at bridge—quite amusing, but it cut six hours out of my week-end working time, which partly explains this wretched note. 'The bloom is gone, and with the bloom go I.' Next week, as I keep reiterating, you'll get something a little better.

22 November 1956   *Grundisburgh*

There is something odd and comic and reassuring in the way both of us are being harried and constricted by encroachments from the external world. Mine are nothing to yours, but to the superannuated man of leisure a prospective committee is a headache, an old boy dinner a heavy and a weary weight. This last is due this evening. The absurd thing is that I always quite enjoy it when it is once started, but that makes it no less of a hang-over. Anyway a speech is always that, and I am expected to be funny. On the way up, the train is about at Colchester when the conviction settles on me that not only can I not think of anything remotely funny, but that there isn't anything funny left for anyone to say and do. By Chelmsford a ray of light dawns, viz that the audience will be mellow enough to regard almost anything as funny, even if none have reached the stage described by Sir Thomas More 'with his belly standing astrote like a taber, and his noll totty with drink'. I am no clearer as to what astrote means than Mr Micawber was about gowans, but the whole sentence has a rich vigour and vulgarity which is surely very attractive. I suspect Sir Thomas More was of the same vintage as Sir T. Beecham, which I had not dreamt of before. *Utopia* is not beside my bed. That S. Smith is *fine* and I have transferred it and return it with many thanks. A rum thing is that S.S. was like old Johnson in many ways, but the latter in a letter to Boswell expressly commands him to be entirely silent about his mental and physical ailments, and then he will think about them less and 'then they will molest you rarely'. S.S's advice to talk freely about them postulates a long-suffering audience. Of course the best bit of advice would have been 'come and sit in a corner when I am in good form'. And what boisterous fun he would have had with Leavis!

My mouth always waters when I hear of your company at the Lit. Society. Did you ask Roger about that bull? I imagine the conversation round the table to be of the finest vintage. I suppose like the Junior Ganymede, of which Jeeves was a member, the club rules forbid you to retail any of the *bon mots* lavishly begotten.

There is something very incongruous in A.P.H's being on an anti-obscene committee, or perhaps he is all for abolishing the present checks. As on many other questions (e.g. hanging) I find myself continually dashed by the opinions and personalities and (often) appearance of those on the same side. I shout 'down with hanging' confidently till I read the speeches of Silverman and Co. I want lots of freedom for books until I find myself marching in step with a cargazon of arch, self-consciously broad-minded swaggering females—shall we say like the daughter of a certain professor who was passionately keen about the right pronunciation of Latin and devoted half one lecture to showing the different sounds of 'qui' and 'cui'. But for each he gave a coot-like whistle which left them indistinguishable. He was a dreary little pedant, hirsute, bloodless, dusty, and was bumped by Housman for the Latin chair to his lasting chagrin. I believe no one knew more about those points in the Latin language which have the least imaginable interest. He couldn't have written and wouldn't have read 'Once in the wind of morning . . .'[1]

25 November 1956   *Bromsden Farm*

All occasions do inform against us. Sunday December 23 would be the perfect day for you and Pamela to come to lunch, but now you won't have your car, I suppose, and our petrol will be too tight for a double journey—damn! Or have you a solution?[2]

[1] By A. E. Housman.
[2] Petrol was now rationed as a result of the disastrous Suez expedition and the closing of the Canal.

I read of your Old Boy dinner in *The Times*, but they did not mention the witty brilliance of the Guest of Honour: taken for granted no doubt. Our dinners will not, I fear, survive Jelly[1], and although they were pretty dull I grieve at the breaking of yet another tradition. My uncle Duff used to make excellent speeches at the old dinners. Anthony Eden never once turned up.

The conversation at the Lit. Soc. is mostly confined to groups of two or three: the table is a long narrow one: later in the evening people circulate a little and change seats. Roger, who lunched with me last week in excellent form, says he always deliberately sits next to Cuthbert H., because he finds the awfulness so exaggerated as almost to be enjoyable. Also Roger much prefers him to Dunsany!

Tonight I must somehow write a review of six detective stories for *Time and Tide*: it should be eight, but I haven't had time to read the others, even in bed.

Yesterday I drove to Oxford and spent four hours in Magdalen library, checking and copying the Wilde letters there. Tom Boase, the President, gave me an excellent lunch in the middle. At the end I had twenty minutes in Blackwell's before they shut, and picked up a few scraps of Wildeana—that job is the greatest fun, if only I had time to do it properly. 'We work in the dark—we do what we can—we give what we have. Our doubt is our passion and our passion is our task. The rest is the madness of art.' I expect you know where that comes from.[2] Like you, I copy out for the pleasure of doing it.

Last week was much occupied by Harold Nicolson's seventieth birthday present. John Sparrow started it, but very soon the whole of the organisation devolved (as they say) on me. Getting from his secretary a copy of his address-book, we circularised more than 350 of his friends. Eventually 253 of them contributed £1370! Getting the cheque to him on the right day, with an alphabetical list of donors was a great nuisance. I also circularised them all again, telling them the result. On the evening of the birthday (Wednesday) Sparrow gave a small dinner for H.N. in the little private room at the Garrick. (I had to order food and wine—what next?) Apart from H.N., J.S. and myself, the party consisted of Raymond Mortimer, Jonah, Alan Pryce-Jones,

[1] Nickname of my Eton housemaster E.L. Churchill.
[2] From Henry James's short story 'The Middle Years'.

16

Jim Lees-Milne (contemporary of mine at Eton) and a young friend of Harold's called Colin Fenton. It was an agreeable evening, and H.N. was moved almost to tears by the whole day: he wrote me a charming letter afterwards.

Hardly had the fumes dispersed when the Duff Cooper Memorial Prize cropped up again in a big way. Constant telephone calls to Diana at Chantilly about getting Winston as prize-giver (which she did), a drive across London to look at Enid (Bagnold) Jones's drawing-room where the ceremony is to take place, much more telephoning to devoted ladies and champagne-providers, drafting and sending out a press release, etc, making sure the cheque (£200) is ready—phew! Enid Jones lives next door to Winston, which is a help, since they say he's not good for much more than twenty minutes now. Her drawing-room was built by Lutyens out of some old stables and is like an attractive stage set—at that moment another devoted lady rang me up here to say that Winston was going to speak only of Duff and would I get one of the judges who awarded the prize to say a few words about the *book*. Also, who is to marshal the press photographers? Unfortunately Hamish Hamilton (the publisher of the prize-winning book, Alan Moorehead's *Gallipoli*) is not on speaking terms with Randoph Churchill, who is now interfering actively—phew again! Oh for an ivory tower stuffed with books! All this takes place at 6 p.m. on Wednesday in Hyde Park Gate. At 7.45 I am supposed to be dining with the Priestleys in Albany in a dinner-jacket. No taxis, no petrol, no time.

29 November 1956   *Grundisburgh*

All is not entirely lost. We *mean* to go to Eton by car and, when there, may find the twenty-odd miles to Henley quite possible. Let us wait and see—as indeed one does every mortal day in more or less of a dither. How utterly repellent our days are, compared with those, say, of 1897, when nothing of the smallest importance happened the other side of the Channel, still less across the Atlantic. Still it cannot be denied that it is all beastly interesting. I shall continue to maintain that, even in the workhouse. And I shall have R.H-D's letters with me, which no one else will have, and what do all the little debits count against that? Do you remember Morris Finsbury's balance-sheet *à la* Crusoe beginning '(Bad) I have lost my uncle's body' '(Good) But then Pitman has found it,' and then realised that the spirit of antithesis was running away with him? I would bet on your loving *The Wrong Box* but may be wrong. Some very good men cannot stomach that corpse being bandied about, e.g. old Scott Holland who was about as good a man as you could find.

'Old Boys' are rather hang-overs, and one can have some very blush-making moments at them. Luckily this year John Verney was in the chair, and did the job perfectly. I caught a dreadful glimpse of myself now and then behaving exactly like that emetic Mr Chips, but the opposite number to him would I suppose be someone like Cyril Connolly or Jack Haldane, so what will you? Have you, by the way, read Hollis's *George Orwell* and if so, or even if not, can you tell me why he is so important? It is not fair to answer *1984* or *Animal Farm*, because he is regarded as very fine outside them and I can't quite see why. I like a good deal of his thinking aloud, but is it very profound or illuminating? I am rather on the fence about him, as about many things and people.

The slogan in literary London is obviously 'Who shall we get to do this? Oh of course R.H-D.' The dinner to Harold N. on the top of everything else. I really think somebody else might have ordered the menu—which I bet you did with great care. You don't tell me what it was—I always like to know that. J.M. Barrie, recorded by Tuppy, once said that the great merit of Phillips Oppenheim's books was the excellent eating in all of them. Another comment was that P.O. always tired of his book soon after the middle and then 'merely kicked it along to its end'. Tuppy had a complete set of P.O., which must have been as hard to collect as the whole of Trollope, of whom one has *never* read all.

Your account of the D.C. Memorial Prize preparations is delicious. Do tell me in full how it went off—all those non-speaks. The literary world sounds as full of envy, hatred, and malice as the academic. Winston, I heard last week, refused to speak to his constituents, not, as was said, because he had a cough, but because he is so sunk in gloom that he just cannot speak to anyone. I wonder how you found him. I suspect that his vision of England's future goes near to breaking his heart. What *little* men are governing us and everybody else at this time!

I am in labour with a speech at the King's Founder's Feast on Dec. 6 —answering the toast of *Floreat Etona amicabilis concordia*. You see the difficulty at once. No Oppidan within living memory has been remotely conscious of any special affection for King's. And if I say much about Eton, well, there are very many non-Etonians at King's now, so that note must not be stressed. In fact I shall be skating on a pond full of patches of cats'-ice. But how can one refuse these flattering invitations some six months in advance? I have not the nerve to refuse, as a Trinity don did, an invitation in September to a dinner on Jan 31 on the grounds that it was always in that week that he caught one of his worst colds. Claud Elliott reassures me by saying that the audience is pleasantly tight, so it doesn't much matter what one says, but that is rather a dangerous line. Tightness may leave their critical faculties unblunted but remove the barriers to freedom of comment. Then home to a batch of exam-papers and silence—a good moment. Marking papers soon becomes as mechanical as knitting, and I *believe* each script brings in two shillings (it used to be one and ninepence). But of course the world *may* have come to an end by then.

P.S. Here is W. Cory on public school education—the last word, *me judice*.

[WILLIAM JOHNSON CORY ON EDUCATION]

At school you are engaged not so much in acquiring knowledge as in making mental efforts under criticism. A certain amount of knowledge you can indeed with average faculties acquire so as to retain; nor need you regret the hours you spent on much that is forgotten, for the shadow of lost knowledge at least protects you from many illusions. But you go to a great school not so much for knowledge as for arts and habits; for the habit of attention, for the art of expression, for the art of assuming at a moment's notice a new intellectual position, for the art of entering quickly into another person's thoughts, for the habit of submitting to censure and refutation, for the art of indicating assent or dissent in graduated terms, for the habit of regarding minute points of accuracy, for the art of working out what is possible in a given time, for taste, for discrimination, for mental courage, and for mental soberness.

2 December 1956   *Bromsden Farm*

I applaud your courage and persistence in the matter of driving to Eton for Christmas, and live in hopes of your both lunching here on the Sunday. Detailed instructions will follow shortly. On Friday (St Andrew's Day) I played truant from the office and spent most of the day driving people about—my wife to and from the school where she teaches, my boy and the Linklater child back here to lunch (their tutors having sensibly agreed), back to Eton for tea in my boy's room —altogether more than a hundred miles. And I was promptly rewarded for my altruism, since the Henley petrol-supply, which till then had been flowing normally, abruptly gave out yesterday morning, with the announcement 'No more till the 17th'. We have two gallons in our tank and are five miles from anywhere. How my wife is going to get to this infernal school of hers I simply don't know. I'm sure there is already a black market in coupons, but what use are they when the pumps are empty? A fortnight of the sort of hardship that this is going to mean, exactly coinciding with the P.M.'s last fortnight at Goldeneye (shade temperature 86), is not calculated to strengthen his popularity.[1]

Naturally I love *The Wrong Box*: how could you be wrong? Almost the nicest thing about it is that the details of the plot escape my memory fairly promptly each time, leaving only the Health Boots, and William Bent Pitman, and 'The *Athaeneum*—golly, what a paper!' and the Maestro Jimson—so that after a year or so I can read it again with fresh delight. I wish I could *now*, but if I ever have a moment (which seems unlikely) *Annals of the Parish* is first in the queue.

That passage of Cory is magnificent: exactly where does it come from? All this editing has produced a passion for exactitude in references. Copying it into my book I came on these two extracts, which I

[1] Anthony Eden was recuperating at Ian Fleming's house in Jamaica.

copied out many years ago. What do you think of them? And do you know who wrote them? I fancy they matched some feelings of mine at the time of copying. Here they are:

(a) I am a willow of the wilderness,
Loving the wind that bent me.

(b) As the bird trims her to the gale,
I trim myself to the storm of time,
I man the rudder, reef the sail,
Obey the voice at eve obeyed at prime:
'Lowly faithful, banish fear,
Right onward drive unarmed;
The port, well worth the cruise, is near,
And every wave is charmed.'

Write only on one side of the paper, and give your reasons for your verdict. The examiner examined!

I have *not* read Hollis's *George Orwell*, and I don't propose to, unless it is my only book on a desert island. Orwell is of no importance from the literary point of view, but for some I daresay he has the fascination of litmus paper or a chameleon: he was (slightly to change the metaphor) a sort of barometer of the Thirties and early Forties, going through and writing about *all* the experience of young left-wing intellectuals during those troubled years. If you and I cannot read him with pleasure, my dear George, let us be certain, even if ridiculous to boot.

I too always like to know what people had to eat: wasn't Galsworthy good at it? Do you remember *Old English*? At Harold N's birthday dinner I ordered hot lobster with rice, roast pheasant and *soufflé surprise*, with sherry, meursault, claret and port or brandy. When I was a boy I too had an almost complete set of Phillips Oppenheim (over ninety vols),[1] but at some moment I grew ashamed of them and gave them away. Nico Davies has a superb collection (he must have inherited the taste from J.M.B. or from Tuppy), to which I have occasionally added something. I chiefly remember a proliferation of cocktails, usually described as 'amber-coloured fluid'. I met the old

[1] I now (1979) have 153.

21

boy once on the Riviera and sat goggling at his feet. He was old, with a young and pretty 'secretary'.

The Duff Cooper Prize was duly awarded on Wednesday, in the presence of what the *Manchester Guardian* rightly called 'a small but glittering assembly'—all Duff's friends, so much so that it almost seemed as though he was there himself. My calling in Harold Nicolson to open the proceedings and mention Moorehead's book was immensely successful: he did it beautifully and briefly. Winston was terribly frail and tottery. Although his little speech was all written out, one couldn't feel sure he'd get through it without losing the thread. However, he did. (Beforehand he rather sweetly showed his script to Moorehead, to make sure he'd got his name right.) Moorehead replied in a few, very good, words, and then Winston, like an old hunter wanting more than a sniff of the chase, got up and said another sentence or two. It was all very moving and exactly right. Champagne flowed freely, and the old warrior drank some as he beamed round at his friends. Even in the grip of withering age he makes all our present rulers look like feeble pigmies. I couldn't stay as long as I'd have liked, since I had to rush home and change before dining with the Priestleys (scampi, partridge and delicious vanilla ice with lumps of ginger in it). A funny little party—two architects (Lord Mottistone, Jack Seely's son, and Paul Paget, who is a cousin of mine) and a lady from B.B.C. television—all very nice but the party seemed curiously pointless. After the others had gone I stayed on for an hour's cosy gossip with the Priestleys. I like him very much (a very old friend) and she is beautiful, as well as very intelligent. Now I must get on with my proofs.

5 December 1956   *Grundisburgh*

Does anything pleasant *ever* happen? Really this combination of humiliation, impoverishment, hideous inconvenience and insecurity in the near, middle, and distant future is very hard to bear. It is a very inadequate silver lining that Ike should be improving his putting, and Eden his tennis, breast-stroke and complexion. Surely he will be out in the twinkling of an eye, and his Government. No Govt can survive such hideous results, whether the action that produced them seemed at the time to be right or wrong. And the alternative is Gaitskell and Co. Assuredly 'we are for the dark'—except that nothing turns out quite as dreadful as one expected. I fear and suspect there may be exceptions. But, as a tiresome and sensible friend of mine says, 'There is nothing we can do about it, so why talk about it?' Like all such statements, it doesn't hold quite so much water as the speaker thought.

That is good about *The Wrong Box*. I wonder how true it is that Lloyd Osbourne wrote practically all of it, also that the *Athenaeum* never forgave R.L.S. for 'Golly, what a paper' and always gave him snooty reviews. *Pauvre humanité!* Some—many—good men have enjoyed *The W.B.*, Stanley Baldwin among them. Alington knew it really by heart, and M.R. James too, I believe. *His* memory was simply uncanny.

I do not know where that Cory passage comes from—I *think* from some 'Notes on Education'. John Carter would know, if you ever come across him. Cory was something of a genius, but he was very dogmatic in his opinions and often obviously wrong, e.g. when he said Tennyson's *Queen Mary* was 'altogether nobler' than *Hamlet*, that *Christie Johnstone*[1] was immensely superior to *Vanity Fair*, that Campbell would outlive Shelley, that Jane Austen's novels, except *Persuasion*, were in 1884 mere 'worsted-stockings'. Do you think that in seventy years someone will record as one of the aberrations of great critics that R.H-D thought nothing of Orwell? I don't think so; in fact what you say chimes in with my own doubts and suspicions. How a small and persistent clique can bolster up a writer's reputation. Landor's remark hits the nail firmly: 'We admire by tradition (or fashion) and criticise by caprice.'

I like your two passages; I suppose our moderns would condemn them as romantic? subjective? smooth? what? I wish I could place them.

Old English!! or rather 'A Stoic', i.e. story, not play. Just like *The Wrong B.* with you! It has always been one of my favourites—Germane soup; filly de sole; sweetbread; cutlet soubees; rum souffly, according to Meller, and old Heythorp added hors d'oeuvres (oysters as it turned out) and a savoury (cheese remmykin), and you remember

[1] By Charles Reade (1853).

'cook's done a little spinach in cream with the soubees'. This from memory; I don't *think* it is inaccurate. Your Nicolson menu pleases me; was it a really *fat* pheasant? There is *nothing* so good. By the way Meller told old H. he had 'frapped' the champagne a little. What exactly does that mean? I have never dared to ask anyone, because obviously one ought to know. I am no man of the world. I remember being quite ignorant what 'bortsch' was long after everyone else knew; I am not quite sure how to spell it now.

Your account of Winston fits in with what others have said. One would not be surprised at his going any day. He is the only man in public life with the undeniable insignia of greatness about him.

To-morrow I go to the King's Founder's Feast ('Doctors will wear scarlet; orders and decorations, medals or ribbons, will be worn'). Well that all sounds rather tremendous, but when I told them my tail coat had long been one with Nineveh and Tyre, they came down to earth and said half the company would be in tuxedos and quite a number in corduroys and jumpers. My speech is assembled, morticed, dovetailed, planed, polished and dried. Sometimes I think it will prosper, at others a swift and easy death is my only wish. Do *your* feelings on such occasions behave in so volatile a fashion? I take comfort from Roger's (I think) telling me that a Lord Mayor of London told him a few years ago that he had no nerves before a speech, and that he never prepared but said what came into his head, implying that his head could transmute anything into gold. He then, an hour later, made the worst speech R. had ever heard. You saw, no doubt, of Roger's windfall from the *Evening Standard* for his Suffragette book.[1] Very heartening news, and I suppose his sales will swell for all his future writings—just as Gerald Kelly's fees soared after he had painted the Queen Mother or one of them. Does the Chancellor pinch half of it? I shall be sitting next to Provost Annan at the Feast. Do you know him? They tell me he is very amiable.

Your Priestley party sounds poorly chosen. I expect he is good fun. I like his writing. I think I must re-read *The Good Companions*. Has it weathered the years well? And what a very good play *Dangerous Corner* was. Do you think a house-party at Hawarden eighty years ago would have shown much the same sort of imbroglio if the lid had been

[1] *Votes for Women* (1957) had been given a £5000 prize by the paper.

removed—Lord Acton a pansy, Mary Drew a mere Rahab, the
G.O.M. himself a successful embezzler, etc? No, but I suppose quite a
number of house-parties would have. One of the oddest things was
the immense respect for old Devonshire, though everyone knew of
Skittles and the Duchess, etc. And yet Dilke, who was immensely
able, never lived down *his* amatory scandal. Was it merely that one
mustn't be found out?

I am reading Basil Willey's *More Nineteenth Century Studies*, and
enjoying it. Do you agree with me in always faintly but persistently
disliking Cardinal Newman? That air of saintliness wears rather thin,
when his (very sharp) temper was roused, and he had no width of
sympathy. In disliking him I am in the dubious company of George
Moore. You remember that delightful passage, in *Vale* I think, where
he proves to his brother the colonel how badly Newman often wrote.
Maurice Headlam, who was not at all like G.M. in all other ways,
went so far as to say that Kingsley had the better of the argument
which led up to N's *Apologia*, but I can't really believe that. Cuthbert
H. asked me to write a little appreciation of Maurice in *The Times*, but I
refused; although we corresponded pretty regularly, I didn't really
know him well, and there wasn't in truth much to say about him.
His letters were illegible and, though interesting in bits, had too
many dull patches, when he would describe at length a house I had
never heard of, belonging to some man I didn't know, with particular
mention of how his elderly wife had kept her figure and looks, neither
of which I had ever seen. He was latterly much depressed with the
way of the world, and (like Tuppy) as really '*felix opportunitate
mortis*'.

9 December 1956   *Bromsden Farm*

This morning I unaccountably woke up with a splitting headache,
and despite repeated doses of aspirin it is still with me: so you must
forgive a short and dreary letter. Several hours at work on the proofs
of the Henry James bibliography have perhaps not helped, though it's
the sort of work I usually enjoy. Jonah has sent me the first four
chapters of his new book, which are delightful, especially one on

stalking.[1] He has abandoned a strictly chronological and consecutive narrative, in favour of set pieces, scenes, incidents or character-sketches, with a chapter devoted to each, and so far it's working out very well. I've also got the first fifty typewritten pages (all she's written) of Diana Cooper's memoirs: they are enchanting, and if only she can keep it up, her book will be unique and altogether *her*. She's coming to London tomorrow and I must encourage and stimulate her to continue.

Those two passages I sent you last week are both by Emerson: surprising, don't you think? I have been reading Hardy. I love the old boy's poetry more every year—it's not primarily youth's cup of tea, I should say, but one of the consolations of middle age. I'm sure you know his 'On an Invitation to the United States', but nevertheless I copy out the first stanza for pleasure:

> My ardours for surprize nigh lost
> Since Life has bared its bones to me,
> I shrink to seek a modern coast
> Whose riper times have yet to be;
> Where the new regions claim them free
> From that long drip of human tears
> Which peoples old in tragedy
> Have left upon the centuried years.

I had exactly that feeling when I first visited New York, built on a rock without roots of any kind. How splendid that you are such a *Stoic* fan: 'frapped' simply means 'iced', from the French '*frappé*', which means the same.

I'm sure your King's speech was a huge success: pray describe the scene in full detail, with ample quotation from what you said. I do know Noel Annan and like him very much. He's well under forty, for all his baldness—very quick and intelligent. His wife (née Ullstein) is pretty, clever and amusing. I'm sure he'll be a successful Provost, and only hope he doesn't stop writing. His book on Leslie Stephen (his only one so far) is badly constructed, but has excellent things in it. I wrote to congratulate Roger—tax-free, I trust?

[1] *Georgian Afternoon.*

Fancy, Emerson! He is one of those men whom it is somehow difficult to read, but are devilish good whenever quoted. I read most if not all of the *Essays* at Cambridge and have his correspondence with Carlyle, but the thrawn old Scot was a better letter-writer—in fact one of the best there are, though I am almost alone in knowing that. There *is* another, much better man, who has said so in print, but I cannot remember who it is. Leavis, perhaps? Good God, how dreadful if it was. I am *quite* sure it wasn't.

The King's feast was immense fun. They were very welcoming. The Provost seemed to me entirely charming; he is on the way to being an outstanding success, which, in the most censorious community in the world, i.e. dons, is a remarkable start. The Vice-Provost, I fancy, was responsible for all the arrangements—an affable little man with whiskers of the *exact* shape, colour, size, and I suspect consistency, of mutton-chops, name of Saltmarsh. There was an old drunk of that name at Harlech (and if you come to think of it, it is hard to imagine a *thirstier* name) but I didn't quite dare ask him if he was a relative. I sat between George Rylands and John Carter, and nothing could have been more enjoyable. And only last week I asked you if you knew him (J.C.)! Really the lapses of the septuagenarian brain, because I had already noted that you had published his last book, and had rejoiced—because there is always satisfaction at seeing two good men come together. He was up to me about thirty-odd years ago; I had seen him very little since, but he is one of those rare and refreshing souls with whom one goes on from the exact place where one left off. He was interesting about the old villain Wise—shocked at the tales of his sordid thefts from the British Museum, because, as he very aptly put it, there was a certain loftiness of style about his forgeries which the other crimes altogether lack. Do you know George Rylands too? I expect so; in fact I shall give up asking you that otiose question. G.R. has what they call oodles of charm—and excellent wits too. And he is also very kind to me, which Tuppy used to say was all that mattered.

I agree T.H's poetry is immensely satisfying to the mature. Why did old Moore so dislike him? Not perhaps that old Moore's caprices matter. Didn't he also put Landor above Shakespeare and say that *Agnes Grey* was the most perfect prose narrative in existence? I suppose he often just made up his mind to play the *enfant terrible*.

I have just finished the Strachey-Woolf letters. Not fearfully good are they? Good things here and there of course, but Strachey is often trivial and V.W. often shows off, and on the whole one sees why many people spit at the name of Bloomsbury. And I suspect they would spit even more if all the names were given. Neither had any *humility*, and I am more and more blowed if that isn't the *sine qua non* of all goodness and greatness. The trouble is that if you are very clever and don't believe in God, there is nobody and nothing in the presence of whom or which you can be humble. For instance, Milton and Carlyle, for all their arrogance, were fundamentally humble, don't you think? Here endeth the epistle of George the Apostle.

I think we shall manage the motor-trip to Bromsden F. Your itinerary is fool-proof. 'Keep Left' seems the slogan. How does one avoid going round in a circle? There isn't a right-turn anywhere. But I must warn you that there is no way I cannot miss. I claim to be the only man who after going many miles on the Great North Road, and meaning to keep on it, suddenly found himself off it. Can you beat that?

I am temporarily swamped in exam-papers. What *is* the point of examining on the *Midsummer N.D.*? The candidates have all been told by their palsied beaks that the plot and the character-drawing are masterly—the plot being absurd and the c-d perfunctory. Not *one* of those flatulent impostors has told his candidates that nothing in the play is of the smallest importance or merit except a great deal of celestial poetry—oh yes and of course Bottom. One young woman—not in my lot—wrote that the two best characters were Pluck and Button. She passed all right. The exam was run by the Welsh Board.

Don't stand any rot from that headache. Bed for all ailments however small; that is how Lord Quickswood lived to eighty-seven, though always delicate.

My wife (her name, by the way, is Comfort—a New England name, which I believe she alone possesses in this country) is preparing an enormous joint of *spiced beef* for your and Pamela's visit. Apparently it has to be massaged with a different herb every day for a week— we'll hope for the best, and fall back on the Christmas ham if need be. You will also find here my two sons—Duff (20), who is flying home from Düsseldorf at hideous cost, and Adam (13), your great-nephew's messmate. My daughter Bridget (21) may not be home by Sunday. I rehearse all these names and facts so that you know what to expect. Wear old clothes, for nothing here is smart in any degree. We shall expect you between 12.30 and 1. What fun!

I saw Tim Munby last week at my bibliographical dining club, and he reported enthusiastically on your speech at King's. I wish I'd been there. Lord Quickswood seemed to receive a disproportionate amount of space in *The Times*—all about dim Church squabbles of long ago. Was he any good as Provost? I too have just read the Strachey-Woolf letters—very disappointing, I thought. Full of arrogance, and all the spice removed with the people's names. This scrappy book cannot enhance the reputation of either of them. I'm not sure I agree that it's impossible to be humble in spirit unless you believe in God—in fact I'm sure I disagree, and if I weren't so proof-weary would quote examples to prove my point.

The Lit. Soc. on Tuesday was good fun. We ate fillets of sole, roast turkey and roes on toast, with potable wines. I again (God help me) sat (or rather *was* sat) next to Bruce Lockhart, but on the other side of me was Laurence Irving, a wholly delightful chap whom I hadn't seen for ages. (Did you ever read his huge life of his grandfather? So far I've only read *in* it, finding it good and hoping for leisure enough to en- compass the whole. Now it's so relevant to my Oscar Wilde investi- gations that I'm thinking of devoting the Christmas recess to it.) Anyhow Laurence and I talked for most of the evening about O.W., H.I. and kindred subjects.

My sister and her husband were dining next door in the big coffee-room, and I went in and sat with them afterwards. One day I spent an amusing hour in the National Portrait Gallery—seeing much that was new to me. I can stand museums and galleries for a short time only—do you find it the same? Soon one becomes overwhelmed by fatigue, air-conditioning and general surfeit. One of the merits of the N.P.G. is that the pictures are not, as in many galleries, hung so close together that one can't look at one without catching more than glimpses of its neighbours.

Most of to-day, except for garden duties and picking high branches of holly in pouring rain, I have spent wrestling with Fleming's proofs, partly alone and partly with their author. This is the *fourth* time I have read the book and I'm heartily sick of it, as I so often am of even the best books before they're finally printed. If only Peter had taken more notice of my remarks when I read the first typescript, we should have been spared many hours of irritating work. Now he has made so many major corrections on the page-proofs that I shall have to call for yet another revise before the indexes can go smoothly ahead. Years of contributing to *The Times* have introduced into P.F.'s prose woolly constructions like 'It would seem'—which to me is unacceptable in any context, and which I have now removed at least twenty-five times from this book. I daresay that all this trouble is quite unnecessary, since few realise or notice what has been done, but I hate to publish sloppy writing if it can be improved. And all the time I'm longing to get on with Oscar Wilde, and all the detective work it involves. Recently, for example, I got hold of an undated letter (most of them are) to Clement Scott, the dramatic critic of the *Daily Telegraph*. The only clue was a phrase saying, roughly: 'I liked your Ode very much, and thought it much better than Lord T's.' No verse by C.S. in the London Library, but luckily I have two devoted friends who are often in the Reading Room of the British Museum, and I asked one of them to get out all books of verse by Clement Scott (he published several) and see how many odes he wrote, and when. There turned out to be one only—a valedictory ode on the retirement of the Bancrofts, which was recited by Irving from the stage of the Haymarket Theatre on 20 July 1885. As soon as I got down here I rushed to the big life of Tennyson, and found that his lines on the marriage of Princess Beatrice were published in *The Times* on 23 July 1885—which means that I can date that letter within a week or so. See what fun it is!

But now I must turn aside to write a pithy footnote on the French novelist Huysmans for my George Moore book—not a dull minute!

Meanwhile the demolition of the next-door house in Soho Square is crashing on, with hellish noise and dirt. God knows how long it will take, or whether my house will stand up alone. Anyhow I hope to be here to welcome you on Sunday.

20 December 1956   *Grundisburgh*

'Counting fish as nothing': you remember the actor Elliston's parenthesis in his inventory of a good dinner. That is how this letter is to be regarded in our correspondence, for in four days we shall meet. I say, *spiced beef*! Are we in *The Arabian Nights*, or *Vathek*? How many dishes were there at the Caliph's feast, when the poor man was rather seedy, and could taste no more than thirty-two? But where is the spiced beef in that delectable banquet on your Christmas card which arrived yesterday afternoon? There is turkey, and duck, and ham and much else; and what a brave, new, *Old English* note the card altogether strikes. I shouldn't wonder if one of the dishes contained cheese remmykin.

'Comfort'! What a lovely name to have. Is it common overseas? I suppose the Puritans knew it. Milton would have liked it surely.

Old Quickswood was not a good Provost—so arbitrary and capricious, and quite sure that he was right. He loved argument, but Provosts aren't there to be argued with. But he was good with the boys and they flocked to the lectures merely to hear him introduce and thank the lecturer. He made very clear indeed the gap between the born speaker and the rest who after much sweat produce something that passes muster. He was about the readiest and wittiest I have ever heard. But he had nothing like the delightful friendliness of Monty James which put everyone at their ease, and never made one feel that one was unsound about the Holy Ghost.

I have followed up the Strachey-Woolf letters by reading Clive Bell on his friends. He questions the existence of 'Bloomsbury' as a one-time centre of culture, but, however hard to define, it was surely recognisable all right—like Housman's terrier and rat.[1] Does anyone deny that V.W. and L.S. and Co were exclusive, and fastidious, and highbrow, and contemptuous of past greatness, and mutual admirers, and if that isn't Bloomsbury, what is?

We shan't be able to talk about humility over the spiced beef, but it *is* exciting to find you disagreeing about it. You will I am sure produce some cogent evidence, but I warn you that an 18-pounder I sooner or later shall bring into action is to maintain blandly, infuriatingly, irrefutably, that a great number of people think they don't believe in God, who, in fact, *do*!

P.S. Unless the petrol situation is entirely *bouleversé* we shall arrive on Sunday at about 12.40—a little giddy from so much left-turning, but *all agog* for you and yours and SPICED BEEF!

30 December 1956   *Bromsden Farm*

Your and Pamela's visit was an *immense* success with all ranks, and we're already looking forward to your next. I only hope you didn't use too much of your precious petrol. Our festivities passed off smoothly, and the rationing-enforced isolation, added to the fact that I unbelievably had five consecutive days here without other publishing work, got me so engrossed in the dating, arrangement and annotation of the Oscar Wilde letters that I now look on all else as a gross and deplorable intrusion.

I was at the office only two days last week, and spent most of one of them looking up things like the Oxford Sports of 1877 in the London Library. *The Times* index for those years, while omitting all mention of music in any form, is full of sport and bankruptcies and suicides. Our rude forefathers liked their game well hung, I can see. Tomorrow I suppose I shall have to buckle on my full publishing harness: the Spring List (which will soon reach you) isn't too bad, but one always feels that the next list will be barren and impotent. The great thing is

[1] Housman said that he could no more define poetry than a terrier could define a rat, but he thought they both recognised the object by the symptoms which it provoked in them.

to work up a string of willing horses, each producing a saleable book a year, and so doing most of the work for one: most of my winners have been by one-book men, with all to do again. I lunched at the Beefsteak on Friday, with John Hugh Smith, who is utterly deaf, and three other dullards whose names I didn't know. That shows what comes of trying to be sociable! Next week, dear George, you shall have a longer letter. Meanwhile a happy new year and all blessings.

3 January 1957   *Eton*

I thought of writing a 'thank-you' letter after that Sunday, but then the fear that *you* might think it a trifle gushing prevailed and I didn't—probably wrongly, as it was disobeying both Arthur Benson and Dr Johnson, who said such impulses should always be followed. We did enjoy every moment of our visit enormously, and shall certainly pay another on a less grim day when the sunshine is external as well as internal. And I want to fix in my mind that study of yours where— *inter alia*—you write your letters to me. If you follow your usual practice you will next be writing on my birthday, Jan 6. Had I been a girl I should have been called Stella. The nurse of that day rose to still more rarefied heights and said to my mother 'You could have called her Etwol' (*Etoile*). But alas 'shades of the prison-house' etc, and when I got to school the star in the east had disastrously fallen from these and other such gracious associations, for it was a synonym for a visible fly-button. (Is that still so and was it in your day?) Attlee was born in the same week as I was, but any inferences to be drawn from that are, so far, jejune.

I had four days at Cambridge last week. Every day we walked through Downing College ('the first college you come to and the last you go to', as some wag put it) and I resisted the temptation to heave half a brick through the window of Dr L--v-s. One of my colleagues is Colin Eccleshare, who says you and he have met but no more. A good man. You probably know his chief at the Press, David. I may tell you that I gather from Colin E. that the general opinion in Press circles is that R.H-D is 'a very able fellow'. The Cambridge University Press column in *The Times* always seems to me to consist of books selected for their unreadability, but I suppose they are exempt from the normal vicissitudes of publishing. I have been reading with great pleasure in the Newman selections. So far my favourite is his masterly trouncing of Sir R. Peel and Brougham in *The Tamworth Reading Room*. It is superb in its ease and force—which come out particularly well when one reads it aloud, as I do when all have gone to bed.

John Hugh Smith I have known since 1892. He was at the same prep. school and house at Eton, and college at Cambridge, but we were never particular friends, though when we have subsequently met we have had an amicable crack. As a boy and young man he made rather a point of saying the wrong thing, and came in for a good many snubs—by which he was entirely unaffected. An able fellow and I suppose, like all Hugh Smiths, possessed of a sixth sense where money is concerned. A nice thing to have, but few nice people have it (epigram!).

We have had a very pleasant time here and seen a good many old friends; hardly any family men go away in the Xmas holidays and it is a good place and time for the children. When I was a boy only about six masters were married and their wives knew their place. Now practically all are, and some of the wives—well this is the season of goodwill and charity, so let us leave it at that. I am occupying the Dame's room. Her bedside literature is *all* the books about the Queen and a novel by Vicki Baum of quite startling indecency—all about an American faith-healer. He is said to be a saint and marvellous healer, but I don't know. His chief job (or 'assignment') was to cure a schizo, and one is led to suppose he has done so when the schizo strangles his sister (whom some time before he had raped). A very odd book. Queen Victoria would have hated it.

5 January 1957   *Bromsden Farm*

Many happy returns of the day. I have no suitable birthday present ready, so you will have to have it serially, as the books arrive from the binders. Did I ever send you the John Carter? I know I said I would, but perhaps Christmas fatally intervened: you must forgive my dotty incompetence.

It's fine to know that you and Pamela enjoyed your visit here and will come again—if we ever get petrol. Your reference to A.C.B. and Doctor Johnson reminds me of the stage-door-keeper at the Lyric Hammersmith in 1928–29. He was clearly a failed actor and looked like an aged pocket-Irving, small with long grey hair and a wonderfully histrionic face. I forget his name. Anyhow, he was always very nice to me, and at Christmas I gave him a present (I forget what). He wrote me the most charming letter, which I hope I've still got somewhere, in which he said: 'Always follow such generous impulses, dear lad'. He must be long dead. Now that you remind me, I remember hearing 'star in the east' applied to a fly-button. I expect you know the story of Winston in later years in the House of Commons. When a colleague tactfully told him that several of his fly-buttons were undone, he said: 'No matter. The dead bird does not leave the nest.'

Last week I miraculously found in Foyle's an almost complete set of bound volumes of a monthly periodical called *The Theatre* which Clement Scott edited from 1876 to 1896 (just the years I need). It includes lengthy reviews of all new plays and revivals in London, with the exact dates and full casts, as well as articles and theatrical gossip and excellent photographs of the leading performers of the day. It will be invaluable for my notes, particularly since I can refer to it in the office: I simply haven't time to spend hours in libraries, alas.

Now I must go to bed, and you are having your last read of the Dame's Crawfie and Vicki Baum—more tomorrow.

Sunday evening, 6 January.

Today has been soft and sunny, and I spent some hours agreeably extending the new brick path. I trust you had the same weather for your drive home.

I have just been struggling with a 200-word 'blurb' for the large selection of Edmund Blunden's poems which I did for Collins—a hideous task, which I have botched up unsatisfactorily. Tomorrow I'll have it typed out and then try to improve it. Generally I find that things read better in typescript, and best in print: which is encouraging while it holds good. Meanwhile the notes to Oscar absorb me. The trouble with footnotes (and this book will contain several hundred) is that they tend either to be bald, dull and severely factual, or (when one tires of that) to be full of fascinating but almost wholly irrelevant matter. For instance, I must have a note about the Roman Catholic church of St Aloysius in Oxford, which O.W. frequented as an undergraduate with R.C. leanings, and when I find that its architect was Joseph Aloysius Hansom, who also invented the Hansom cab, I can't resist putting that in. Anyhow, in the later stages it's easier to cut than to amplify, so I continue to indulge my fancy now and then. When this job is done, I shall know every kind of marginal detail of the history of the last quarter of the nineteenth century.

Now I must rewrite my Will—a largely worthless document, but it might as well be up to date—and prepare a manifesto about the Collected Edition, in twenty vols, of the works of S.T. Coleridge, for which I hope an American foundation will pay. If they don't, the whole thing is off. Tomorrow, God help me, I have to take the chair for a very intelligent female don called Kathleen Tillotson (her husband, also a Prof, edited my *Newman*). She is going to address the Dickens Fellowship—at least I think so, but I've lost the letter about it. Goodness knows what it's all about, or what I shall say. Perhaps luckily, I can't prepare anything without knowing what she's going to speak on. They asked me about eight months ago, damn them.

What splendid news about your nephew Charles.[1] 'Go out and govern New South Wales' no longer means what it did in Belloc's early days. I imagine this will at any rate postpone a final decision about Hagley? My elder boy used to mess with Norrie, son of the retiring Governor of N.Z., and spoke lyrically of the food-parcels from the Antipodes: too bad that Adam won't benefit likewise.

Oh yes—I had occasion yesterday to look at Henry James's biography of William Wetmore Story, the American artist (Oscar wrote to him), and was charmed by the beginning of the book's final sentence: 'Death came to him, as with a single soundless step, early on the October morning . . .' What more could one ask? But I have lots to do first: the teeming brain must be gleaned a little more thoroughly—just for the fun of it.

[1] Viscount Cobham, who had just been appointed Governor General of New Zealand.

It would be tedious and otiose—my favourite adjective, as 'sombre' and 'squalid' are Winston's—to tell you in every letter what immense pleasure yours give me, but I think perhaps it should be done each recurrent season. This is the winter declaration.

You say you 'have no birthday present'. Gosh! As that great man Humpty D. said, it is those who get non-birthday presents who are the fortunate ones, and who gets more of them than G.W.L.? And, my dear Rupert, the Prince of Darkness should go to you for lessons in temptation. Your catalogue makes St Anthony's ladies look like nuns ('blots upon the landscape' as Mrs Cornish said, but, suddenly realising they were R.C's as she was, added 'But what *dear* blots'!). I look forward eagerly to John Carter's book, especially after meeting him again at King's after many years. After a long spell in Suffolk my relish for good talk is positively morbid. Cyril Butterwick tells me J.C. is now at Sotheby's, and a major influence in increasing the prestige of the firm. J.C.B. is himself glossy with prosperity—Brigg umbrella, Poole trousering, Thomas footwear, etc. But he is one of those who are not spoilt by prosperity and was particularly pleasant and easy. I urged him to put on paper his experiences in the book-china-silver market, but he hates the pen, I fancy, and the world will never hear how he failed to notice something unique in a Byron volume he had bought, or how some dealer asked £5 for something he *knew* was worth £200.

That is a fine Winston you send. New to me. I do hope all these gems are noted down somewhere, otherwise half of them will be ascribed to Bevan. Not to Eden, I think, who has (as Winston feared) fallen to myxomatosis. It reads genuine enough, though no doubt the *Mirror* and *New Statesman* etc will be ready with their innuendoes and sneers. Did you read that enormous *T.L.S.* leader, which—I thought admirably—dealt with the fundamental fallacies of Socialism? I read it aloud to Pamela. It took one and a half hours—and how the leisure implied by that must make *your* mouth water. I don't believe you ever let up, and the columns and reviews in the Press leave me with the impression that you deal with a book a day. And yet you write long and lovely letters to decaying old jossers in the back-woods of Suffolk.

Your acquisition of Clement Scott sounds very good news. Old Agate would have revelled in it. And if your Oscar W. isn't a best-seller—but I don't know. What about that adolescent pretentiousness of Colin Wilson's going through, is it *nine* editions in a few months? If Tennyson were writing now, he would surely, if honest, revise his famous line to 'We needs must love the lowest when we see it': certainly, if referring to public taste. Of course you must not leave out such notes as the Aloysius one. All good men will like it. Have you in your O.W. and 1890 researches come across this poem of R. Le Gallienne, two stanzas of which I enclose?[1] It is presumably not a joke. Those were undoubtedly the days.

Thank you for your Belloc line apropos of Charles. Very happy. It will go to him forthwith; I am not sure that he doesn't think the appointment *is* like Godolphin Horne's (was it? I need hardly say my copy of those poems was lent to a boy and never returned), but he thinks, and I am sure, he is right to go. Anyway it is better that than settling down at Budleigh Salterton. The main crux has not been mentioned in the Press, viz that Charles is already sixteen to seventeen stone, and the standard of N.Z. meals is much higher than in England. He goes for five years, and I must prepare for the shock of seeing a nephew of twenty stone in my eightieth year. I don't know what the Hagley plans are; in any case it won't survive another Labour Government, like a lot of other things.

I have just embarked on Ervine's *Shaw* and expect a good deal of fun from it. I met E. once at the H.M.'s table at Eton, and he was good value, so robust and vivacious and full of flavour—and refreshingly and unrepentantly *wrong* in many of his judgments. He laughed us all to scorn for not pronouncing the letter R in words like 'four' and he was

[1] BEAUTY ACCURSED

> I am so fair that whereso'er I wend
> Men yearn with strange desire to kiss my face,
> Stretch out their hands to touch me as I pass,
> And women follow me from place to place.
>
> The sleepy kine move round me in desire
> And press their oozy lips upon my hair,
> Toads kiss my feet, and creatures of the mire,
> The snails will leave their shells to watch me there.

genially insulting—as in his book—about the trifling difference that there is between Eton and Borstal. But why, in his book, does he say that Flora Finching is in *Great Expectations*, and why does he insist on the spelling 'humourous'? I suspect that that springs from Shaw's spelling of 'humor' and 'color', which I always found irritating, especially as he claimed that it would save millions of man-hours.

I hope your speech at the Dickens fellowship lecture went well. Remembering your little impromptu oration about some pretty dim guests at a Johnson Club meeting, I feel sure it did. You were perhaps less pithy than old Powell, who myopically read out the names, *sans phrase*, and omitted that of his own guest.

P.S. I say, Rupert, *dare* I tell you? Yes I will; you said I was to. An odd but very strong taste of mine is books about large wild animals, and in your list I see Muldoon's *Leopards in the Night* and my mouth waters. To which your *right* answer should be. 'Your mouth can go to hell and you with it.' But you won't. What you *can* do is to look away and be silent as if I had said something unforgivably indecent —which I have!

12 January 1957   *Bromsden Farm*

I don't think of you as a 'josser', though I love the word: one degree less opprobrious than 'buffer', do you think? The long-delayed Carter volume will positively go off to you next week—also *Leopards in the Night*, if it isn't out of print. If it is, its successor, *The Trumpeting Herd*, will follow in due course. Fancy your being such an ardent carnivoro-phil—at last a taste we don't share!

The new Prime Minister[1] I greet with unqualified approval. Eton, Balliol, the Brigade of Guards *and* a Publisher! What more could one desire? Between the wars I served on various publishing committees with him and always admired his courage and common sense. In 1945 I very diffidently suggested to him that *faute de mieux* I should write the life of Hugh Walpole for him to publish (he was back in the firm

[1] Harold Macmillan.

39

then, being in Opposition) and he immediately and forcefully said: 'An excellent idea. I can't think of a better person to do it.' So my contract was signed by the future P.M., and my morale enormously enhanced. I first met him in 1927, when my sister and I stayed with the Richard Cavendishes at Holker. The only other members of the house-party I can remember were Lord Robert Cecil and old C.P. Scott of the *Manchester Guardian*. How I wish I had kept a diary—then and elsewhen.

I don't remember meeting the Le Gallienne poem before: the whole work must be sought out. It was not Godolphin Horne, but Lord Lundy:

> We had intended you to be
> The next Prime Minister but three:
> The stocks were sold; the Press was squared;
> The Middle Class was quite prepared.
> But as it is! . . . My language fails!
> Go out and govern New South Wales!

I did a lot of work on the Nonesuch Press collected volume of H.B.'s verse, and will look out for a copy for you, though it's hard to find, being a limited edition.

If you start listing the errors and misprints in Ervine's *Shaw*, you will wear your pencil down to a stub, but I enjoyed the book thoroughly—even as I was enjoying Laurence Irving's great tome until everything else broke in. Now goodness knows when I shall find time to finish it. The proofs of the Blunden poems came in last week, and I airmailed a set to the poet in Hong Kong, beseeching him to do the correcting. The indexes still have to be checked. It should be a lovely book: I'll send you a copy in June or so.

Today I cut down some large hazels with an axe, and the unwonted exercise has half-paralysed my arm. On the other hand I can begin to see why Mr Gladstone cut down trees whenever he had time: the action fulfils some primal instinct: do you agree? Now I must go to bed. More tree-felling, George Moore and letter-writing tomorrow.

I've felled some more trees, corrected some more George Moore, spent some time going through P. Fleming's proofs with him for the fourth time, read part of a manuscript (a biography of the Burnaby who rode to Khiva), slept for an hour by the fire (most enjoyable), and here I am again. The lecture at the Dickens Fellowship last Monday was a curious occasion. The Swedenborg Hall is a depressing *venue*—a grim room surrounded by long-dead, unknown and vilely painted Swedenborgians. Some sixty or so Dickensians turned up, mostly elderly and hard to rouse from apathy. The only person I knew was Angela Thirkell, whom I questioned about her Burne-Jones relations and Oscar Wilde. She was all smiling helpfulness. My introductory remarks made up in booming clarity for what they lacked in sense and preparation, and then Kathleen Tillotson spoke for well over an hour. Dickens's revisions in the various editions of *Sketches by Boz* were her theme, and very ably she handled it, quoting many amusing passages previously known only to the readers of *Bell's Life in London* in the early 1830s. But my chair was hard, and being cruelly exposed on the rostrum I was compelled to sit up and appear to be listening intently. 'Any Questions' produced the usual pin-drop silence, which I ended by asking a few myself. All was mercifully over by 9.30 (we got there at 6.45) and since Mrs T. refused all offers of refreshment I walked gratefully home to Oscar.

At the Lit. Soc. on Tuesday I sat between Donald Somervell and Harold Nicolson. The latter talked entertainingly about Swinburne's love of being beaten (if possible by muscular ladies), which he had learned from Gosse. Donald Somervell reminded me of Sydney Smith's saying: 'I had a wonderful dream last night. I dreamed there were thirty-nine Muses and only nine Articles.'

On Wednesday I went to a party in Robert Lutyens's studio for the unveiling of his recently painted portrait of my sister, which is a wonderful likeness. I spent most of the time talking to darling old Lady Emily. She is getting very old and frail, and I pray that her third and last book (now at the printers) will be published in time for her to enjoy it. Jonah and Evy were there, also my ex-wife Peggy and many other old friends. The news of Eden's resignation increased the jollity still further.

Two parcels on the breakfast table this morning, viz my new suit of clothes and John Carter's book—the latter obviously promising a great deal of pleasure, the former very little, because the only time *my* suits ever look nice and new is before I have worn them even once, and to open *this* parcel is on all fours with the sad little experience of a kindly butcher as he contemplates the happy piglet whose throat he is about to cut. That ironed and spotless tweediness in the box is full of reproach. You, I suspect, if not exactly dressy in your garden, somehow manage to give your shabbiness an aristocratic air. I shall never live down the Southwold vet telling my daughter that he had given a message for her to 'your man', who in fact was her father sawing wood. Did the chap expect me to saw in spats? J.C's book will on a rough reckoning give me about the 400th hour of enjoyment I have had from the firm of H-D. More really, because I often look again at books like the Cockerell letters, and the Moore, and the Newman— and of course *Hugh Walpole*, not from the firm. My brother Richard knows the P.M. quite well and thinks highly of him. But can *anyone* succeed as P.M. nowadays—times that are entirely revolutionary except (here) in the mere matter of bloodshed? But at least H.M. is sound in wind and limb. Grundisburgh has a firm belief that Eden has cancer, but like many other communities, it revels in what Mr Gladstone used to call the 'grubous'—a good blend of grim, gruesome, and gloom. I suppose that in history he will be relegated to that dim stratum where Perceval, Addington, Lord North and Co lie in dusty oblivion. And no doubt the archtwerp in Egypt finds no difficulty in convincing the simple-witted Arabs that it is *he* who brought Eden down.

Do you really tell me, Rupert, that you are not thrilled by lions and tigers and leopards and gorillas, or is it a relic of infantilism that I am? Jim Corbett's books are often looked into, and the page describing the appalling fury of the 'Bachelor of Powlgarh' tearing a tree to pieces about four yards away from J.C. flat on his face behind a prone trunk and eventually dragging himself away by his *toes*, still lying on his face, till he was out of earshot, and finding next day that the tiger, though silent for half-an-hour before J.C. dared to stir, *had* been there all the time—well that gives me more delicious shudders than any ghost story, or even Madame de la Rougierre in *Uncle Silas*.[1] A lion who carries in his mouth for four miles a dead buffalo, a gorilla who with *one* hand can pull seventeen men over in a tug-of-war, or, when vexed, grips a rifle-butt so tightly that it is *dented* by his finger-prints—well, as Faustus said, these things feed my soul. But I expect you, who face authors and Nancy Spains and such without blenching, do no doubt find lions and tigers very small beer.

Newman's writing is continuing to give me the deepest of all satisfactions—great thoughts, beautifully expressed, and springing from a manifestly great mind and character. What I *always* miss in B. Shaw is this feeling of *depth*. Churchill's speeches had it—echoes of great waters in the mainstream of English history and tradition—more than that, of *man's* history as he 'rolls darkling down the torrent of his fate'. I wish I could write. These metaphors roll and wallow about like cattle, but you see what I mean. I have just finished Ervine's great book, crammed, as you say, with misprints but vastly interesting. It leaves me with a greatly enhanced admiration for G.B.S's character and much less for his intellect. His toughness and patience and cheerfulness all the first half of his life were surely quite outstanding, as were his generosity and good temper. But I do find his pontifications maddening; so many even of the better ones are no more than emphatic and well-phrased half-truths. One of the oddest of St J.E's amusing kinks is his apparent belief that all Shaw's ladies were of outstanding beauty—a belief completely *bouleversé* by a page of pictures of the big four—*not* of course the enchanting Ellen Terry, and presumably Mrs Pat had plenty of allure. Curious, by the way, that both Mrs Shaw and Mrs Chesterton were allergic to conjugal intercourse. Not Mrs H.G. Wells apparently, but then, as one of his extra-mural women said, his body smelt like honey—which I find faintly repellent.

Fancy your meeting old C.P. Scott—did he strike you as formidable as many found him? I wonder what he would have said if N. Cardus, on the mat for writing 'from whence' instead of 'whence', had closed the interview by saying 'I will lift up mine eyes unto the hills from whence cometh my help'. It would have finished him no doubt.

[1] By Sheridan Le Fanu (1864).

Richard Cavendish. Was Lady Moyra there? Half a century ago she was the most attractive creature in mind and body and soul that I ever saw.

Thank you for your Lord Lundy correction: one should be accurate about these things. I had a pupil once who knew all B's cautionary tales by heart. Did they collect *every*thing of his, e.g. those tiny things about Lady Meyer etc and his inscriptions, some perhaps hardly printable, but I like:

> I am a sundial, and I make a botch
> Of what is done much better by a watch.

But the men of letters in the coming age will have no time for engaging trifles. More's the pity.

Tree-felling. Did I never tell you that it has always been a favourite exercise of mine, since the age of about fourteen, and even now I will on the smallest provocation fill my discourse with words like 'kelf', and 'spurning' and 'helve'. There is no exercise like it, though for the ageing the scythe is less exacting, the only trouble there being that unless you start young, you never get that razor-edge which makes the actual cutting ludicrously easy—just as there is nothing in carving but a really sharp knife—like your lady's ham-knife on that Sunday. My father was an expert with the axe, and indeed about trees altogether, and never could really forgive W.E.G. for being such a philistine about them; he only liked felling them and didn't do it very well. My father said you couldn't regard yourself as a really good axe-man if you could not 'throw' a tree to within a foot of where you wanted, without a rope. As to the scythe, a Cumberland mower cuts a swathe ten feet wide. The normal mower is perfectly pleased with one of six feet. I do about five (when in form). The oldest mower in Grundisburgh is ninety-six.

Where the devil is Swedenborg Hall? Those societies—Dickensians, Baconians, *Johnsonians* etc—are always dreary affairs. Do you remember how Henry James shuddered—in about a thousand words—when John Bailey asked him to address the English Association? The notion that creative literature, or indeed literature of any kind, could be in any way helped or profited by an association clearly seemed to him sheer indecency. Your Dickens evening sounds pretty grim. Have you ever known anything but a 'pin-drop' silence when questions are asked for? At the Ascham Society meetings at Eton the same sequence was always in evidence. After a minute or two, Broadbent would utter a complicated sound composed in equal proportions of a snore, a belch, and a groan. Toddy Vaughan then gallantly saved the tottering situation with a question which proved, instantly and without a peradventure, that he had been unconscious throughout the paper. But what did it matter? In those spacious days the refreshment afterwards was toothsome, various, and unstinted.

I really must stop. Thank you for the Sydney Smith dream. Arthur Benson used to have marvellous dreams, full of wild fun and monstrous and irrational cruelties, e.g. himself about to be beheaded or one of his colleagues actually being hanged, inside a sort of cupboard, whence came a horrid noise of bumping and kicking.

19 January 1957   *Bromsden Farm*

So glad you've got Carter at last. I'm hoping to send you the *Leopards* next week, though I still can't share your enthusiasm for those great beasts.

Eden's cancer is widely discussed in London too: poor man, I wish him no ill, though I doubt whether he'll be as clearly remembered as Perceval (murdered in the House) or Lord North (lost us America). Addington is nearer the mark. And how many people could instantly say who was P.M. at the time of the Battle of Waterloo?

Reverting to your passion for wild animals, have you ever read *Elephant Bill* and *Bandoola*? If not, I will unwillingly encourage your aberration by sending them along.

C.P. Scott, as I remember, struck me as an object of compassion rather than awe. He was old, and his great qualities, unknown to me, were not immediately apparent in that huge rich house. Lady Moyra was a brisk and managing hostess, Lord Richard a dear old round-faced sheepdog.

Yes, the Nonesuch volume included all Belloc's printable verses, including many never printed before. I have often longed to assemble his unprintable ones, which are now available only in the memory of his friends. Did I tell you (I fear I did) of the time at luncheon at Duff's when he quoted his parody of A.E. Housman? It began:

> When I was one-and-fifty
> I found him at it still.
> His eye was just as shifty,
> He made me just as ill.

But how did it go on?

Yesterday I scrambled the George Moore letters off to the printer, but I fear the proofs will need some attention. Old Sydney Cockerell (he's dead but he won't lie down) has sent me a large bundle of letters between himself and my beloved Viola Meynell, who died the other day. They are naturally most moving and interesting to me—but to others? I simply don't know. And all the time Oscar is waiting for his annotation. For one short footnote one may easily write several letters and spend hours (albeit enjoyable ones) looking things up. P. Fleming left for Canada to-day after giving me a parting pheasant. If you read his piece in the current *Spectator*[1] you will learn of *some* of my difficulties with his proofs. My military son has sent us a letter of twenty-three quarto pages, describing goose-shooting on the Baltic. After standing waist-deep in liquid and icy mud for four days he brought down *nine* geese and drove back to Düsseldorf exulting. I've never much cared for goose anyhow.

Sunday, 20 January

I can't remember whether you take both Sunday papers. If so you will have been amused by the two reviews of *Newman*: Raymond all for N but against this book, Toynbee all for this book but against N. Oh well, reviews almost always cancel each other out neatly, but since we also got Harold Nicolson on *Margaret the First* (would you like her?) I can't complain of the amount of space, which at advertising rates would have cost the best part of £500.

The tree-felling is over, and two big bonfires have consumed all but the log-worthy stems. My brick path, which should be finished next week, has lately developed a strange curve, but I tell them they're

[1] 'A Goldfish's Farewell to his Bowl', reprinted in P.F.'s *The Gower Street Poltergeist* (1958).

lucky to get any path at all. Adam is preparing for his first half at Coleridge's and seems quite unperturbed. Next Thursday I have to preside over a 'Literary Brains Trust' at Rossall, whose exact locality I failed to look up before idiotically accepting the invitation. Hours in the train, a sherry-party in the Headmaster's study, a dinner in Blackpool, a sleepless night, more hours in the train—you shall have all the grizzly details next week. By contrast, last Monday–Tuesday I spent a delightful twenty-four hours at Brighton, visiting a friend who was recuperating there. I have always loved the place and felt well there: also its air contains a delicious feeling of truancy, for when I was a boy I was constantly ill and my mother always took me to Brighton to recover. As I forced my pennies into the slot-machines on the pier I rejoiced at not being at school. Even to-day that feeling persists, lending an extra zest to what is agreeable enough in itself. We sniffed the icy ozone, ate excellent meals, saw a rattling good film (*The Battle of the River Plate*) and made an exhaustive tour of the secondhand bookshops, of which there are a delightful number. I bought a dozen books and returned reluctantly to Soho Square, where the air is loud and dusty with the adjacent demolitions. I dined out on Tuesday, Wednesday and Thursday, all quite enjoyable, but when am I to do my Wilde editing? Sometime in February I shall go on a fruit diet for a week (my weight is steadily mounting), which means that I *have* to stay in all the time, since the sight of others eating is unbearable. *Then*, perhaps, I shall get some work done. What am I reading, you ask? Proofs and manuscripts and detective stories and Lily Langtry's memoirs (of great Wilde interest). The great Irving tome is still unfinished, chiefly because it's too large to carry about or read comfortably in bed.

24 January 1957   *Grundisburgh*

The *Leopards* have arrived—what is the collective noun, a 'slink', or perhaps a 'cruelty', though I think that is bagged for cormorants or something—bless them and you. They will accompany me to bed to-night and I shall dream of one coming at me 'like a torpedo', though covered with blood. You clearly regard my taste for them with tolerant derision, as if I still retained a taste for scooters or tin soldiers; but I stoutly counter-attack, and say that your indifference to the 'fearful symmetry' of a tiger and its 'deadly terror' is to me so odd as to be classified among the anfractuosities of the human mind, and if that doesn't abash you, nothing will. I am sure Peter Fleming will be with me, but alas he is far away on the billow. But I may be wrong. I remember a passage in one of his books in which he derided the crocodile's formidability and left the reader with the impression that there is little to choose between it and a tortoise, or some other beast which is usually asleep and very slow to anger or action when woken up. I have got *Elephant Bill*, a delightful book, but *Bandoola* is new to me.

Thank you for the Belloc quatrain. I wonder if Housman knew that parody of him by your uncle; he rather enjoyed them, and always said that the best was Hugh Kingsmill's 'What still alive at twenty-two, A fine upstanding lad like you?'

The Ascham Society often entertained a visitor, but one might easily have found himself in for a grim evening, e.g. Broadbent on Beddoes, or old Chitty on Anselm, or Toddy Vaughan on Poggio which extended over two sittings. Arthur Benson was secretary then and there is a pencilled word 'closure?' in the minute-book when he consulted Luxmoore as to what was to be done. L., who had early school the next morning, sternly nodded. Ram told me that the paper began with so long a passage in Greek that the members, convinced that the whole paper was to be in Greek, fell into helpless laughter. However, after six minutes or so Toddy stopped, looked severely round and said 'So wrote Plato'.

Your tale of your son among the geese is good, ending with your delightful anticlimactic-paternal comment 'I never much cared for goose anyhow', but you cannot conceal your pride in a son who spends four days up to the waist in mud and then writes twenty-three pages on it. Have all H-D's this unresting energy?

I only see the *Sunday Times* and of course read R. Mortimer on Newman. Like many of us, he clearly feels, when reading a vol of selections, that he could have chosen better. But I am not well enough up in Newman to agree or dis- in this matter. I found some of *The Idea of a University* rather hard going, but at such times I remember

Carlyle's contemptuous comparison of some man who decried Goethe to him, who 'complained of the sun because it would not light his cigar'. But one can always skip. Were N's letters so good? I have never heard or read of anyone else saying so, but perhaps they have. Why does Toynbee dislike N.? He had an unchristian temper, and I suppose a good deal of the Socratic capacity for making the worse appear the better cause, but somehow he is one of those who are outside the reach of our superficial, *prima facie* judgments, and he often said things which hit one, if I may coarsely say so, plumb in the wind. And it is worth remembering, but I hesitate to say with what feelings, that D.H. Lawrence called 'Lead Kindly Light' and 'Abide with Me' 'sentimental messes' as compared with what he called 'healthy hymns', viz 'Fight the Good Fight', which is to put *Marmion* above the Nightingale ode. Why must our geniuses so often be patently and infuriatingly *asinine?* Old Shaw and his alphabet for instance. Anyway it looks as if the sum of money at issue will all be wasted (or, as the solicitor corrected it, 'absorbed') in the costs.

I have just had a bit of luck—turned off a lot of muck from English stations and tried a foreign one and *at once* they began to play Bach's Air for the G. string, than which—to use the favourite ecstatic aposiopesis invented by Mrs Gladstone or her sister. And another bit of luck yesterday (this letter is ending like the majestic river Oxus, and is now 'shorn and parcell'd') I picked up a book by Margaret Mead—not at all a favourite author of Mrs Boffin's—and found among the bibliography 'A Study of the Pelvic Type' by *Ruth Christian Twaddle.*

Saturday night, 26 January 1957   *Bromsden Farm*

To-day I write triumphantly, for my brick path is at last completed! My daughter (who is home for the week-end) says it looks like a switchback railway, but Comfort, delighted and astonished that I should have accomplished anything so useful, is full of praise. Oscar Wilde has suffered of course: I must push on with him tomorrow.

The Housman parody was by Belloc, not Duff. My syntax must be at fault. Not that Duff couldn't turn a pretty set of verses when the mood was on him. One of the weeklies set as a competition a sonnet to be called 'On first hearing that Wordsworth had had an illegitimate child', the first line to be 'Byron! thou should'st be living at this hour.' Duff won it with this spirited entry:

Byron! thou should'st be living at this hour,
    We need thy verse, thy venom and thy wit
    To castigate the ancient hypocrite.
We need thy pith, thy passion and thy power—
How often did that prim old face turn sour
    Even at the mention of thy honoured name,
    How oft those prudish lips have muttered 'shame'
In jealous envy of thy golden lyre.
In words worth reading hadst thou told the tale
    Of what the lakeland bard was really at
When on those long excursions he set sail.
    For now there echoes through his tedious chat
Another voice, the third, a phantom wail
    Or peevish prattle of a bastard brat.

Not bad for an amateur, I should say.

Oh yes, another of my books has just been chosen by the Book Society—Vincent Cronin's new book, which comes out in April.[1] You shall have it when it's ready—a lovely book. We should now sell 30,000 copies instead of 6000—a great help to the firm, and to the author, who is an altogether admirable and charming person. How satisfactory it is—and how rare—when the prizes go to the right people! Since P. Fleming's book is also due in April, we shall have our hands full just then.

Sunday night, 27 January

Last week was exhausting. On Monday I dined with the Selwyn Jepsons in Bayswater and worked till 11.30 on Max Beerbohm's letters to Reggie Turner, which they own and I am to publish. On Tuesday I lunched most agreeably with Peggy, my ex-wife, at Wheeler's excellent fish restaurant in Old Compton Street: do you know it? That night I attended a disastrous dinner of my bibliographical dining club at the

[1] *The Last Migration.*

Garrick. Carter, who pretty well runs it, had run into Roger F. and asked him to come as a guest. The general rule is that there are no guests, except on occasional Guest Nights or by general agreement. Roger was, I think, unaware of this, and the slight *gêne* caused by Carter's solecism would soon have evaporated, had not *two* members, quite separately, *arrived* heavily inebriated. Michael Sadleir, poor lamb, is I fear in constant pain from cancer or some such and drinks to dull the pain: most pardonable but not conducive to good conversation. The other, a bookseller you wouldn't know, was sullenly aggressive and in his studied but only partially coherent rudeness to one after another of his fellows a seething mass of Non-U inferiority was quickly apparent. I managed to insulate Roger between Carter and Sparrow, but the rest of the round table was hideous. If Carter hadn't made the mistake of putting us in the big coffee-room instead of our usual private room, we might have been able to cope better with the situation; as it was the dinner dragged interminably, and I slipped away as quickly as possible, swearing 'never again'.

On Thursday morning, as I was boarding the train for Preston I saw Roger, and after lunch walked along and talked to him and Sybil, whom before I had seen only for a moment at Paddington. I liked her so much, and we had a delightful gossip. I was travelling First at W.H. Smith's expense, in company with their two publicity managers and my fellow-Brainstrusters, Dilys Powell, John Connell, and Hugh Ross Williamson—all very friendly and easy. At Blackpool, where we were lodged in an excellent hotel, we were joined by Frank Singleton, an old friend who edits the *Bolton Evening News*. Rossall is three miles along the front: luckily the H.M. was out of action with a slipped disc and it was raining so hard that we were let off a full tour of the school. After tea and drinks we faced 650 boys in Big School. They had prepared the best set of questions I've met and seemed to enjoy it all. The B.B.C. were everywhere recording, and half an hour of the programme is to be broadcast: I'll let you know when if they tell me. Then a six-course dinner, with appropriate wines, at the hotel. I sat between the School Chaplain and the Second Master's wife, both very nice. To bed exhausted at 1 am, and up in time to catch the 8 am train back. Dilys typed her *Sunday Times* film article all the way back while Hugh R.W. and I gossiped. I really must stop wasting time so frivolously. They pay fifteen guineas and all expenses, but the wear-and-tear alone comes to more than that. Goodbye till next week.

I enjoyed the *Leopards*, as I knew I would. Muldoon doesn't, I imagine, know quite as much about them as Jim Corbett did, and his were mostly not so much man-eaters as cattle-eaters. Both had very narrow shaves, as no doubt anyone doing that job must have. The great Selous's advice to elephant-hunters was 'get *one* and be content, for elephant-hunting, if continued, must end in the hunter's death.' Two days ago I found myself at a film, *The Slave Girl*, a tale of ancient Babylon. Superb pictures (technicolor) of buildings and Assyrian dresses, armour, etc and a magnificently impossible story. The hero was shot a good many times through the heart, and tortured, and surrounded by scores of men thirsting for his blood; he leapt into a pool full of the largest crocodiles, wrestled successfully with two of them, and slit their throats. The heroine (whom everybody would call Semi-Rammis) was burnt at the stake but rescued just in time. The villain of course, after hitting the hero's sword, and having his own hit (no one but Lewis Waller ever made a stage-fight look convincing) was pushed into the crocodile-pool and they took—in every sense—tea with him. It was glorious rubbish but I enjoyed it.

I like your uncle's poem 'Byron! thou should'st' etc. As do so many, he strongly disliked the man Wordsworth, who must have been uniquely dried-up, stiff, dull, self-satisfied, arrogant, but at his poetic best—Who was it said 'He stumps along by your side, an old bore in a brown coat, and suddenly he goes up and you find that your companion is an angel', i.e. is at home in a region where Byron saw only George III and Southey having their legs pulled. I see the latest Byron book puts everything down to B having been a homosexual. But haven't we always known he was, remembering his own description of his feelings at school about Lord Clare? He must have been grand fun in company when not showing off, or on the defensive. Poor B., we must always remember he was a Harrovian.

I say, your bibliographical dinner! Is dear John Carter a bit arbitrary sometimes? I suspect he might be, like many another good man of strong character who has been strikingly successful. An odd co-incidence that when your letter arrived, one of my bedside books was M. Sadleir's *Fanny by Gaslight* which I greatly enjoyed. I suppose *Esther Waters* started that genre?

I am glad you met Sibell Fulford, Pamela's favourite sister, but her large heart holds all of them. I expect you know S's last husband was my brother Caryl who died in 1931. Their boy—particularly promising—was killed at Anzio, not many yards away from Humphrey.

3 February 1957   *Bromsden Farm*

I fear you won't get your double letter to-day. Last Thursday I was walking briskly down Frith Street, on my way to the Beefsteak Club to lunch with the head of Scotland Yard (R.L. Jackson—perhaps you remember him—a huge boxer at Piggy Hill's—incidentally he never turned up for lunch, but that is beside what little point there is). The pavement was wet, I slipped on a thin film of dog's mess, and fell heavily forward, grazing and bruising one leg nastily. I don't need to tell you how heavily large men can fall: I was momentarily stunned, and had to be helped up by passers-by. Apart from a sore and stiff leg I suffered no ill-effects until yesterday (Saturday) morning, when (*post*, but I can scarcely think *propter*, *hoc*) I woke with a temperature of 101.4. Struggling up I spent the day muzzily by the library fire, and after a good sweat last night achieved subnormality this morning. Tonight I am feverish again: no other symptoms: it's all very mys-terious: but you will understand why my usual plan of correspondence has gone awry, together with most of the work I brought down with me. I shall go up to London tomorrow, come what may. Not having had a temperature for *years*, I feel outraged.

Yes, Carter is a bit arbitrary at times, though I'm very fond of him. How delicately you corrected my misspelling of Sibell, bless you. Now I shall know!

Don't get up till your temperature is what it should be. My nephew Charles was tempted by a fine day to go and play golf too soon. Result six or eight months in South Africa to save his lungs. It is true that it was pneumonia that he was convalescing from, but the moral is the same. You are right about big men falling. Old Gladstone of course had a theory—rather like his thirty-two chewings of every mouthful —that to avert shock after a fall, one should remain some time *in situ*. So more than once passers-by were rewarded by the sight of a venerable statesman prone in the gutter, and returned home more than ever convinced that the G.O.M. was insane. But how dull it would be if great men had no foibles, like Barham writing *The Ingoldsby Legends* with a cat on each shoulder, or Dumas putting on woollen socks whenever he had a love-scene to write, or Johnson touching every lamp-post he passed.

By the way I have just been re-reading the *Lives of the Poets*. How full they are of good things! Anything approaching the nonsensical always evoked some delightfully weighty irony. When someone timorously suggested that *The Beggars' Opera* would encourage crime they were put in their place with: 'Highwaymen and housebreakers seldom frequent the playhouse, or mingle in any elegant diversion; nor is it possible for anyone to imagine that he may rob with safety because he sees Macheath reprieved upon the stage.' That should do much to restore your temperature.

My daughter Diana, let me tell you—though it won't interest you at all—is engaged to be married—to one Alexander Hood who moves in high circles among government officials and is a very good fellow. He is forty-two and she is thirty-seven next week and all seems just as it should be. The news is being broken to the Queen[1] at just about this moment and will appear in *The Times* on Saturday, being till then one of those secrets that about 150 people are well aware of. She will have a good life, travelling from time to time all over the world. He is a descendant of the great admiral, and Pamela was pleased to find in the *D.N.B.* that *he* owed his initial rise in the Navy to 'his friendship with the Lytteltons and Grenvilles'. She read no further, being daunted by

[1] Diana was working as Press Secretary in Buckingham Palace.

the extreme dryness of the author's English. Old Leslie Stephen's motto for contributors, 'No flowers', was often interpreted by them to mean 'Nothing but potatoes and cabbages'. They are less austere now I fancy.

10 February 1957   *Bromsden Farm*

I'm happy to say that my fever of last week-end vanished as suddenly and mysteriously as it came—some sort of safety-valve to make me rest a little, perhaps.

Yes, the *Lives of the Poets* are superb, and once again your words make me long for the leisure to re-read such splendid stuff. 'By the common sense of readers uncorrupted with literary prejudices, after all the refinements of subtlety and the dogmatism of learning, must be finally decided all claim to poetical honours.' Them's my sentiments, and yours too, I know. My beloved Edmund B. knows chunks of this book (as of most others) by heart, and is fond of quoting, as though it applied to himself (I copy for the pleasure of it):

> His morals were pure, and his opinions pious: in a long continuance of poverty, and long habits of dissipation, it cannot be expected that any character should be exactly uniform. There is a degree of want by which the freedom of agency is almost destroyed; and long association with fortuitous companions will at last relax the strictures of truth, and abate the fervour of sincerity. That this man, wise and virtuous as he was, passed always unentangled through the snares of life, it would be prejudice and temerity to affirm; but it may be said that at least he preserved the source of action unpolluted, that his principles were never shaken, that his distinctions of right and wrong were never confounded, and that his faults had nothing of malignity or design, but proceeded from some unexpected pressure, or casual temptation.

That's the stuff! What an epitaph! And how cunningly I pretend to write you long letters which are mostly copied out of books!

I read admiringly yesterday of Diana's engagement: your quiver of grandchildren will soon overflow. When is the wedding?

55

My soldier son returns to civilian life in about a week's time, and I'm hoping he'll feel in the mood for some active gardening. Oh yes— I read a nice remark the other day, a boy's apology for not returning a book to the School Library: 'Awfully sorry, sir, but I was waiting for it to dry off.' Last week I went to a small party given by a young author of mine called Michael Alexander, at which were gathered four of the most beautiful girls I've ever seen. Mostly 'models', it transpired, and aggressively illiterate.

I spent one afternoon in the London Library, happily compiling footnotes for Oscar Wilde. I met Rose Macaulay in the stacks, gropingly seeking the Theology section. 'You'll find yourself alone there,' I said. 'Yes', she answered; 'I always do.' And yet once I dare say that section was besieged by bearded scholars and earnest doubters. I am supposed to hand in a review of eight detective stories by tomorrow, but I've read only six and a half, so they'll have to wait a day or two. This afternoon I read in manuscript a new novel by another of my young hopefuls. It's no good at all, but I felt bound to read it all before telling him what's wrong with it—which is pretty well everything. That's how my time is spent, you see.

It's ten years this month since my firm published its first book (*Fourteen Stories* by Henry James) and the occasion gives me pause. Altogether I've published 310 books, including quite a few that I regret. Was it worth all that sweat? I suppose so, though if I could afford to, I'd pack up publishing tomorrow and just be a freelance literary bloke. As it is . . .?

When I at last met my friend Jackson, head of the C.I.D., last week he told me he'd recently met his old tutor Piggy Hill, who greeted him with the words: 'Hullo, Jackson, I understood you were dead.' Characteristic, I should say. There can't be so many eccentrics among Eton beaks in this egalitarian day. My second-half Adam has been asked to play chess for the School! Fred rightly forbade it, since the match was scheduled to last four hours.

Very glad to hear you are well again. I expect, as you say, that it was a sort of safety-valve. I was interested to read that old Shaw had severe periodical headaches all his ninety-four years. Let us charitably assume that they were responsible for some of his pronouncements.

I am pleased to hear of this further feather in E. Blunden's cap, viz that he knows Johnson's *Lives* so well; and thank *you* for your quotation 'His morals were pure' etc. *Who* is being so majestically dealt with? It must be someone I have not yet re-read; I am mainly browsing among the Sprats and Garths and Blackmores, not, so to speak, tackling the whales—Milton, Dryden, Pope. Do you, or does E.B., know the place in the 'Milton' where the Doctor splits an infinitive? The passage you quote would be a very good example to show the difference between the pompous and the powerful and precise—'long associations with fortuitous companions will at last relax the strictness of truth and abate the fervour of sincerity'. Every single word pulls its weight—which makes it all the more surprising that he wrote that Blackmore's prose was 'languid, sluggish, and lifeless' and that Shenstone's landscape gardening might seem absurd to 'a surly and sullen' spectator. But perhaps the adjectives have shed some of their associations over the years.

I say, Rupert! The Literary Society![1] And your *wicked* cutting away of *all* my just misgivings! Won't all Cuthbert H's acidities ('What's *he* ever done to be a member?') be abundantly justified? Though I grant you I feel the honour as much, every bit, as the misgivings. Let me be flanked by you and Bernard F. and dear Tim N. at any rate at first. Though I am bound to tell you, all my letters recently from Sir Cuthbert about his brother Maurice have been particularly gracious.

Pamela and I met on Monday all or nearly all Diana's in-laws-to-be, and very pleasant they all seemed. It really does seem to be one of those arrangements in which it is hard to find a flaw—a remark to which I can hear the Doctor's ghost countering 'Depend upon it, Sir, the history of man shows that no such flawless felicity. . .'

You among the mannequins! What *do* you talk to such lovelies with their empty heads about? Themselves I suppose. Do they enjoy their

[1] George had been elected a member.

lives? Are their 'morals pure, their opinions pious'? And do they pass 'unentangled through the snares of life'? What is Rose Macaulay doing in the theological department? There are so many things to talk to you about. You must have begun publishing roughly when we came here, i.e. your life's work began as mine ended. I remember getting James's *Fourteen Stories* and enjoying them. And in the ten years you have made a big name of R.H-D in the publishing and literary world. I too wish you had time to write.

In the train yesterday I was *thrilled* by *Moonraker* by Ian Fleming. Is he any relation to Peter F? It is very well written, so perhaps he is. Are his other books good? The book I read on the going-up journey was *Paradise Lost*—the creation of the animals, Book VII. It is immense —'the river-horse and scaly crocodile,' 'the parsimonious emmet' etc. How right the Russian Moujik was who told Maurice Baring that he liked *P.L.* because 'it makes me laugh and cry'.

Yes, that is Piggy Hill all over. Grizel Hartley and a friend once called on him at Ledbury, and finding him out, left a note in which they apologised for pinching a 'pair of Worcester Pearmain' apples. Two days later she got a p.c. 'They weren't W.P's., they were James Grieves,' and nothing more. There are no more Piggy Hills at Eton. But let me tell you, in your day there were nothing like the great eccentrics of my day. So the smoothing and flattening-out goes on, and soon Eton beaks will be as indistinguishable from each other as ants.

17 February 1957   *Bromsden Farm*

Yesterday morning I began a week's thinning cure. This consists of drinking nothing, and eating only fresh fruit three times a day. One feels alternately blown out and hollow, also feeble and ratty, but it worked when I did it before, and I hope to lose a stone. The one thing that becomes intolerable is to see others eat, so I have thankfully refused all invitations for the week, and hope to do a lot of work. Inevitably one becomes, for the time, obsessed by weights and measures, but at least I am not paying fourteen guineas a week, as at Tring for orange-juice. I'll report results next week.

I'm so happy at your joining the Lit. Soc. It wasn't even necessary to rig the voting. I don't say I would have done so, but I very easily could have. As it was, you romped home top of the poll. The others elected were Alan Moorehead and John Piper. There were six candidates for the three vacancies. As you will see, the electoral system is more complicated than the Papal one, and takes far longer. I fear that at your first appearance you will be bidden to sit next to the President, but thereafter I shall shanghai you to my end of the table. Last week's dinner brought Cuthbert to my side, with Ivor Brown on my other. After a few introductory prophecies of six weeks' hard frost Cuthbert mellowed considerably, and with a mixture of flattery and teasing I managed to keep him jolly until, when it was time for him to leave, he discovered we were thirteen, and refused to move until everybody rose together. Since half the members were out in the lavatory, this took some time to arrange, and in the meanwhile Cuthbert (looking himself like death slightly warmed up) told me of all the people he knew who had died through defying the superstition.

I rejoice in having found a scrap of Johnson which pleased you anew. It refers to William Collins, of whose works E.B. edited the best edition. Did I tell you that he (E.B.) is coming home in May for a six-months holiday with all his family? Goodness knows where they'll find to stay.

How splendid that you enjoyed *Moonraker*. Ian is Peter's younger brother—one year younger—and a most engaging character, though quite different from Peter. His other books are good too, though the bridge-game in *Moonraker* is his high spot so far. Originally he was in Reuter's, then a stockbroker, then in Naval Intelligence, now Foreign News Editor of the Kemsley Press. He writes a good bit of the Atticus column in the *Sunday Times*.

Last Wednesday I attended a luncheon-party at the Ritz, given by the A.P. Herbert (Obscenity) Committee for Tony Lambton and Roy Jenkins, who are going to try and get a second reading for our Bill on March 29. Six of us are going to watch from the Strangers' Gallery. After lunch I went on to the Royal Literary Fund, where, during the interminable reading of the minutes, I gossiped with Frank Swinnerton by writing notes on the back of the order paper, like boys in school. That evening I went to *At the Drop of a Hat*, an entertainment given by two men, one of them in a wheel-chair. I can't remember when I laughed so much. During one turn, an imitation of a tennis-umpire at Wimbledon, I became almost hysterical. Do go to it if you have a chance: I know you'd love it.

Tomorrow my elder son returns to civilian life, with two years' accumulation of kit, and I fear an overdraft at the bank. He has just spent a week-end in Berlin and reports that in the East Zone a gramophone record which here costs 37/6 can be bought for 4/6. My daughter reports from Wales that the latest trade-name (among Evans the Hearse, Dai the Pub, etc) is the Hire Purchase agent, who is known as Trevor the Never. More hot news next week.

21 February 1957   *Grundisburgh*

The last man I knew who took a thinning cure had a curious experience. He weighed 19 stone 10 lbs and for one exact year he ate and drank nothing *at all* that had a particle of fat in it. He kept up what he admitted was an intolerably severe régime, and on the 365th day he weighed himself again. The answer was 19 stone 11 lbs. So he went angrily and thankfully back to porridge and ham and 'cheese remmykin', and was quite happy for a year or two before passing out very much in the same way as old Heythorp did. On the other hand I used to find taking off a stone or so in the summer holidays quite easy. In doctors' jargon I have, or had, a very rapid metabolism—which cuts both ways. The sylph who faced a new division in Sept was the Boniface of December. What was unbearable (as you say) was to see Marsden breakfasting on porridge, sausages, cold ham, buttered toast *ad lib*, and continue positively stylitic.

The Lit. Soc. prospect fills me with pleasure, mingled with diffidence on realising the intellectual distinction of my fellow-members. I am interested to see A.P.H.'s name *crossed out*. Is there a tale behind that? Did he assume that the Lit. Soc. shared the tastes of Sir Gerald Kelly? Tommy Lascelles, whether deliberately or not, achieved a master-stroke of tact in telling me that among the original members was poet-laureate Pye, of whom all I know is that he put into rhyme several episodes in my ancestor ('the good Lord')'s *History of Henry II*,

60

and of course Byron's 'Better to err with Pope than shine with Pye'. T.L's mention of him had the effect on me that, according to Miss Reynolds, Goldsmith's bow had on everyone in the room—it put them at their ease, because at least they knew they couldn't possibly make a worse bow than *that*. My excellent ex-pupil Bernard Fergusson has asked me to drink with him at White's and proceed thence and, thus fortified, to face Sir Cuthbert and Sir Malcolm and (I hope) Sir Terence. Any chance of *you* being there too—I mean at White's? Then I could face even his lordship of Dunsany with a cheer, as Browning did the unseen. I love your vignette of Sir Cuthbert refusing to rise till all the rest had, and retailing the fatal results he had known following thirteen at table. Why, in any case, should he mind, if he had been the first to rise? *Joie de vivre* is not a conspicuous element in his make-up. The picture of e.g. Roger hurriedly emerging from nether regions, hitching and buttoning, in order to restore Sir Cuthbert's peace of mind, is one I shall long treasure.

Confession is, they say, good for the soul. I *had* re-read the Life of Collins and—doltishly—not specially noticed the passage you quoted. I feel as foolish as I did last week when, standing at the bus-stop cross-roads, I signalled all clear to a van coming from Burgh into the Woodbridge-Tuddenham road at right-angles. A moment later there was a crash of ironmongery as a retired admiral in his Morris came down the W-T. road like a driven grouse. Do you know the feeling of not having the smallest vestige of leg to stand on? It is most unpleasant. The only ray of comfort I got was the sight of both of them reduced, if not to equanimity, at least to almost complete silence by my admission that the whole thing was entirely my *fault*. I too, like Hugh Walpole, have a strain of Mr Pooter in me.

Well, the Collins passage I did notice with particular pleasure was: 'A man doubtful of his dinner, or trembling at a creditor, is not much disposed to abstract meditation or remote enquiries.' Good but not as good as yours.

How right you are about that bridge game in *Moonraker*. Few know less about the game than I do, but it thrilled me. I.F. must be a devilishly clever fellow. All the scientific stuff in the book is at the very least immensely plausible. I must get hold of his other novels. I wonder why I never came across him at Eton.

I shall remember about *At the Drop of a Hat*. But the trouble is that I don't now *hear* in a theatre, unless I am very close. Usually humorous plays are the hardest to hear, as apparently all back-chat must go at the speed of a machine-gun, and it is too fast for me. Though, as the curate said, no one likes a bit of fun more than I do. (Do your family ever puncture you as mine do when they talk of some play or film and end by saying to me: 'It's frightfully good: you'd hate it, Father'?) And that can be said to me with perfect truth by practically all our leading critics, as you will realise when I tell you that I am very largely allergic to Jane Austen. I have been reading *Persuasion* on the last three evenings and often exclaiming how bad it is. Pamela, with that feminine commonsense which sees, and misses, so much, says 'Why do you read it if you hate it so much?' and is not at all convinced by my reply that it is because humility is almost the leading trait in a character of which thirty-eight years' experience should have shown her the beauty. Anyway, if your riposte is as indignant and contemptuous as I fully expect, my next letter will have plenty to say. At the moment all the 'demurrer' (legal) I can put in is to say *à la* Byron and Pye 'Better to err with Charlotte Brontë than shine with A.B. Walkley, Maugham, Cecil, and all those women who can't leave their idol alone'.

24 February 1957   *Bromsden Farm*

All is well. I am nine-and-a-half lbs lighter and have just consumed with relish a poached egg on spinach—my first hot food (or drink) for more than a week. I had hoped to achieve prodigies of work, but in fact felt too empty, feeble and *cold* to do very much except browse and sleep after a day in the office. My soldier son arrived back from Germany on Monday, went out to a party without the keys of the flat, and woke me in the small hours to let him in. To cheer me up, E.B. reports from Hong Kong: 'Sad to relate, on the menu tonight at Sea View I observed "Fried Prawns' Balls with vegetables $3.50" I could not explain my laugh to our Assistant Lecturer Miss M. Yee.' Don't you particularly like that 'Sad to relate'? I have written back saying I thought Nightingales' Tongues were the *ne plus ultra*, but clearly the East knows better.

A.P.H. only once attended a Lit. Soc. dinner. He sat next to Roger and never came again, or paid any subscription. How tiresome of Bernard to nobble you first. Never mind: I'll see you for a moment at the Garrick over our pre-prandial sherry, before Tommy nobbles you for dinner. I'll most certainly attend the Johnson Club on March 26 if you're going to be there. I shall probably bring a charming Canadian called George Whalley (a Professor, as they all are), who is an expert on Coleridge. You will certainly like him. What about a drink at Soho Square first? I'll try not to fuse the lights. Or perhaps the Garrick would be more convenient? As for your suggested Johnsonian recruits, Frank Swinnerton can seldom be coaxed from Cranleigh after dark; G.M. Young is, alas, gaga. He was a member for many years, and (goodness knows why) put me up for membership before he withdrew. Tillotson is already a member, D.B. Wyndham Lewis wouldn't get enough to drink, Charles Morgan is not frightfully clubbable. Jonah perhaps: is he an admirer of the Doctor? I must arrange for you to meet E.B. again when he's in England this summer.

You ask whether we disagree about anything. I think not, though I can't share your liking for books about large wild animals. Certainly I'm with you about Jane Austen, who has never been a great favourite of mine. But it's so long since I read her (except for one, of which more in a minute) that I'd like to try again with the cold eye of middle age before finally jumping down on your side of the fence. I see what so many other people see in her, but myself (tell it not in Bloomsbury) if I want to refresh myself in that period I prefer Scott. My uncle Duff adored her novels, and in the last week of his life, when he knew (consciously or subconsciously) that he hadn't long to live, he came to Soho Square on Christmas Eve, and, saying 'I've brought you a Christmas present: I hope you haven't got it already,' he pulled two slim volumes out of each pocket of his greatcoat. They were a first edition of *Northanger Abbey* and *Persuasion* (4 vols), in which he had written 'Old men forget but they are grateful when they remember'. I was much touched at the time, and when he died suddenly at sea on New Year's Day, the books became doubly precious, as his farewell gift. Later that year (1954), still moved by the same emotion, I re-read *Persuasion* in this copy, and persuaded myself (almost) that I shared Duff's admiration for it. But in truth I don't think I did. When, oh when, shall I have the leisure to try the others again and report fully to you?

Last week I had a brush with the Cabinet Office, who suddenly demanded changes in Fleming's introduction to *Invasion 1940*. Since Peter was (and still is) inaccessible in America, I rang up Sir Norman Brook, the head of the place and a very nice man with whom I had tricky dealings over both G.M. Young's *Baldwin* and Duff's *Old Men Forget*. To him I made a strong *ad misericordiam* appeal, explaining (truthfully) that 30,000 copies of the book were already printed, the author couldn't be reached, and his suggested alterations would involve me in hideous expense and untold delay. Audibly shaken, he said he would reconsider the question, and on Friday evening I got a note withdrawing all his demands. Phew! In fact I don't think he had a leg to stand on, but he's not the sort of person one particularly wants to make an enemy of.

All this week-end it has rained pitilessly, and I have gratefully stayed by the library fire, reading manuscripts. I'm in the middle of (a) Speaight's Life of Belloc, which is much better than I expected, (b) the new Michael Innes detective story, which is good uproarious fun. Charles Morgan's novel I have bought but not yet begun. On March 1st my George Moore proofs are due to begin arriving, and I shall have to shelve Oscar while I deal with them. What with those two, and Max B's letters to Reggie Turner, I shall be composing footnotes from now to Kingdom Come. Luckily I enjoy it, but time is always lacking. I envy you your leisure and your summer-house.

28 February 1957 (*Grundisburgh*)
At the moment
I am in Sloane Square
about to attend a meeting.

Your metabolism is in the championship class. Nine and a half pounds in, what is it, two weeks? I never managed speed of that kind. But doesn't that *cold* feeling mean that you are getting it off *too* quick? And I suspect February, even a mild one, is not the right month to start in. But I don't really know anything about it. The faculty itself is pretty feeble about diet—*quot medici tot sententiae.* Some years ago some ass started a campaign against spinach—full of oxalic acid, I think he said it was. Rubbish! It is almost my favourite vegetable, but a lot depends on the cooking. Swithin Forsyte, on his deathbed, was fretful about his cook not producing spinach equal to what he got at his club. How it pleases me to read that you relished a poached egg and spinach because I love it in spite of the sneers of so-called gourmets at the poached egg. Did I ever tell you that in the Hagley nursery each of us chose the dish for luncheon on his or her birthday. My choice was always mince and poached egg—and I like it just as much now. And if possible it should be followed by rice-pudding and rhubarb. I doubt if you will see eye to eye with me there. Of course if in the early Nineties we had known of fried prawns' balls I should have had to think again. I look forward to meeting E. Blunden again. Am I right in thinking he has some tie with Suffolk?

Yes, I too was hoping to drink with you before making my début, but Bernard F. was v. quick—and is such a good chap that I didn't see how I could refuse. And I *will* turn up at Soho Square on the 26th with great pleasure—or the Garrick, whichever you decide.

Your summary of the possible Johnsonian candidates I suggested is full of pathos—and humour too, alas—rather like Crabbe's Suffolk community, 'the moping idiot and the drunkard gay'.

Since my last, I have re-read *Mansfield Park.* It is much better than the insipid *Persuasion.* The Crawfords are interesting, and it is refreshing to find one of her snobbish dolls quite frankly committing adultery; but here again all the characters converse with exactly the same rounded amplitude which demands to be turned into Latin Prose. But some of the scenes and pictures are good. One sails along on smooth and shallow water under a mild blue sky. But I doubt whether I shall feel strong enough for *Emma.* It is very long. I shall have to keep all this *very* dark at the Lit. Soc. I am sure Ivor B., and Harold N. and many others are Janeites of the deepest dye. A sentence I treasure is one of Raymond Mortimer's: 'I am a great admirer of J.A. and therefore a little mad.'

I have with me—and am half through—*Lord Byron's Marriage.*[1] Immensely interesting. The highlight of it is of course the brilliant

[1] By G. Wilson Knight.

Don Leon poem of Colman's—very shocking and all that but as good as Pope *qua* skill. I imagine Lady B. was fairly bloody, and her family and advisers worse. Odd that B. should never for a moment have suspected that she and they might destroy his account of the whole affair, and so did not keep or safeguard a copy. Still, I suppose B. and marriage simply could not combine, whoever might have been his partner. The set-up reminds me of Henry James saying, when he heard Arthur Benson was to write the life of Rossetti for the English Men of Letters series. 'No, no, no, it won't do. *Dear* Arthur, we know just what he can, so beautifully, do, but no, oh no, this is to have the story of a purple man written by a white, or at the most, a pale green man.' I think I have it right; it came thirty or forty years ago from Percy Lubbock.

This will arrive on the same day as the G. Moore proofs and you will not find it so interesting, and you will be right, for I have just re-read it. Remember in mercy that yesterday afternoon I was at a meeting where the main topic was the operation of a sinking fund— which I always associate with sinking spirits. As a topic it is inferior even to *runts* (see Boswell).[1] I finish this at my club. The chairs round me are full of bodies. Some are alive, some not. We shan't know for certain till the rattle of tea-cups is heard.

P.S. I rather think Crabbe wrote 'The moping idiot and the *madman* gay'. Drunkard is better!

3 March 1957   *Bromsden Farm*

The English winter is worth living through if it ends with two such days as yesterday and to-day have been. I imagined you basking in your summer-house and pitying everyone else, though our front

[1] JOHNSON. 'Mrs. Thrale's mother said of me what flattered me much. A clergyman was complaining of want of society in the country where he lived; and said, "They talk of *runts*;" (that is, young cows). "Sir, (said Mrs. Salusbury,) Mr. Johnson would learn to talk of runts:" meaning that I was a man who would make the most of my situation, whatever it was.' He added, 'I think myself a very polite man.'

lawn was a delicious sun-trap and we happily lunched out there. The nine and a half lbs were lost in *one week*, and it *was* much too quick, and February is *not* the best month for such drastic treatment, but all is safely over, another one and a·half lbs lost last week, and I am slowly getting into training for next Saturday, when I am to attend a Feast at King's as the guest of Leslie Hotson. I shall stay Friday and Saturday nights with Madeline House (Humphry's widow) in Cambridge, and return to London on Sunday, in time (I hope) to write to you.

Like you, I always go for minced chicken and poached egg if it's on the menu: never lets you down, does it? I'm crazy about rhubarb too—and rice pudding.

E.B. has indeed a most sentimental tie with Suffolk. He lived there for some years when he was first married, in 1919 or thereabouts. It was during those years that he found all the John Clare manuscripts in Peterborough.

The Byron book sounds extremely interesting. Wilson Knight is a crackpot, but at times I daresay inspired, as so many crackpots are. Does he attempt to *prove* (1) that Colman wrote *Don Leon*: (2) that C. ever saw the famous memoirs? I must read it.

Henry James's remark about A.C.B. on Rossetti is superb, and new to me. If only Percy Lubbock would write his memoirs! A lot will be lost if he doesn't, but I fear he is too old and lazy. I always send him any H.J. books I publish, and he always writes most appreciative letters of thanks. It's more than twenty years since I saw him. Shall I write and suggest a book of recollections? I think I will.

I'm just finishing the Belloc biography. It's a most capable and painstaking work, though I could have done with a few more personal touches (gossip, if you like) at the expense of many pages about Distributism, Politics and the R.C. Church.

The George Moore proofs began to come in on Friday, and I have been through all I've received, delighted with the letters themselves but horrified to find how much still remains to be looked up, checked, cross-referenced and shuffled into shape. My list of notes looks like this:

(1) When exactly did Lady C's mother die?
(2) Did Consols drop to 80 in August 1907?

(3) Who was Harry Lynch?

(4) Is the place in Ireland New Grange or Newgrange?

(5) What and where was the Diploma Gallery (1922)?

And so on. I already (on perhaps a quarter of the book) have enough to keep me in the London Library for an afternoon, and Oscar will have to hang fire while I'm at it. Between interruptions that major work rumbles on. I am now annotating Part IV (of nine), which covers 1883–1890. I keep getting new letters (mostly from America) which have to be interpolated, and often entail a rearrangement of the notes, since each person, book, event or whatnot must be annotated on its *first* appearance. I'm sure when you read the finished book you'll agree that all this detailed work is worthwhile—at least I hope so.

Fleming is back from America, exhausted and with a heavy cold. He reports that Harold Caccia is doing splendidly in Washington, but is increasingly fed up with Dulles, and indeed with Eisenhower, who sees no-one except caddies and reads nothing but brief 'digests' of world news. He is, Peter says, now almost completely insulated from the world and its doings—which is pretty terrifying.

One of my few rules in life is never to refuse the offer of a bookcase, since I never can have enough, and next Friday a *huge* one is being delivered at Soho Square, where there isn't a square foot for it: all would be well if I wasn't guarding E.B.'s 7000 books there for him. They'll be with me at least till 1961.

6 March 1957   *Grundisburgh*

Again from the summer-house, but 'basking' is perhaps hardly *le mot juste*. The sky is the colour of a dead fish's belly, a deadly little breath from the East ('somebody's not using Amplex') is shedding that thin sad sort of rain that looks as if it was never going to stop. But a sweater, a muffler, and a rug enable me to despise its rather toothless moroseness, and a Haydn symphony puts the finishing touch to my equanimity—which in any case is at its height while I am writing to R.H-D.

I have finished the Byron book. Wilson Knight puts up a strong case, though apparently Lady B. still has her defenders, and like so many defenders they fly easily into temper. W.K. refers the reader to his article in the *Twentieth Century*, June 1956, for all the stuff about *Don Leon*. He thinks there is no doubt Colman wrote it; also that 'in all probability' C. had seen Byron's Memoirs (burnt). How prejudice does blind the critical judgment! Ethel Colburn Mayne dismisses *Don Leon* as 'little filthy brochures' telling of 'things unspeakable in villainous Alexandrines'. Well 'filthy' etc is a moral judgment, but as to villainous Alexandrines, (a) they are not Alexandrines and (b) they are frightfully skilful.

Do write to Percy Lubbock, insisting that he must write his memoirs. Of course he ought to. He knows more about Henry James than anyone, I should say. But he feels his years—though his eyes are much better; he writes with his own hand now—and never, I imagine, wrote easily. But he needn't write another *Earlham*; memoirs need not, should not, be so beautifully jewelled, or move with such grace (one really wants so many words to do it justice. Do you remember Keats's line 'Mid hush'd, cool rooted flowers, fragrant-eyed'? As some good man pointed out, he gets four out of the five senses into the line).

I am immensely interested in your remark about Desmond MacCarthy taking such trouble over his writing, because old Gow who had been pro-M. complained that his later reviews were 'shamefully idle'. The censure was mainly based on what he said was excessive quotation from the work reviewed. Gow can be hyper-critical, but he is not as bad as Housman—his idol and indeed model, who used to say things like that about E.V. Lucas, who had at one time attended H's lectures in London and so, said H., 'I am responsible for his education—in so far as he can be said to be educated.' I have heard G. describe someone as 'not a serious scholar,' because though the man could read Plato and Lucretius with feet on the fender he spent no time on emending some text which, when emended, no one could possibly want to read.

I have just got from the Library the Holmes-Pollock letters, as I greatly enjoyed the Holmes-Laski ones. But Sir John P. (whom I suspect to be an ass), who edited them, has left in far too many letters about legal cases which are simply caviare etc. I also suspect that his father (Second Classic and Seventeenth Wrangler, if you please) had a good deal of Dryasdust about him. *All* the good things I have noted so far come from old Holmes. I like: 'Whenever I read Shakespeare I am struck by the reflection how a few golden sentences will float a lot of quibble and drool for centuries, e.g. Beatrice and Benedick.' Not new of course but profoundly true, and crisply put. I am a poor Shakespearean, i.e. I am, like most, overwhelmed by the poetry, but so often bored by the absurd action of the play and the characters, and *always* by the wit. And if to be luke-warm about S. and J. Austen doesn't put one beyond the pale in the Lit. Soc. what will? Probably I ought to have made these confessions to you before you proposed me. Holmes quotes with approval a Frenchman's answer when he was asked if a gentleman must know Greek and Latin: 'No, but he must have forgotten them'. That was in 1892. In 1962 the answer will be 'I don't know what you mean by gentleman; as to G. and L. nobody should know them; to do so would argue that much time has been lost which should have been spent on liquid hydrogen or metal-stresses.'

I am delighted to hear about Harold Caccia—a very good man. What a sinister picture of Eisenhower—at the head of the greatest power in the world. Do you know Winston's latest—about U.S.A. bungling: 'It wouldn't have happened if Eisenhower had been alive'? I have to choose my audience for this; it wouldn't do at the Ipswich Club. The answer might so easily be on the lines of my daughters aged between seven and thirteen say, on about Jan. 4 when I said 'Brrrr! It might be midwinter.' 'But father, it *is* midwinter.' They fell into the trap all right but only once apiece.

17 March 1957   *Bromsden Farm*

No letter from you yesterday—but then you had nothing to answer, and perhaps the Lit. Soc. flattened you out. It was undoubtedly the best evening since I've been a member, and this I can attribute only to your presence. I'm glad you had Donald Somervell next to you: he's most friendly, amusing and agreeable. We were lucky to be spared both Cuthbert and Dunsany. My end of the table was very gay. Eric Linklater told me he recently bought in an Edinburgh junk-shop a fine painting on wood of an allegedly 48 lb salmon. Underneath was inscribed 'Caught by Colonel MacGregor in the Tay, 3 June 1880'. Eric had this removed, and substituted 'Caught by Private Angelo in the Po, 1 April 1943'. Thus adorned, the trophy now hangs in Eric's Scottish home.

My visit to Cambridge was most enjoyable. Saturday morning I spent 'doing' the secondhand bookshops, and in the evening I accompanied Leslie Hotson to the Feast at King's. First-class food and drink, and agreeable company. I had a few words with Arthur Waley and E.M. Forster. Afterwards the whole party, several hundred strong and well primed, was let loose in the Provost's Lodging, where Mrs Annan and five other ladies were dining. What lovely rooms they all are, and beautifully furnished. I got away soon after eleven, and woke unharmed next morning. Moreover, my weight yesterday morning was exactly the same as it had been a fortnight before!

I did write to Percy Lubbock, but so far he hasn't answered.

I am in the middle of reading the galley proofs of the George Moore letters; it is essential I should finish them tonight, the hour is almost eleven, and you must forgive a miserable half-measure this week.

My son's departure for West Africa has been advanced to next Wednesday. When he gets back (in June) he immediately starts for Canada. 'Youth and the sea! Glamour and the sea!'

Last Thursday I paid my second visit to the French actors. Edwige Feuillère is a dream. La Dame aux Camélias was great fun, and I enjoyed the comedies too, though the language was harder to follow. Next week she assaults the Everest of Phèdre, and I shall be there to cheer her on.

The destruction in Soho Square continues brutally, but there are flowers in the garden, and occasionally spring in the air. My youngest was eventually allowed to play chess for the School, but was defeated by an elderly lady in a basement off High Street Kensington! What next?

20 March 1957   Grundisburgh

No, I didn't write because up to the end of the week I was rather up to the neck after the meeting of a G.B. of which I am Chairman, at which the Headmistress could not be present, and I had to write a detailed and careful letter about the meeting, and the numerous questions her absence left unanswered. The carefulness was necessary as the gist of much of the letter was that she was in some matters behaving fat-headedly, and—*inter alia*—that a teacher of biology aged seventy-two, *all* of whose eight candidates failed in the G.C.E., might perhaps not be a wholly adequate teacher of biology. Another letter I had to write which did *not* take long was to congratulate an Old Girl on winning the fencing championship in the Olympic Games —one of the five—was it?—English gold medals.

Never have I enjoyed an evening more than that with the Lit. Soc. That blend of friendliness and intelligence which seemed to me the pervading atmosphere is very heartening. Yes, Donald Somervell is one of those who puts one quickly and completely at ease. Tommy Lascelles too was in 'merry pin,' if one may borrow from John Gilpin. I had a good crack—up to 11.45—with Ivor Brown. I liked him.

That is a good tale of Linklater and the fish. Had you no *serious* fisherman at your end of the table? Usually they are rather stiff about such tales. The one I like best (pity you can't stop me if you know it!) is Chauncey Depew's attempt to deflate the story of a gigantic fish described to him. 'Was it a whale, perhaps?' and got a cold look and a calm reply 'We wos baitin' with whales.' Once I charged the beloved Monty James with laughing heartily at a story which I knew he knew, and got the—for him—brusque reply: 'Why not? It is an excellent story, and I was delighted to be reminded of it.' I didn't dare counter with 'Remind, indeed! As if you ever needed reminding of anything you had ever heard or read!' Like the dog Rab, he had a look sometimes of 'thunder asleep but ready'—when e.g. he suspected meanness of any kind or lack of charity.

I am glad Cambridge and King's shewed a gracious face to you. I too thought the college had some very pleasant people in it. Percy Lubbock always (though he is very fond of him) says E.M. Forster is a disappointing conversationalist. Odd, because some of *Abinger Harvest* and *Two Cheers for Democracy* is first-rate talk. I wonder how you found him. Percy, by the way, took *weeks* to answer my Xmas letter, and said that for some time his disinclination to put pen to paper, or indeed do anything, had grown into positive nausea. I think he begins to feel really old sometimes. The way I think it will take *me* is that described by H.G.W. to Frank Swinnerton 'Perhaps that's what old age is, Swinny; a little slower, a little slower, and at last feeling triumphant at getting across a room. It's horrible.' And although old age, like death, has been described a million times, every man finds both full of surprises, nearly all unpleasant.

I am interested to read that Belloc put *Rasselas* at the top of English prose. I have just finished Speaight's Life. How badly, somehow, B. managed his life, mainly through not realising the truth of St Paul's statement that it is not always *convenient* to utter all the truth. I suppose he struck the Oxford pundits as a very brash young man, and sometimes, e.g. the Dreyfus affair, deliberately wrong-headed. Still, why call it *All* Souls if so much brilliance and character is inadmissible. But I don't really know the ins and outs. I took a volume of B's essays in the train and found most of them, alas, very thin—no hint of the rich fun and quality of Godolphin Horne and Co. But, as by now you must know, my literary taste is capricious, imperceptive, antiquated, ossified, you may well disagree. I remember, years ago, setting *The Eye-witness* for Private Business—Hastings, Armada, Waterloo, etc as told by one who took part, thinking they must be exactly what was wanted to stimulate interest. It was a flat failure; the boys thought the accounts were very insipid—and so did I! That last picture of B. with a beard gives a profoundly sad impression.

P.S. Your description of the French play is very appetising. Do you agree with J. Agate that by and large French acting is in a different class from English? One thing I always approve heartily is that any French player who is not heard in pit or gallery is greeted with shouts of '*Parlez*'. They insist on getting their money's worth.

Sorry your son lost his chess-match. Old Ram's uncle never lost a chess match, because, when defeat loomed, he accidentally knocked the table over, pleading a sudden attack of cramp. *Verb sap.* I believe the school chess cup is the largest at Eton, presented by some fanatic. Ram was a chess blue at Cambridge but his Oxford opponent beat him. 'He was better with his pawns than I was' was Ram's verdict in 1950. I always regarded pawns as encumbrances to my dashing sorties.

Once again it's past eleven p.m. and having just spent four and a half solid hours on the George Moore proofs I feel drained of all sense and sensibility. I keep thinking I've finished with that infernal book, but even now I'm short of one illustration and shall have to compile an index as soon as the page-proofs are ready. Poor old Oscar hasn't moved an inch for ages. By the way, do the words 'The forest is like a harp' ring any bell in your well-stocked memory? George Moore puts them in quotation-marks as though they came from somewhere. Shelley? or where?

I got a charming answer from Percy Lubbock: 'I am afraid it isn't likely that I shall ever be younger or brighter than I am—but if such a miracle *should* happen, I will remember your pleasant suggestion.' I fear that's the last we shall hear of the matter.

You're quite right about that fishing story of Linklater's. I told it to Arthur Ransome, a great fisherman, and I could see he was a little shocked.

Yes, I agree with Agate about French acting. *Phèdre* last week was most beautiful and impressive, though I wished I'd had time to re-read and absorb the play beforehand. Like Greek Tragedy, Racine should be known almost by heart, so that the subtleties of acting and phrasing can be relished.

My elder son is now on the high seas bound for Dakar. In a note from Liverpool he reported a comfortable cabin to himself and added: 'The officers hardly speak at all, and eat incredibly slowly, but they are all very well-meaning. The Captain is broad Scottish and awfully nice.'

Yesterday, in lovely hot sunshine, Comfort and I had our first trial of strength with the new motor-mower. Neither of us had ever operated one before, but we found it most satisfying and enjoyable, though we did more than we realised and are stiff and blistered today. Last night we dined gaily with the Osbert Lancasters, who live in Henley. Osbert and I went up to Oxford the same term in 1926, and he hasn't changed *at all*.

Don't you rather like this footnote: 'The remainder of this paragraph, which Coleridge wrote with his gout medicine instead of ink, has faded and is all but illegible'.

I must say our end of the table [at the Johnson Club], under the—
I am sure—approving eye of the Doctor, was very good fun. I was
delighted to find that Christopher Hollis really enjoyed himself and
expressed gratitude to me for getting him into the Club! Of course
he produced a good guest in Muggeridge. What riddles human beings
are! That kindly, civilised, understanding man under the same hat as
the spiky, unbalanced wrong-headed reviewer of Francis Williams's
history of the Press and pretending(?) that he prefers the *Mirror* and
Sketch to *The Times*, the *Observer*, the *M. Guardian*, and that the taste for
a nude bathing beauty and that for a *Times* Fourth Leader are on the
same level. First thought on meeting him 'What an excellent chap!'
First thought on reading his review 'What a Philistine!' But I suspect
he enjoys trailing his coat. I liked him very much.

That paper I believe really to have been a definitely good one. But
wasn't it dreadfully badly delivered? An intelligent Frenchman
doesn't read *his* language like that—any more than a French orator
would. Is it our native modesty? I sympathise with Arnold Bennett's
exasperation when an Englishman sat like a graven image through
Pavlova's swan dance till, near the end, a feather fell from her wing,
on which the Englishman said 'Moulting'. No other word passed his
lips.

What a nice young man your Canadian is; he got on swimmingly
with Roberts. I had a feeling that if in that delightful hour *chez vous*
the conversation had turned on modern poetry, my status as a country
bumpkin with hair full of hay-seed would have been even more firmly
established. I should not wonder to find that *Finnegans Wake* is an
open book to him. Meanwhile I fight a stout rearguard battle.

Yesterday my main contribution to the G.B. deliberations about
Woodbridge School was to have the word 'finalise' deleted from the
minutes and 'complete' put in its stead. I was supported by the local
archdeacon. The rest of them—sanitary inspectors, small builders,
shopkeepers, auctioneers—were apathetic, till I said it was 'bastard
American', when a prim shudder ran through the room and I realised,
too late, that the lady-secretary was present and her face was scarlet.
However 'finalise' *was* deleted.

I am in the summer-house surrounded by daffodils and my heart dances with them, and across the lawn is a cherry-tree in blossom, about which all I can say is what the historian of Solomon's reign said about the almug-tree, i.e. 'No such almug-trees were seen in the land' (which Monty James said was crossly interpolated by the scribe who was bored by the raptures being dictated to him). But of course every spring the earth's beauty is something new, never before seen. But how ludicrously brief it all is. Four or five days and the cherry-blossom one morning is merely white compared with its first days, for which there is no word. Daffodils do last longer, though not so long as I want them to. Few things do.

Dr Adams had a poorish day yesterday.[1] I don't see what his counsel can make of that Harley St Dr's evidence. I gathered in London that the conviction that he is guilty is widespread. Still *vox populi* is not always *vox Dei*, though it may some day be so regarded.

I am almost certain that line you ask about, 'The forest is like a harp', is in Shelley, but cannot place it. I shall have an exploration this evening; in fact I *have* just re-read *Prometheus*, and if anyone says it isn't tremendous, I shall have the greatest of pleasure in recommending their instant relegation to the nearest asylum. There was, by the way, one bright spot in Muggeridge's *New Statesman* article, where he indicated hatred and contempt for the man L--v-s.

31 March 1957   *Bromsden Farm*

Let us get one thing straightened out once and for all. I have been to far more dinners of the Johnson Club and the Lit. Soc. than you have, and I know, beyond, as they say, a peradventure, that it is *your* presence that makes these occasions *go*. So let us have no more pretence of its being to my credit—except in so far as I am stimulated to greater enjoyment by your being there. Incidentally, you had a tremendous success with George Whalley, who when I saw him again on Friday could talk of nothing but your wit and charm. No mention

[1] Dr Bodkin Adams was accused, and later acquitted, of hastening the death of some of his elderly female patients.

of S.C.R.'s conversation, or the speaker's dim delivery—just praise of G.W.L. So you see, I am not alone in my judgment!

I spent most of Friday in the Strangers' Gallery of the House of Commons, and though our Bill got its second reading, and we were given a good lunch at half-time, I was *appalled* at the abysmal level of speaking. Admittedly the big shots were absent, but we must have listened to twelve or fifteen speakers, on both sides of the House, and most were lamentable by any Eton House Debate standard. Goodness knows what made some of them choose politics as a profession. I can think of no more appalling punishment than to be compelled to listen to every so-called debate in the Chamber.

I adored your story of the Englishman watching Pavlova. I expect you saw her, but to me she is only a mythical bird, just as Nijinsky is a legendary faun. Actors—and even more dancers—can survive their last admirer only if they have been written about by a genius. Gordon Craig I consider a very phony genius, but his move-by-move description of Irving playing a scene from *The Bells* is immortal: do you know it?

I forgot to tell you that on Tuesday I had a most agreeable lunch with Jock Dent. We talked hard of Max and Agate, and books and the theatre. He is a charming fellow, but now I fear rather disappointed. Dramatic critic to the *News Chronicle* isn't much of a job in the public estimation, and his fortnightly cinema page in the *Illustrated London News* can be read only by people waiting to have their teeth out. Jock recently read through (or at any rate turned every page of) the first hundred years of the *Manchester Guardian* and he has kindly sent me a few references to Oscar which he had noted down. He can be extremely scholarly and assiduous when he's interested, and it seems a great pity he can't be harnessed to some solid literary or theatrical task.

Yes, most people seem to think Dr Adams guilty, but many believe he will get off: his counsel certainly seems very adroit. What else? On Thursday I went to see the Dean of St Paul's about putting up a memorial tablet to Duff Cooper in the Crypt. The Deanery is an exquisite house—red brick, 1690, Grinling Gibbons carving round the front door, full of pictures of old Deans—including one of the only two authentic portraits of John Donne. But of course it's much too big and cold for to-day, and I found the Dean very understandably recovering from a feverish chill. Previously I had met him only on committees, where he never speaks. At home he shyly talked about poetry and literature, in which he is obviously interested. He spoke at length of St John Ervine's Life of General Booth, and I must confess made me want to read it. Have you?

On Thursday night I dined with Reggie and Joyce Grenfell in their new flat in Elm Park Gardens—a gay and cosy evening. Have you ever seen or heard Joyce perform? She has just written another whole one-woman show which she is to give in the autumn.

My daughter has been home for the week-end, and luckily she is fascinated by the new motor-mower, so I was spared that this week, or rather liberated for other gardening activities, which have left me stiff and ready for bed. An old and dear writer-friend of mine has sent me the typescript of a 350-page novel about a juvenile delinquent in an Italian quarter of New York. I have struggled past page 100 and must somehow finish. But what *am* I to say to him? This sort of thing is the most painful of publishing hazards. You couldn't say the book was *bad*: it's just *dull*, and who on earth wants to read such stuff? By contrast, Ian Fleming's new thriller, *From Russia, with Love*, I got through in a flash. Put it down on your library list. Also the new Michael Innes, *Appleby Plays Chicken*. Or do you only get 'serious' books from the library?

4 April 1957   *Grundisburgh S.H.*
                                                          (summer-house)

I am not going to pretend that the first sentences in your letter did not give me great pleasure—nor would you believe me if I did. All I would say, as what I believe the lawyers call a 'demurrer', is that I can easily be as dull as Dulles in many companies. I read your opening sentence to Pamela; she was undoubtedly pleased, but I am not sure I did not detect in her attitude some tinge of resemblance to Hugh Walpole's vis-à-vis Wodehouse apropos of Belloc's eulogy.[1] But

---

[1] See *Hugh Walpole* by Rupert Hart-Davis, p. 403.

what wife of thirty-eight years' standing could ever see her husband as other than the humdrum old bore and egoist that he is? I always think Chesterton's crack one of his best: 'Every good wife will support her husband through thick and thin, though she is perfectly aware of the thickness of his head and the thinness of his excuses.'

I observe that the modern note is to be rather sniffy and patronising about G.K.C. Let them! He wrote much that was wise and much that was witty. I wonder if the anthology of him just come out is any good. I have again been reading in G. Tillotson's *Newman*—with a good deal of satisfaction, but with a growing feeling that he could have made it much better. Surely it is the sword-play of the *Apologia* and what led to it which is *now* the most interesting thing about it. It is all very well for Newman to deprecate the literary aspect of his own writing, but that is what appeals in 1957, not wire-drawn theological problems. What I like about *The Tamworth Reading Room* bit is the skill with which the argument and the language are handled. But as we saw ten days ago, these university professors don't think enough about their *audience*. We at Trinity in 1904 were lectured to by a very great philosopher who spoke throughout with his face turned to the wall. On the other hand Verrall was the last word in brilliance and fun—though what I chiefly remember is his crow of laughter when calling over the list of his pupils and finding that 'Shufflebotham' was followed at once by 'Sitwell'. Or probably I only remember being told that. He was what Joxer Daly would have called 'a lovely man'.

Percy Lubbock is not at all well—bronchial, cardiac, etc, can do nothing, even walk upstairs, sees no one, writes no letters. And I suspect he is rather a rebellious patient, especially as his wish to live is not very strong. I have known him for sixty-two years, i.e. longer than any non-relative. Who was the good man I met recently who shared my opinion of *Earlham*, i.e. as a book of almost unique beauty? It is about the only thing of importance I am quite sure of—much surer, that is, than I am of the existence of God or that a point has position but no magnitude. Though I quite see what Desmond MacCarthy meant when he said it would have been even better if now and then Percy had just let his narrative scamper along in any old words. I said—it was at the H.M's at dinner—'You mean one doesn't want all one's water filtered,' and D.M. looked at me as if thinking

'This chap isn't such a fool as hitherto I thought him' and said 'Yes; exactly.'

I am glad all goes well with Joyce and Reggie Grenfell (my old pupil). I have only met her once, and, like everybody else, liked her immensely. I particularly appreciated the cleverness with which she prevented dear Reggie from feeling and looking as does Mr Summerskill in the presence of Edith. Joyce must be almost of the calibre of Ruth Draper.

I note what you say of books to read. Do not think 'a God's name that I only read 'serious' books. I am fastidious about novels and thrillers, but love good ones, e.g. M. Innes. I ask weekly at the library for another Ian Fleming, but they are always out. There is some very succulent tasting in your Spring List; surely a winner or two among them. Does G.L. Watson come into the open on Housman, i.e. (need I say it?) as a homo? The emphasis on that side of humanity is really becoming alarming. This month's *Contemporary Review* has a review of a book on the negro problem in U.S.A. It contains the sentence 'Mr Furnas misses what is perhaps the deepest psychological reason for the tension in the South, the white man's fantasy that the negro has a bigger penis than the European male.' The author of the review is 'the grand-daughter of a slave now studying psychology at Bedford College'. I find the mental picture of her hurrying round the dormitories with a tape-measure faintly nauseating. On the other hand it is refreshing to picture Queen Victoria reading the *Contemporary Review* in Elysium.

I can see that these Lit. Soc. Tuesdays are going to interfere with our letter-writing if I don't look out. It would be absurd if you got this letter *after* our meeting, so I shall post it here tomorrow, and hope it will reach you in time.

I agree that Chesterton is greatly undervalued just now, though I am told that his first editions are much sought by collectors. Certainly time will winnow away a good deal of his minor work, but much will surely remain. I can't help pointing out that Joxer's phrase was 'a *darlin'* man', *not* 'a *lovely* man'. *What* a good play that was, and what a pity that O'Casey left Ireland and so cut himself off from his true source of material. But perhaps he'd already said all he had to say. Now he's just an ould grouch, doubtless the literary bully of the Totnes area, with a chip on his shoulder the size of the Nelson Column.

Gordon Craig's description of *The Bells* is in his book on Irving: I'll bring it up to lend you on Tuesday. Also the new Ian Fleming, if I get it back in time from another friend.

I am repeatedly amused by the Eton habit of writing all reports, except the Housemaster's, before the results of Trials are known. Both my boys are natural examinees and somewhat idle in class—which makes the reports on them amusing. For instance, Adam, after ending up *bottom* of D.2. got a Distinction in Trials, *and* the Trials Prize *and* Science Prize (ugh!) for Lower D—all this in his second half at Eton! Secretly I hope he will keep it up and be made O.S. as his brother was.[1]

Yesterday he came to London and I took him to a film called *Doctor at Large* (simple fun but no pain to sit through), followed by dinner at the Garrick, at which he knocked off a glass and a half of claret. To-day he has been delightedly working the motor-mower. Mercifully all three children love using it, but I foresee many summer weekends when none of them is here, and there's the best part of a day's work in the job. I have worked so much in the garden to-day that I have practically seized up in all limbs. Goodnight, more in the morning.

Sunday morning, 7 April

The skies this morning, my dear George, are ashen and sober, the air bites shrewdly, and I fancy that Oscar Wilde will get more of my attention than will the garden. Adam, after striking a few lugubrious and tuneless notes on a large guitar which Leslie Hotson left here, has bicycled off to play with a friend.

Last week was wonderfully restful, since I managed to dodge all engagements, and so got through a pile of manuscripts and other work. I twice saw Elisabeth Beerbohm, Max's widow, who is a charmingly warm-hearted and intelligent person of great integrity. She is much

[1] In due course he was made Oppidan Scholar.

pleased that Merton have agreed to institute and maintain a Max Room, containing his books, drawings, letters, etc. I have promised to do all I can to get it going. Next Thursday I am going to the London first night of *Zuleika*—which Max insisted should be pronounced *Zuleeka*, though for singing reasons they call it Zul*i*ka in the play. You know, I expect, that Hardy said Dy̆nasts like that.

I shall soon have to spend an afternoon in the B.M. Reading Room, having collected a list of O.W. queries which I cannot answer elsewhere. Oh yes—about the 24th of this month I shall have the final (page) proofs of the George Moore letters. Would it amuse you (or rather, perhaps, could you bear) to read a set of them for me, looking for errors of fact, taste and syntax? It's not a long book, but I have spent so much time on it that I feel I may at this stage miss almost anything through over-familiarity with the text. So your help would be a great blessing.

11 April 1957   *Grundisburgh*

Anyone who thinks the Lit. Soc. is going to interfere with our correspondence must think again. Who was it who said 'the good is the enemy of the best'?[1] I am not *absolutely* sure what it means but I think the man meant something like e.g. your not writing because a Lit. Soc. meeting was approaching. How good and timely therefore was your letter last week arriving Monday *vice* Tuesday just to show. That was a very good evening again. The Duke and he whom the irreverent Roger always calls the holy fox[2] were most affable, and Tim and I had a good crack with H. Nicolson, who, *inter alia*, told us that Tennyson in his last years drank far too much and was often muzzy. Do you know at all who the 'small nervous Eton master' was who tried to talk to Tennyson in a high wind and came, no doubt, to a dead end, when T's first response was 'I don't know who you are, and I can't hear what you say'? It must have been before Toddy Vaughan's day. Pecker Rouse and Hoppy Daman were both mathematicians, and would have had nothing to say to him—or anyone else

[1] Voltaire said *Le mieux est l'ennemi du bien*.
[2] Lord Halifax.

—outside sine and co-sine. Arthur Benson once told me that small collegers hated being fagged to Rouse's because, though you could avoid some, you couldn't avoid *all* the empty bottles that were thrown at anyone who came into the house—i.e. the level of Rouse civilisation was that of the mining districts 150 years ago. A bad beak does *a lot* of harm. I never really lied without a twinge until I was up to Rouse, when I learnt nothing about x and y but all about how to lie. Perhaps some might say this is a very valuable lesson—essential for Etonians, of whom so many go into politics—but I doubt if we shall find it approved on the Judgment Day.

Were you up to me when the task was to describe the Judgment Day in the style of O. Henry or some Yank like that, and one colleger, remembering the sheep and goats of scripture, called it 'that day when the all-wool babas put the half-Nelson on the bearded Williams'? Not a bad try? I occasionally got a gem or two, and ought to have collected them. Do you recollect the Alington poodle—exactly like a typhoid-germ magnified? The boys had to suggest what Dr Johnson would have said about it: 'Sir, it is evident that the microscope has no monopoly of horror' seems to me an inner if not a bull's-eye.

How right you are not to allow my miscue on Joxer Daly to pass. Never, please, be tolerant to any such blunders I make. How curiously apt Ivor Brown is to misquote—so, equally oddly, was C.E. Montague. As to 'darlin', I feel almost inclined to say, like that conceited ass Clement Shorter, 'Fancy my forgetting that!' when he was taxed with some blunder about the Brontës.

I have enjoyed Roger's *Votes for Women* immensely. Tommy Lascelles once complained that R. could not resist making irrelevant and slightly indecorous jokes, and ditto smacks at Tories and aristocrats, but I see no sign of that in this book, though it is often extremely funny. It seems to me very well done, though it has one odd defect, viz extraordinarily sloppy punctuation. He seems to be very vague about the functions of the comma. Ought not the publishers to have pointed this out? You will know. He says calmly that he expects sour reviews, as the book has been a good deal boosted. We shall see.

The Lit. Soc. certainly hasn't spoilt your epistolary charm. I loved the remark about Alington's poodle. There is nothing whatever to be said for Clement Shorter, a snuffling, go-getting louse in the locks of literature. His grabbing of the Brontë papers was typical: did you read Margaret Lane's admirable book *The Brontë Story*?

Do you know a long, pedestrian, unique poem called *The Setting Sun* by James Hurnard? It was published in 1870. I have never seen the original edition, though I believe it's in the London Library, but in 1946 the Cambridge Press brought out a volume of selections from it, made by G. Rostrevor Hamilton. It's largely autobiographical and descriptive, flat and heavy-going, with occasional flashes of deliciousness. Here is one:

> Davenant was born upon the third of March,
> Waller was born upon the third of March,
> Otway was born upon the third of March,
> And I was born upon the third of March;
> But that affords no proof I am a poet.
> Thousands of blockheads in the lapse of time
> Were also born upon the third of March.
> Milton was born in Sixteen hundred and eight,
> And I was born in Eighteen hundred and eight;
> But what a mighty interval divides us
> Besides the simple interval of time!

Isn't that fun? I'll send you the book of selections if you'd like to see it. Also Gordon Craig and Ian Fleming.

Today I have gardened in the sun—'sweated in the eye of Phoebus' —and only hope that all night I shall sleep in Elysium. Also I opened the cricket season by bowling my youngest a few creaking overs in the meadow. Alas, at thirteen and three-quarters he already makes hay of my googly, which used to baffle him regularly.

On Wednesday I was one of sixteen at a stag dinner in the Garrick, given by Hamish Hamilton for the head of Harper's (American publishers). I was well placed between Fleming and Priestley, who was at his nicest and most amusing. Remind me, when we next meet, to tell you of the dentist in Didsbury: it's a story that needs to be told rather than written. J.B.P. also said, of the Adams trial, that the most sinister words in the whole business were those used by the Doctor when he was set free: 'Now I must get back to work'. Others at the dinner included Julian Huxley, Quennell, Pritchett, Connolly (ugh!), Brogan (on the wagon these two years and much the better for it), John Hayward, Rattigan the playwright, and some smaller fry. It didn't last too long, the food was good, the speeches brief and amusing, and I enjoyed it more than I had expected to.

On Thursday evening I went with Elisabeth Beerbohm and two other friends to the first night of *Zuleika*, which is delightfully gay and tuneful, although the leading lady is quite without looks, charm or talent. With someone looking like your friend Marilyn Monroe it would run for ever. Most of Max's subtleties have been 'ironed out', but here and there a genuine line pops up:

'The owls have hooted, Miss Dobson; it's too late for love.'

I must read the book again. We were in a box, and Elisabeth spent most of the time singing and dancing the relevant 'numbers' in the shadows at the back. She is the sweetest person, and we are firm friends. When I got home on Friday I slept for eleven and a half hours.

The demolitions in Soho Square have now reached a Wagnerian crescendo with the introduction of *three* electric drills working at once. Several times last week I was driven to dictate letters in the flat, and on Friday afternoon I took refuge in the Reading Room of the British Museum, where, among the rustle of black clergymen and wild-eyed researchers badly in need of a bath, I spent three hours looking up this and that scrap of peripheral Wilde information. Thank goodness the London Library and my own shelves save me from most of such drudgery. I adore literary research in fact, but I find the atmosphere of the B.M. both enervating and distracting.

In bed I am reading the new detective story by Nicholas Blake (Cecil Day Lewis). The scene is laid in a publisher's office (C.D.L. is a partner in Chatto & Windus) and I'm enjoying it greatly. Have you read his earlier ones? *The Beast Must Die* is the best. You must forgive so much of my letters for being literary—that's the way I am. What *should* I do without books? Turn jobbing gardener, perhaps, and rush home (as the Yorkshire Dales farmers do) to catch the latest instalment of The Archers?

Now I must write a footnote about Lionel Johnson (who introduced Oscar to Lord Alfred Douglas) and the terrible poem he later wrote to O.W., beginning: 'I hate you with a necessary hate'. How interesting and infinitely complex everything is!

17 April 1957Grundisburgh

Peter Fleming's book[1] is enthralling! I know literally nothing of the public taste, but if it doesn't sell many thousands, then I shall mutter à la Carlyle 'The public is an old woman. Let her maunder and mumble!' I do hope the pleasant mental picture I have of shekels *pouring* into 36 Soho Square is according to the facts. Surely P.F's book is immensely good—so close-knit without ever being stodgy, and all his comments so full of wit and wisdom. Of course it was *his* luck to have such a story to tell, but *ours* that he had the telling of it. My *pulse* kept on changing its tempo as I read—not only at the hair-raising, touch-and-go happenings but also at his unfailing felicity of language. This last I put, with your letters, and the talk at the Lit. Soc.—and what else? not much—as the chief pleasures of my old age.

The Setting Sun has not come my way, but your quotation from it at least shows that James Hurnard must have been a good man—just as any ten lines from anything autobiographical from Mr—? would show him to be a man of four letters.

You are having the humbling experience of all fathers. Your googly is treated as poor Mr Pope's underhand service was by his daughter Marjorie.* He retired, feigning a sprained ankle, but the irreverent offspring of 1957 would see through that. But let me tell you when Pamela was teaching Humphrey divinity, and was emphasizing the incredible goodness of Christ, H., finding the wings of his imagination tiring in the void, asked 'Was he as good as Father?' When P., as is

---

[1] *Invasion 1940.*

* Cryptic allusion is the besetting and infuriating failing of beaks. Mr Pope *et fille* come from H.G. Wells's *Marriage*. I love Wells's novels when he isn't bullying, or girding, or putting us all in our places. G.W.L.

supposed, answered that he was even better, H. gave up and has been an agnostic ever since. (Do you remember how Birrell hearing someone decry George Eliot, prayed that God would smite him, and when God failed to do so, B. from that moment ceased to believe in Him?)

I say, Rupert, what company you do keep! That 'stag' dinner at the Garrick among all the wits. How you can put up with, and even show signs of welcoming, the senile droolings of an old usher is passing strange. Does V.S. Pritchett talk as well as he writes—or perhaps you agree with those who think his cleverness is a bit too thick? I suppose nearly everyone is convinced of Dr Adams's guilt, and that if those nurses' evidence had carried weight, he'd have been for it. I cannot help thinking his practice at Eastbourne will have shrunk a good deal these last weeks. Wherever he 'gets back to work' he had better manage that none of his patients dies, or heads will wag. He has not got a conspicuously attractive face.

How pointless, surely, that Zuleika should not be extremely lovely. Whoever cast a plain and charmless young woman for the part cannot have been in his right mind. I must read the book again. I remember delighting in it, but thinking—no doubt blasphemously—that it went on just a little too long. I expect you have got a lot of interesting stuff from Elisabeth B.

This is a lamentably disjointed letter, and the main reason is that I started doing my income-tax return this morning, and my mind, till that is off it, is the mind of a Suffolk yokel, threatened with melancholia. Why do all the shares I sell—at a small loss—start booming next day? Among the sayings which the late Geoffrey Madan claimed to have culled from Chinese literature and which some thought he composed himself there are three pleasing but grim items under 'The Three Illusions'.

(1) To think investments secure.

(2) To imagine that the rich regard you as their equal.

(3) To suppose your virtues common to all and your vices peculiar to yourself.

But I probably put his *Livres sans nom* by your bedside.

Fancy your saying that I must 'forgive' so much of your letters being literary. That is what I particularly enjoy, because there is no better topic for the pleasantest gossip—especially when it is interspersed with so much else of shrewd comment on men and things. Why does one's wife, when one says x is very dull, *always* assume that one's judgement is based on x not being at all *literary*. In vain I say I merely want him to be intelligent. I don't believe even the best wives understand more than a fraction of their husbands. Not that it matters that we are all 'in the sea of life enisled'. I shall look out for N. Blakes, having had *no idea* that he is Day Lewis.

Easter Day, 21 April 1957   *Bromsden Farm*

I was sure you'd enjoy Peter's book: he took infinite trouble with it, and (as you may remember) I read it in manuscript and two sets of proofs, correcting and commenting mercilessly. Alan Bullock's review in to-day's *Observer* is the first one that has seen the point, and The Critics were sensible this evening. Do write Peter a line—he'd be so pleased. His address is *Merrimoles House, Nettlebed, Oxon.*

You don't have to read all the Gordon Craig book unless you want to. The best thing by far, as I remember, is the detailed account of that scene in *The Bells*.

Tomorrow Elisabeth Beerbohm and two other friends are driving down for the day, and since Friday all ranks have been mowing, clipping, sweeping, uprooting and setting to rights. I am again stiff and aching, but pleasurably.

As well as Roger and a detective story, I am reading (for Oscariana) Whistler's *Gentle Art of Making Enemies*. Have you read it? A hotchpotch of paragraphs and angry letters to newspapers, from which the Butterfly emerges as most dislikeable.

Now I must limp up to bed. I fear this won't get posted till Tuesday, so I'll add a page or two tomorrow. I hope to goodness this wonderful weather holds for another day. I heard my first cuckoo yesterday, and lots to-day. How I love it! I imagine you surrounded by grandchildren, dispensing Easter eggs and seeking refuge in your summer-house.

Monday night, 22 April

Edmund B. announces that he will arrive in London on June 1st with his wife, four small children, and two Chinese nursemaids, and will I see whether I can get them accommodation for a few days. Having lived most of my life in London, I am totally ignorant of its hotels (I last stayed in one in 1917) and scarcely know where to begin.

I also learn that the aged American poet Robert Frost is to visit England this year. Did you hear him reading some of his poems on the wireless the other day? I think very highly of them, and more than twenty years ago I prevailed upon him by letter to allow them to be published by Jonathan Cape, for whom I then worked (they still publish the poems, curse them). After much correspondence the affair was settled by a telegram reading:

THE POEMS ARE YOURS AND SO AM I FROST

I have never seen him, and had given up hope, for he is over eighty, but now perhaps I shall have my wish.

Have you looked at that book of poems called *Union Street*?[1] I did send it to you, didn't I? I think it has the real stuff in it, and I'm delighted to see that two critics have already said so—*Times* and *Sunday Times*. The poet is a Cornish *schoolmaster*, and funnily enough a delightful chap.

25 April 1957   *Grundisburgh*

I *will* write to Peter F., and if he thinks my letter is otiose, supererogatory, ambivalent and many other adjectives whose meaning I am never *quite* sure of, well no irreparable harm will have been done.

Whistler always seemed to me the prize sh-t, though he wrote and said some good things. Was he ever nice to or about anybody? There is a big book to be written about sh-ts, there being such an infinite variety. It should be done by Hart-Davis and no other.

Your two books will be returning as soon as I get back. I read Ian Fleming's till far into the small hours. What an extraordinarily vivid touch he has whatever he touches—people or things. One is always holding one's breath or shuddering or agog in some way or another

[1] By Charles Causley.

about what is going to happen. I put it to you that, on thinking it over, the main flaw is that Bond never really does anything to show *why* the Russians rated him so high. Are not both he and M. *rather* easily bamboozled? I enjoyed it greatly, but was always expecting some brilliant coup by B., and didn't mind as much as I should have when he was bumped off. All his cleverness seems to consist—rather illegitimately—in his capacity to gather from people's faces what they are thinking. In cold fact jolly few people do that.

Craig's book *is* a curate's egg! The *Bells* chapter immensely acute and convincing, but I found much of the style so restless and high-pitched. Of course Irving was a genius; old Agate makes that clear enough again and again, but I thought it was generally agreed that—like Edmund Kean—it was *in spite* of his defects and mannerisms, whereas Craig sees them all as virtues, viz that '*God*', pronounced as you and I do, is 'deadly and hard', and 'Gud' is in the ripe old English tradition. Bilge, my dear Rupert! And Irving's walk was a dance, and preserved 'the last tingle of the mighty Greek tradition'. Will that really do? Finally it is surely silly to sum up *any* play of Shaw's as 'an accursed sermon in jam'? Shaw's not *very* harsh hint that one evening H.I. had drunk too much (which hint his son Harry approved of) is dubbed a lie, somehow proved by Craig saying that he once saw H.I. 'apparently intoxicated after eating a small steak and drinking nothing'. What a rum world these great actors live in—never seeing, hearing, reading anything except as providing an idea for the theatre. Thank you very much for the loan. Also for that little book of *first-rate* poetry. Who is Causley? and why have I never heard of him? He really *has* something to say and his own way of saying it. Pamela made me read *Under Milk Wood* recently, but I couldn't do much with it. Perhaps it demands to be heard. I gather many people love it. Do *you* read it with your pulses bounding? Is it well thought of in the Lit. Soc.? Does Sir Cuthbert know it by heart?

We have just bowed off the last of eleven grandchildren with attend-ant parents and nurses, and I revert from the role of Abraham to that of St Simeon, the summer-house being my pillar. I love them twittering and hopping and scampering and rolling about the place, daily missing homicide or suicide by a hair's-breadth, but there *is* a certain com-pensatory relief in finding the soap in its dish and not in the bath, and the ink in its pot and not on my cushion. I made the mistake of trying to read *Justine*[1] while the family played Racing Demon and uttered the screams and curses that appear to be part of the game—and I found that after twenty pages of *Justine* I had not the faintest idea what it, or he, or she was really at. And I have tried it again. No result! And they say it is superb. In ten years' time I shall be left high and dry by modern literature, and in writing to me you will feel you have joined the spiritualists and are communicating with a ghost.

By the way, I was told recently that poor old Percy Lubbock is in a bad way—physically better than a month ago, but very gloomy, and short in the temper, and self-absorbed—and immensely tiresome about politics, if you please, rather airing communistic views and contemptuous and angry when opposed. That does happen, I know; something hardens or softens in the brain, and the character changes. Nature is so far from being a lady that she is not even a gentleman. This is no way to treat the man who wrote *Earlham*.

Remember you said you might fix up a meeting with E. Blunden. Perhaps just before he goes back to China. Then he will go happily, feeling that whatever nostalgia may come over him, at any rate he doesn't meet retired pedagogues in China, lacking in hair, teeth, hearing, sight and understanding. You know all about it, adding, after saying Causley is a schoolmaster, 'funnily enough, a delightful chap'.

28 April 1957   *Bromsden Farm*

I fear you won't get much of a letter to-day, for at any moment we are to be invaded by three supper-guests, and there's no knowing how long they will stay. Meanwhile here is a photograph of Duff Cooper's tomb, which may interest you. With a magnifying glass you should be able to read the words. It cost £600 and a lot of to-and-froing, including a journey to Belvoir to inspect the site. Have you ever been there? The Castle is spectacular—a towering Victorian-Gothic building, castellated to infinity, on a hill in the middle of a huge flat plain. Next time we meet, remind me to describe Duff's funeral: it was most dramatic. Now I hear our guests arriving—

[1] By Lawrence Durrell.

So *I* am the man to write a history of sh-ts! A backhanded compliment, if ever there was one. Frank Harris and Lord Alfred Douglas would bat high up the list.

Which reminds me—tomorrow is the last day of Adam's holidays and I have promised to take him to Lord's to see M.C.C. v Yorkshire. Snow is bound to fall.

Last week a friend told me (and I believe it) that when Ian Fleming mentions any particular food, clothing or cigarettes in his books, the makers reward him with presents in kind: 'in fact', said my friend, 'Ian's are the only modern thrillers with built-in commercials.' I too thought the behaviour of Bond and M. in this book puerile, but that Turkish chap was good, and like you I couldn't put the book down. I asked Ian if Bond was dead, and he said NO—after a long sojourn in the School of Tropical Medicine he will be fit for Opus VI, which in fact is already written.

You're right about Gordon Craig: he is one of the great frauds of our time, a poor actor, an impractical designer, hideous wood-engraver, and amateurish writer—but just occasionally he pulls it off, as with *The Bells*.

So glad you like Causley's poems. Up to last week I had sold 140 copies—and then, after two good reviews, I sold 200 in one week and may have to reprint. (I printed only 1000). No one has heard of him before, and you are assisting, midwifely, at the birth of a poet. Wasn't that a splendid review of Peter's book in the *T.L.S.* Peter says that, on internal evidence, it must have been written by someone in M.I.14 —and who am I to contradict him?

2 May 1957   *Grundisburgh*

I put it to you that one of the main defects of continental education —so much more *efficient* than English—is that so many are educated above their ability. They all learn at school to talk about levels of awareness and integrity and where to 'place' x and y, and the rest of the horrid jargon. It is odd how that sarcasm of eighty years ago of some German professor, who said he approved of English education because it was so good for the mind to be 'fallow till the age of nineteen' is much nearer to the truth than was supposed. Or it was till these scientists began laying down the law about their intolerable lore. I see too that some important ass has been saying that three years' training is essential for every teacher—when nobody really knows what education should be aiming at. When old Q.[1] came to Eton he told us how refreshing it was to find a staff which didn't profess to know exactly how English should be taught. Years ago I was a member of the English Association Committee, on which Professor Edith J. Morley held forth interminably, her face radiant and moist, on the theory and practice of English teaching, and old Bradley, walking away with John Bailey, murmured 'It is a pity, besides being rather strange, that poor Miss Morley herself cannot write a paragraph of tolerable English.' Her *magnum opus* was an edition of Crabb Robinson's diary, which, after much enquiry, I am quite sure the libraries have joined into a conspiracy *never* to buy.

We are now at peace after Diana's wedding, and contemplate remaining so for some weeks. The wedding and the two previous cocktail parties produced great armies of London's brightest and best, and I had a number of fortissimo, amusing, but of course much too brief conversations with intelligent people, and much unsuccessful flight from bores. I gave Diana away—rather an irrelevant bit of ceremonial in 1957 surely—in the wedding finery I wore at my own ceremony in Babraham Church in 1919, and seam and gusset and band all stood the strain bravely. To-day's *Daily Sketch* mildly sneers at the number of 'cops' on duty outside the Royal Chapel and puts it down to the bride's 'hush-hush' policy throughout her engagement. They clearly resent anyone having a quiet wedding. 'Such a fuss about jazz-man's sister's wedding' (headline). Of course the police were nothing to do with her, merely routine for anything in that chapel. Does the Press *ever* get its facts quite right?

Thank you very much for the Duff Cooper photographs. I am glad you got Reynolds Stone to do the design. Did you compose that excellent inscription, the only word I don't feel quite sure about is 'trammels'. But I expect I am wrong—'which happens too often,' as Linky[2] said to and of Edward Halifax.

[1] Sir Arthur Quiller-Couch.
[2] Nickname of Lord Hugh Cecil, later Lord Quickswood and Provost of Eton.

Byrne ('Fuggy') once modestly disclaimed omniscience, but said he thought he knew pretty well where he could find anything he wanted. How delighted Alington was when I told him of Gow's saying that he had noticed that whenever we had in chapel the anthem: 'Where shall wisdom be found,' Byrne always looked self-conscious. A vain old peacock!

Yes A. Douglas and F. Harris certainly—and of course Baron Corvo, —and A.W. Carr, captain of Notts, and Colonel Repington, and old Rogers the poet. There will be 'fine confused feeding' in the book. You really must think about it when you have finally polished off Wilde and Moore.

That is amusing about Ian Fleming living via his books on Fortnum and Carreras and Moss Bros. I am glad Bond has recovered, but he must do more than a little easy fornication to get my vote. I.F. is too good a man to risk reminding one of Peter Cheyney.

I wonder who *did* write that *T.L.S.* review of Peter's book. Do good reviews sell books? I have heard that reviews make little or no difference, but I don't know whether it is true. I wrote to P.F. but forbade him to answer. At least three members of the Ipswich Country Club are about to read it on my urging. I can't promise they will buy it, but I think one will. Causley is by my bedside—with Shakespeare, *Earlham*, *Irish R.M.*, Ivor Brown's word-books and Humphry House, who very easily bears re-reading. I love re-reading. Each night from 10.30 to 12 I read Gibbon *out loud*. I read slowly, richly, not to say juicily; and like Prospero's isle the room is full of noises—little, dry, gentle noises. Some matter-of-fact man of blunt or gross perceptions might say it was the ashes cooling in the grate, but I know better. It is the little creatures of the night, moths and crickets and spiderlings, a mouse or two perhaps and small gnats in a wailful choir, come out to listen to the Gibbonian music—'Twenty-two acknowledged concubines and a library of 62,000 volumes attested the variety of his inclinations'—what sentient being, however humble, could resist that?

Did you say you'd read a set of proofs of the George Moore letters? Or didn't I ask you? Anyhow, will you be so angelic? They should be ready tomorrow, and I'll hopefully send them along. I'm deep in them myself already, preparing to compile an index (poor Oscar is shelved again). The whole caboodle should go to press in ten days or so. Meanwhile new manuscripts pour in, including a volume containing all the remaining correspondence between Henry James and H.G. Wells. This I shall certainly publish, but it must be *read*.

To-day, with no children at home, all the mowing fell to me, and I got it done in two and a half hours. Is your garden parched and cracking like ours?

G.L. Watson (whom I have never seen) is an American of (I imagine) independent means. The *Housman* is his first book, and he is now working on a biography of Mrs Jack Gardner the great Boston hostess and literary Mrs Leo Hunter of the late nineteenth century.

The words on Duff's tomb were composed by Diana and slightly revised by me. 'Trammels' was hers, but it seemed to me all right.

You ask whether reviews sell books. Single ones don't, but a con- catenation of good ones at about the same time certainly does. Assuming that all literary-minded people read at least one daily, one weekly and one Sunday paper, a good review in all these within a week will probably stir them. 'I have said it once, I have said it twice, what I say three times is true.' Pinero always said that the only way to get anything across to an English audience was first to say 'I'm going to hit this man on the head', then 'I'm hitting this man on the head', and finally 'I *have* hit this man on the head'. This technique in a slightly subtler form he used in many of his plays.

I'd love to watch the creatures of the night listening to you reading Gibbon. Where exactly does that superb sentence about the concu- bines come? Of whom was he speaking? On the 14th I have to speak at the annual dinner of the Antiquarian Booksellers Association, and I could surely quote Gibbon to them. I haven't thought what to say yet, but perhaps I'll begin by saying that when I was a child I thought 'antiquarian' meant 'very old', and it wasn't until I became a book- buyer that I realised it really means 'very expensive'.

We didn't see the finish of the Lord's match, for we were there only on the Monday, but the sun shone incessantly, we saw Graveney bat, Trueman bowl, and Adam loved it all. To my horror I found that my favourite stand, the low white one between the Press Box and the Grandstand, has been removed, the Green Mound behind it levelled, and the whole space given over to concrete and a huge hideous two-tier cantilever stand, which clearly won't be ready this year. As is now usual in London, the only work on it was being done by West Indians, for whom the cricket naturally took first place. Of the Lord's of my boyhood only the Pavilion, the Tavern and the Mound Stand remain. What I particularly dislike about the new stand is that it entirely obscures those lovely trees. An old wiseacre I encountered told me he was sure it would affect the wicket by impeding the advent of drying winds from that quarter.

I have begun to read that new life of Sargent, and find it most interesting. He impinges on H. James, G. Moore and others of my favourites. The author is an American painter,[1] who writes decently and has taken great pains: there is an admirable catalogue of S.'s pictures.

Did I tell you Causley's book has been selling like hot cakes and is *reprinting,* which few volumes do these or any days. On the 15th I am to attend a lecture by Edith Sitwell, at which she is to read one of C's poems. Afterwards there is to be a dinner-party in her honour, given by the P.E.N. Club. See what lofty jinks you are happily missing!

9 May 1957   *Grundisburgh*

The G.M. book has arrived and I will begin my scrutiny at once with great pleasure and interest. You had mentioned it at the Lit. Soc. and I was delighted to do you a tiny service in return for the numerous blessings you have showered on me. Though I must tell you that a book I once went through, merely to discover the misprints, proved on publication, to have, I think twenty-nine left. But I will do what I can. (By the way for Causley's second ed. 'Eckermann' on p. 8, and 'star sown' on p. 27, though I am quite prepared to hear that the

[1] Charles Merrill Mount.

author *meant* sewn. He often moves in worlds unrealised by me, but that is because I am seventy-four, and anyway I found myself enjoying again and again what I didn't wholly understand. But as my kindly and intelligent old pupil John Bayley used to say, that doesn't at all matter, poetry not being merely for the brain.) You shall have the G.M. book back this week-end.

I expect you are right about 'trammels', and that I have allowed its associations to apply to too lowly a set of things. How on earth *is* one to get *exactly* right, either in use or comprehension, the tone and essence and value of a word? I remember once reading to my division an essay of D. MacCarthy in which he described the gait of an antelope and used the word 'elegant', just the word wanted in the context, but to the boys it obviously was wholly absurd. One in fact said it called up the sight of his aunt's appearance when dressed for church, and I don't suppose that his or anyone else's aunt ever bore much resemblance to an antelope, even in church.

That Gibbon sentence describes the emperor Gordian whose 'manners were less pure, but his character was equally amiable with that of his father'. Then comes the sentence I quoted, which ends: 'and from the productions which he left behind him, it appears that the former as well as the latter were designed for use rather than for ostentation.' I once used it at an M.C.C. dinner, referring to our cricketing ancestors' catholic tastes as evidenced in the almanac in each of the early Wisdens, when material was very scanty. There was easy fun to be got out of such entries as 'Oct 14: Death of Prince Leboo,' and 'May 7: Hippopotamus born at the zoo,' and 'July 21: Sir Moses Montefiore lands at Tangier on his way to S. Africa'. All genuine entries though I have not verified the dates. Now of course every year in May a solid little *cube* in brown paper arrives and turns out to be Wisden. There is no mention of Sir Moses in it. But most of the letterpress is very poor stuff compared with that in the Wisdens of cricket's golden age (1892–1912). It is disillusioning to one with my youthful loyalties to realise that the majestic MacLaren, with his 'superb crease-side manner', was an extremely stupid, prejudiced and pig-headed man, even in cricket matters. Plum always says he had the worst fault of a captain, viz pessimism about his team, expressed in their presence: 'Just look what they've given me—half of them creaking with old age, George Hirst fat as butter' etc etc. But let us remember that when Wainwright gave him a long-hop to leg to get his century off in a Gents and Players, he kicked it away and sternly ordered him to bowl his best.

But Good God, when I get onto cricket I drool like any old fathead in an M.C.C. tie (but just one more. A boy running h. for l. at Winchester cannoned head-down into E.R. Wilson on his way to school, looked up, and in horror gasped 'Good God,' to which E.R.W. gently replied 'But strictly incognito').

Will you please *swear* to tell me when I am a bore—not just when I strike a boring note, which all human beings do—but when the disease shews signs of taking hold. One's wife ought to, and sometimes does, but probably realises that after a certain age the poor man's alternative will be total silence. (Who was it, by the way, who, seeing outside a fried-fish shop 'Cleanliness, economy, and civility, always hot and always ready', remarked 'The motto of the perfect wife'? Gibbon would have liked that.)

I saw the beginnings of that stand at Lord's months ago, and augured the worst. It should impress you to know that *my* Lord's memories go back to *before* the Mound Stand. But I think you omit the Grandstand which hasn't altered except for Father Time at the top. The first Eton v Harrow I saw was from a box above the Grandstand in 1895; a waiter had an apoplectic fit just outside. We—my brother and I—felt we were seeing life.

Last week began with a daughter's wedding and just missed ending with a son's death. Humphrey with wife and son travelling about sixty on a one-way (i.e. double) road had a lorry right-turning just in front of him to get into the other lane. He has two black eyes, four stitches in forehead and three in hand, deep cut in knee. His wife bruised all over, child of one and a half unhurt, though its chair with tray in front was smashed. But somehow nothing affecting the trumpet is affected and he is playing it to-morrow night in Lancashire or Staffordshire. The police intend to sue the lorry-driver. He seems to have made what Belloc used to say was a very common mistake of army commanders, viz thinking your communications are safe because you hope they are. Humphrey was patched up at a hospital in Colchester, where they seem to have done everything fairly perfunctorily, didn't offer him any tea, though he had shed a good deal of blood, but two nurses, hearing who he was, begged for his autograph.

P.S. Do work in that Gibbon sentence in your speech. I assure you it is always a winner. Even antiquarian blood quickens and vents itself in hoarse salacious chuckles.

11 May 1957   *Grundisburgh*

Herewith my poor little gleaning.[1] But I don't really feel at all ashamed, because I never have come across a book more thoroughly and intelligently edited. It puts such old codgers as Aldis Wright and Colvin, who edited the letters respectively of FitzGerald and Keats, in the corner, faces to the wall. The amount of work you get into your day is positively staggering.

I find it a fascinating book, with some delightfully humorous episodes and touches (e.g. the 'Maud Emerald' pages) and very moving in places. What a pity he didn't keep *her* letters, and it seems odd that he didn't—though perhaps not odder than many things about him.

Of course, I rub my Victorian eyes at the frank revelation—approved, apparently, by relatives and friends—that for some years the bed played an important part in the relationship, but in connection with all that there is a gap between the generations.

I have a feeling that G.M's bedwork, and what he ever said about it, is regarded by most who read and love his books as mainly comic, but (a) I may be wrong and (b) it may not matter, though some reviewers have a clumsy touch. What a lot of luck there is about whose hands a book may fall into!

Many thanks for letting me do this tiny job. I thoroughly enjoyed it. And now some 'capable Scot' will come along and find another score of misprints.

This is *not* a reply to your week-end letter.

[1] Of misprints in proofs of the George Moore letters.

I hate to think what a nuisance the G.M. letters are being to you, but I shall await your strictures eagerly. Yesterday in six hours I compiled a rather sketchy index for the book which I think will serve. Goodness knows how long the Wilde index will take me when it turns up.[1]

Today produced thunder, hail and torrents of rain. Mowing was impossible, and next week-end I shall stand breast-high in tears amid the alien weeds. A bullfinch and P. Fleming have been the only visitors: thank goodness few 'drop in' unexpectedly here.

The trouble about the exact meaning of words ('trammel', 'elegant' etc) is not only that they mean subtly different things to different people, but also that their meaning and undertones actually change with the passage of time and alteration in manners. I daresay that Gibbon's broad blade carved out his meaning with more force and exactitude than did the bending rapiers of latter-day swordsmen. And what are you to do about America, where the *sound* of words is differently interpreted? I remember a rather good Galsworthian play about the iniquity of cutting down the copse in front of some country house. It pleased in London, but on Broadway they thought cutting down the copse meant a reduction in the size of the police force, and were baffled.

I shall certainly use that fine sentence in my speech, which I don't mind telling you I am dreading, together with the dinner that precedes and the dance (ugh!) that follows it. Can you imagine dancing with a female antiquarian bookseller? Nor can I. Nor shall I attempt the feat. Were you taught never to begin a sentence with the word NOR? I was, and I think wrongly; sparingly and judiciously used, the construction can be most effective. In *The Cruise of the 'Nona'* Belloc wrote: 'God sent me a pilot. Nor was he a pilot, as the events shall show.' Don't you rather like that?

I'll certainly tell you if I see any signs of your becoming a bore, but it does not seem to me a very likely contingency. I think that excellent remark about the motto of the perfect wife was made by Edward

[1] It took six months.

Thomas and reported by E.S.P. Haynes in his *Lawyer's Notebook*, though I suspect that you have improved the wording a trifle. If it wasn't so late I'd find the book and look it up.

I hate to question anything you say, but I could have sworn that the Grandstand at Lord's had been entirely rebuilt since I was a boy: how can the point be settled? Or are you unshakeably certain that you are right?

Adam writes from Eton: 'I find that if you are a "student" you can get *The Times* for twopence, and I am now doing this.' I doubt whether he penetrates further than the cricket news and the crossword puzzle, but it seems to me quite good for thirteen.

My elder boy, Duff, seems to have been engulfed in some Conradian heart of African darkness: we have had no word for weeks. His twenty-first birthday is looming (June 3), and I have neither money nor ideas with which to celebrate it.

Next Saturday I am to lunch at Merton College, to discuss the Max Beerbohm Room which they are planning: altogether the week is hideously full and I should have some fine confused impressions to pass on to you next Sunday. Now it is midnight and you have had enough, I'm sure.

15 May 1957   *Grundisburgh*

Can you tell me if it is true as I read somewhere that Lloyd Osborne wrote practically all *The Wrong Box*? He must have been good fun, if that is so. But did he write anything on his own—or was he devitalised by what one suspects the husky, dusky Mrs S. to have been—the terror that walks by day? A sort of Frieda Lawrence—though I never quite remember whether she was at the receiving or the discharging end of that plate-throwing.

That 'copse' story is lovely. It is all wrong, I know, but I *cannot* ever take Americans quite seriously—I mean their tastes and judgments and values, though now and then one strikes an absolutely Class I man, e.g. the late Judge Wendell Holmes. But either I always have bad luck with their novelists, or I just don't know my way about. I remember liking Steinbeck's first best-seller, but last week, seeing his name, I wasted half-a-crown on his *The Wayward Bus* to read in the train. Not a single character who was not either loathsome or silly. The blurb calls it a ruthless picture, showing what people are really like, i.e. all in need of an ounce of civet. Is the whole of U.S.A. thinking of nothing but the female bosom? We too shall be soon, judging by the cheap Press. It is all very rum. (By the way, how endlessly and overwhelmingly delicious is the last scene between George Moore and Mrs Craigie, when he dismissed her with a terrific kick on the behind —'or at least on the bustle'.) He would have relished the thought of you treading a measure with 'a female antiquarian bookseller'.

I hate all those rules like 'never begin a sentence with "nor", or end one with a preposition.' Once at Eton I was aware that the young prigs in College had a tremendous down on the split infinitive, so I showed them the list of great writers who sometimes used it— including Dr Johnson. They were shaken—which is all one can ever do with a young K.S. But I approve of a dictum of Judge Holmes mentioned above, viz 'All right to end a sentence with a preposition, but not a paragraph. That should end with the blow of an axe.'

Yes, of course that perfect wife story is in E.S.P. Haynes. I have found it this morning. When in doubt about a word or saying, look it up in Hart-Davis. I read the book when it came out, and was rather disappointed. Several good things but fewer than one expected. I think his palate was rather a coarse one; he did not know vintage from wood.

There are signs of cricket coming to life again—a twitch here and there, a faint clouding of the glass held over the mouth. But there are very few who can bat on a turning wicket. I will find out about the Grandstand. I may be wrong. I am not quite like E.V. Slater (rather an inferior man) who said that while his facts were often wrong, his opinions never were, but I have learnt that, at seventy-four, something one could swear was white, turns out on investigation to have been black as the night from pole to pole.

I can't resist sending you Charles Morgan's letter about the G.M. letters: you might send it back. An American friend also writes enthusiastically, saying: 'A law should be passed compelling you and you alone to be the biographer of all bitches and bastards and all flawed celebrities.' Which, as you will quickly realise, chimes in with your own suggestion!

I've no idea how much of *The Wrong Box* was written by Lloyd Osbourne, but judging by the dreary novels he afterwards wrote on his own, I should say jolly little. I remember him as a lugubrious and rather forbidding old boy in the Garrick Club. I wish now I had scraped acquaintance with him and heard something first hand about the great man. By the way, Oscar particularly disliked *Vailima Letters,* and made fun of the book in several letters. Frieda Lawrence I just met, and remember as a jolly, stout, overflowing woman.

Meanwhile my programme last week was endlessly exhausting. The Antiquarian Booksellers' 'do' lasted from 7.15 till 11.30. Mercifully I was next to an extravagantly good-looking film-star called Phyllis Calvert, whose husband was in the chair. She was charming and gave me strength to cope with the honest bookseller's wife on my other side. The first speaker was W.S. (Lefty) Lewis, the American millionaire who has cornered Horace Walpole and is producing (with a team of editors) an endless edition of his letters. He told one or two anecdotes of book-buying. Then came the President (the film-star's husband), who was fluent and quite amusing. By the time it came to my turn the company (about 180) was desperate with boredom and ready to laugh at anything. I started off with a brisk joke: they roared approval: and thereafter I had them captive. The Gibbon quotation stopped the show long enough for me to consult my scrappy notes, so really I owe it all to you!

On Wednesday I put on my dinner-jacket at 5.30 and attended Edith Sitwell's lecture on Poetry in the Church Hall, Westminster, which was *packed* to the ceiling. She is a poor lecturer, and the poems she read were largely inaudible, despite a loud-speaker in front of every seat. It lasted an hour, and then I repaired to the I.M.A., a musicians' club in South Audley Street, which has just about the best food in

London. Our hosts were the secretary of the P.E.N. Club and his wife. I was happily placed between two beloved old friends, Rosamond Lehmann and Veronica Wedgwood. Opposite us were Dame Edith and John Lehmann. Charles Morgan was on Veronica's other side. The old Dame was most affable, not to say amusing, so the whole thing was highly enjoyable.

On Thursday I was Donald Somervell's guest at a dinner in the rebuilt Inner Temple—very like dining in an Oxford or Cambridge college, though lawyers in the mass are not exhilarating. Donald himself is good company and very nice. When I got down here on Friday evening I slept for eleven hours.

Yesterday I drove to Oxford and lunched in the Common Room at Merton. The Warden (a philosopher called Mure) was most friendly, as was the young librarian. Basil Blackwell was at lunch, which, though exiguous after my three banquets, was sufficient. Then I was shown the room which is to be devoted to the permanent Max exhibition and discussed the arrangements. Then to New College, where I had a long talk with David Cecil, also about Max. Then a delicious hour's browse in Blackwell's, and so home. To-day has been devoted to mowing, clipping, uprooting and all the rest of it. Osbert Lancaster drove over this evening, bringing a jacket (five weeks overdue) for Peter F.'s new volume of reprinted pieces.

21 May 1957   *Grundisburgh*

Of course I *knew* I was right about your editing of those letters; anyone could see it was masterly, but it is always pleasing to be corroborated by one of the real pundits like Charles M. It so happened that the next day I embarked on a huge book which cried out for editing, and—but not only for that reason—bored me a good deal. Henry James's life or picture or what not of Mr Wetmore Story. It is full of letters containing sentences like 'Tell Gilbert not to bother about that commission, and certainly to pay no attention to whatever the wretched — says about the reasons for it, which no longer apply.' Not a ray of light on Gilbert, the commission and its reasons, or who or what 'the wretched —' was. A very mealy-mouthed anonymity, surely, after a gap of nearly a hundred years? I suppose the really faithful Henry James fans love the slow wheelings of his mind behind the scenes of Mr Story's doings, but I felt like wading through treacle. And how solidly uninteresting Browning could be in his letters! Of course every man is two men or more, but the poet and the diner-out ('Who was that too exuberant financier?' as a lady said) reached the limits of incongruity, surely. And is any great man so hard to get a clear notion of as Browning? I cannot imagine him walking, or talking, or smiling—and least of all in love with that bony little spaniel-wife, or father of that futile little bounder his son.

I send you (*not* to be returned) Gow's letter about Watson's A.E.H. book, and add to it two riders (1) that I doubt if G. is any judge of the intensity of Housman's emotional life in youth. However reticent H. was to other friends, to G. he would have been still more so. And after all some of H's lines and stanzas surely could not have been written by a man who did not feel deeply. 'Hectic' rather begs the question. And (2) Why *should* W. be in sympathy with H's kind of scholarship? Who ever was, except a parcel of dry-as-dusts? Gow himself, as Auden shows, was puzzled by H. devoting all that time and brain to fifth-raters, and suggests as the reason what really amounts to vanity.

I have met Rosamond Lehmann once or twice at Grizel Hartley's. Excellent company, and very pleasant to look at. John Lehmann was in my Extra Studies. So (of course!) was Mure K.S. What a red-letter day you had at Oxford! What, by the way, about Provost J.C. Masterman for the Lit. Soc.? I am full, you see, of bright suggestions—generally met by you with bland declarations that they are inebriated pederasts, and—what is worse—bores of international calibre. I look forward to these dinners with what can only be described by that horrible word 'gusto'. Is there better company to be found? Not in the Ipswich Country Club or even among the governors of Woodbridge School, though I rather *like* grocers and sanitary inspectors. As Walt Whitman said in praise of animals, they 'do not make me sick discussing their duty to God', and though on occasions they do sweat, they don't 'whine about their condition'. The grocer retired some months ago, and had a month in Italy, where he enjoyed everything 'except all those old ruins'. The U.D.C. of Rome, he thought, deserved very little credit in view of the state of the Forum. The U.D.C. of Wood-bridge (of which he is a member) would have cleared it up years ago.

The hour is late and I am far from bright. Thanks so much for sending back those items. Tomorrow from the office I will send you a typescript of Max's superb broadcast on George Moore, just given me by Lady B.—send it back sometime. Perhaps you listened to it? Anyhow it reads exquisitely.

A woman friend whom I consulted (she is a keen cricket-watcher) says she remembers the Grandstand at Lord's being rebuilt in the 1930's, only Father Time remaining of the old building. This supports my view, and you have not yet counter-attacked in any strength. With this same friend I dashed to Lord's on Monday and we were well rewarded. Tyson, I fear, is a spent force, but the batting was first-class—Walcott, Sobers and Close. The latter started off as though he'd already made 50 and I detected no mistake in his play. The W.I. fast bowler Gilchrist looks made of india-rubber. At the end of his pro-digious run he leaps into the air, but alas, his length and direction were mediocre. They have made haste with that revolting new stand, and I daresay it *will* be ready for the Test Match—which unfortunately I shall miss. I plan to lie hidden in Yorkshire from June 7 to 28. In fact, dear George, I don't know *when* you'll get a proper letter from me again, for next week-end I have to spend at Blackpool (my second visit this year) with a hideous mass of booksellers. On Saturday I plan to escape for the night to a beautiful poetess (a good one) called Phoebe Hesketh, who lives in the country near Bolton. Perhaps I shall be able to write from there: I'll try.

I've long possessed a copy of the original edition of H.J.'s *Life of W.W. Story* and have often dipped into it with pleasure—and even with profit, though I have never steeled myself to reading it right through.

You're right on the beam in suggesting Masterman for the Lit. Soc. He was in fact elected two or three years ago but refused membership on the grounds that he would never turn up. The same, only more so, would I fear apply to Noel Annan, who would also be an excellent member. So go on thinking of other possibles. Not perhaps one of your good grocers. Some Frenchman said *'On nait demi-dieu et l'on meurt épicier'*, so perhaps we shall all come to it.

What else of last week? On Tuesday Jonah dropped in for a cup of tea and gossiped happily for an hour. He hopes to finish his new book in a couple of months. That evening Eric Linklater turned up from his Ross-shire home and offered to take me to a theatre. I told him that what he (as a bucolic barbarian) needed was a spot of culture, but he said he'd prefer a 'leg show'. By the time I picked him up at his club at seven he had failed to get seats for *Grab me a Gondola* or anything else, so I reverted to culture and dragged him unwillingly off to the Arts Theatre to see Genet's play *The Balcony*, which takes place in a brothel. The theatre was half-empty, and when the lights went down a scruffy, unshaven Central European came on to the stage and announced that Miss Something had been taken suddenly ill, there was no understudy, and the part would be read by Miss Somebody Else. Anyone who asked for their money back could have it. No one did. Needless to say the part was the chief one—the brothel-keeper's pet—and it was read by a nice homely girl from Bagshot, desperately trying to follow the dialogue in a script the size of the telephone book. When she had to help the other woman to dress she fell behind through having to put the book down. The other actors were all appallingly bad, and the play pretentious and windy—rather like the reverse of a Maeterlinck medal—instead of 'moonshine' they repeatedly said 'sh-t' and 'bugger'. We stuck it to half-time and then repaired to the Ivy for an excellent dinner. Next day, fresh as paint, I travelled to Bath and took part in a Brains Trust at Monkton Combe prep. school (which is in *lovely* country). The others were Hugh Ross Williamson, Noel Streatfeild, W.E. Johns (whose *Biggles* books—he has written a hundred!—are enormously successful) and George Cansdale, recently Head of the Zoo. He brought along a python in a Gladstone bag, which delighted the boys. Tea-party, sherry-party, dinner-party, called at 6.45, and back to work.

Yesterday I drove to Reading University to see an excellent photographic exhibition concerning W.B. Yeats. When I get to Yorkshire I shan't *move*!

That M.B. talk on G.M. I listened to it *twice*—as they were sensible enough to repeat it—*and* cut it out of the *Listener* to preserve it for ever, and then of course lent the cutting to someone who hasn't returned it, and whose name I cannot remember. I can only hope that the Almighty does remember, and so directs my curses on to the right head, which I hope by now resembles that of the Emperor Nero, according to Suetonius, i.e. 'pustular and malodorous'. It (the M.B.) is *perfect*—and gave me the same degree and intensity of pleasure that some music, e.g. the Pastoral Symphony, does. I shall read it two or three times more before returning it—and let me tell you, Rupert, that to return it at all is proof of outstanding beauty of character. When they ask on the Judgment Day about my good deeds I shall say 'I returned M.B. on G.M.' and a few centuries of purgatory will at once be docked, which won't happen to the old man of Saxmundham:

> *Qui habuit ventrem rotundum;*
> He borrowed £5 from a master of hounds
> And flatly refused to refund 'em.

A favourite limerick of Tuppy Headlam's—composer unknown. I like the Gibbonian echo of line 2, where some imaginary indecency is 'veiled in the decent obscurity of a learned language.'

I have a horrible suspicion that you may be right about the Grandstand, but I *am* pretty certain that Father Time was *not* on the old G.S. I shall find out at the Test Match. The English Test side is rather *dull*. I have seen nearly all of them so often—Statham and Trueman with those immense and needless runs which waste so much time, and the batting of Bailey, which always recalls the writing of Professor Edith J. Morley of the Reading High School, or the Yorkshire pudding made by the hotel-cooks of southern England. But I want to see the three W's—the only time I saw Worrell, the shade of Trumper was a 'hover over the scene, smiling and nodding his head. And Ramadhin, whose bowling obviously costs him as much effort as breathing. Hutton put him very high last time he was over, on the odd and amusing ground that while it was hard enough to play a ball of which you didn't know the way it was meant to turn, it was still harder when the bowler didn't know either. He also said that he wished he had made the 200 he did make in the last Test in the first, because the W.I's are very temperamental and easily depressed by a big score against them.

Blackpool! I was once there on a fine August Bank Holiday. No sand was visible because of the people; there were eleven mechanical bands playing, fortissimo, different tunes along the front, and whatever lull there was in the din was at once filled by the hilarious yells of *homo sapiens*. If, say, Housman or Gow have to spend any years in Hell, old Nick need only plant them down at Blackpool on endless Bank Holidays. Gow will be forced to read Ethel M. Dell, Housman Galsworthy, for whom he had a mysterious but very strong hatred. I have just read Mottram's book about J.G. and wife—interesting but there *is* something baffling about him. It can't *only* be that he was a Harrovian. Why has all that perfectly genuine high-mindedness, humanity, perceptiveness, literary skill, etc so often a sort of *dreariness* about it? Did you know him at all? Why is there so much animus in so many of his critics? It cannot be only jealousy of his tremendous success. They always are particularly down on the *F. Saga,* which I shall always maintain is packed with interest of many kinds—historical, sociological, characterisational. What say they? Let them say.

Apropos of the Lit. Soc. I suppose these College dignitaries are very busy, though I should have thought they could always find some business in London. I liked Annan very much when I met him last December. Charles Tennyson, whom I came across at lunch yesterday, would of course be splendid, but alas, he is seventy-eight and has an invalid wife. Roger favours a man of law, but I don't know if he has one in mind. What rude things people say about grocers! I remember that French saying of yours being thundered at the Hagley congregation (in English) many years ago by the vast rector, who had the suitable name of Manley Power, but as far as I remember, the only effect was that the village grocer never darkened the door of the church again—like Neville Talbot, Bishop of Pretoria, girding at his flock for imagining God to be an angry old man with a beard—'like Mr Jones there', after which Mr J. joined the Anabaptists.

> 'The grocer who has made his pile—
> Does he grow nicer?' 'No, Sir,

He alters not his ways nor style,
But grows a grosser grocer.'

Shakespeare or Milton, I forget which.

Your evening at the modern theatre gives me the shudders. There seem to be a great many degraded plays about. Are any of these Tennessee Williamses any good? It seems to be accepted that sour and confused writing is all right because that is what the times are. But isn't that a fallacy like 'Who drives fat oxen must himself be fat'?

2 June 1957   *Fisher House,*
                                    Rivington, Lancs.

I write to you from the garden of my beautiful poetess, on a blazing summer's day. I have been for two long walks on the moors behind the house—very like my Yorkshire moors, with larks and curlews and plover—and now I am looking through tall trees at a small green hillock—a considerable protuberance, which I am told is described in Domesday Book as a 'toft and quillet of land'. Beyond that is a hill with the agreeable name of Anglezarke. It is all green and sun-drenched and infinitely agreeable—and not a moment too soon, for last week was a non-stop racket. On Monday I dined with an American thriller-writer. On Tuesday I gave a luncheon-party (six men) for the American poet Robert Frost, a wonderful old man of eighty. Twenty years ago I resurrected his poetry over here and got Jonathan Cape to publish it—but this was my first meeting with the poet. He was witty and charming and anecdotal and in every way delightful. After lunch I drove him back to the Connaught Hotel, where he wrote out a poem for me. We were in a large hotel sitting-room, and I suddenly realised that the only other people in it, at the far end, were my mother-in-law (to whom I hadn't spoken for three and a half years) and Adlai Stevenson (whose wife was my wife's first cousin, and whose books I publish). I decided that these two—in many ways the most interesting Americans alive—should meet, so I greeted my mother-in-law and got the two men talking very successfully.

That evening I dined with Elisabeth Beerbohm and a very amusing

American Jew called Sam Behrman (playwright and author of an amusing book about Duveen the picture-dealer). He is a fanatical fan of my Walpole book and said many flattering and gratifying things. Next day I lunched at the Travellers with a young man who is writing a life of Conrad and thought I could help him. At 6 I went for drinks to my friends the Jepsons, where I met Sam Behrman again—also David Cecil and Jenny Nicholson (Robert Graves's daughter)—all friends of Max, about whom there was much talk. Sam is going to write some pieces about him in the *New Yorker*. Just as I was leaving who should arrive but Mr and Mrs Boris Karloff! I had imagined him dead long ago, but no. He is an Englishman (né Pratt) of perhaps sixty, well preserved and so dark that he must have more than a dash of the tarbrush. I quickly discovered that his great interest is *cricket!* and we chattered happily of Surrey and the West Indies. He bemoaned the fact that he would have to miss one of the Tests to make a film. Who, outside a dream, would expect to discuss Ramadhin with Boris Karloff? On I sped, to dine with a nice man who edits the *Twentieth Century*. Thursday was filled with another lunch party, a visit to the Max exhibition (private view), a finance committee meeting at the London Library, and a champagne cocktail party at John Lehmann's. In the throng were T.S.E. with his new wife, thirty-eight years younger than he and very charming. They stood inseparably arm-in-arm in the most charming way, and the despairing lines of his face visibly softened as he talked of his new flat and his great happiness—very touching.

From all this you can imagine the relief of spending most of Friday in the train to Blackpool, where the whole of the Booksellers Conference (several hundred strong, with wives in tow) is lodged in an enormous hydro built like a pseudo-castle with every possible castellation, crenellation and whatnot. After a *dance* I staggered to bed, but the trams along the front are silent only from 12 to 6. Yesterday I attended the morning session of the conference, snatched some lunch, and came over here. Another session there tomorrow morning, back to London after lunch, to Eton on Tuesday, two days of desperate clearing-up in the office, and off to Yorkshire at 4 a.m. on Friday— blessed thought. I make no promises about writing, but have in fact so come to enjoy using you as my diary that you never know.

Did you hear of the would-be-psychiatrist who, when asked why he wanted to be one, said: 'I really wanted to be a sex-maniac, but I failed in my practical'? Now I must get ready for a Lucullan dinner-party in Bolton. What next?

7 *June 1957*   *Grundisburgh*

I have a horrid feeling that this *may* not reach you on Saturday in your northern fastness. All depends on the relevant postmen, and you know what a temperamental lot they are. I have been trapesing about all this week—Malvern for speech-day, then Oxford for a finance(!) committee, the members of which felt no doubt that no decision on those short-term mortgages could be arrived at without my help. But all *my* to-ing and fro-ing compared with yours is like the Vicar's journeys from the blue bed to the brown compared with those of Ulysses (apropos of which *must* I have another try at *Finnegans Wake* in my spasmodic efforts to 'keep up,' and not sink further into codger-dom?). It is yours to command and mine to obey. But how happy I shall be if you say I needn't!

Robert Frost sounds a good man, as I had already half gathered from references to him in the Press—and I have always admired Adlai as one of those really first-rate Americans. The first-rate in any case is rare, and perhaps particularly so in U.S.A. but—well old Abe Lincoln has always been one of my very favourite men. Has Adlai a pleasant voice? How important that is! The Yankee accent is, to me, always something of a barrier, e.g. when the excellent Dean of Christ Church (a Canadian) preached at the Abbey School a moving sermon about Pet'r. How hard he made it for us to take the apostle seriously. And possibly Adlai may come from one of those queer states which make such laws as that forbidding anyone 'to fire a pistol at a picnic except in self-defence', or, in another state, 'to eat scorpions or lizards in public.' The man who produced these in print vouched for their truth.

I read Behrman's immensely amusing Duveen book, which, too, I suppose, depicted the fantastic element in those unhappy, bored millionaires who fell to collecting pictures in order to get rid of the stuff which *would* go on piling up in their banks. B. must be a man of sound literary taste. Is he as right always as he is about your H.W. book? I have sent all my Wisdens—I had a complete set—to my nephew Charles to lighten his lot in N.Z. and I must confess to you that my lavatory reading lately has been your *H.W.* An essential for a book that is raised to this rare eminence is that one knows it and loves it already. Its influence is active and swift and benign, 'noble and nude and antique'. 'All occasions invite his mercies and all times are his seasons' was actually written by Donne of God, but it has other applications. Who wrote that invocation, which begins:

> 'Hail, Cloacina, goddess of this place
> Whose devotees are all the human race . . .' and ends,
> 'Soft yet consistent let my offerings flow,
> Not rudely fast nor obstinately slow.'

But perhaps your sensitiveness as an author and as a clean, decent, high-minded gentleman will strongly resent all this? Somehow I don't think so.

I found, to my great pleasure, that that Test Match really did quicken my old blood. The W.I. morale would have made them very hard to beat, if they had won in an innings, as looked very probable. Ramadhin's ninety-eight six-ball overs in one innings! And now at last, after three disappointing years, we shall see what God meant Cowdrey to be, and the time approaching when E. Blunden will write of him as he wrote of Hammond in that admirable book which arrived this morning, *bless* you. It may even succeed *H.W.* in the lavatory! I should like to have heard you with Boris Karloff; thank whatever gods may be for life's incongruities. That passion for cricket turns up in very odd places.

I enjoyed two days at Oxford, with the Roger Mynors, where was the beloved Mrs Alington—in excellent health and spirits, though nearly blind and lame as a tree (whatever that simile conveys to you). I had a good crack with my old pupil John Bayley of New College who writes novels and reviews and wholly unintelligible tomes about 'Romance', and is a very nice fellow. His wife Iris Murdoch was there, coruscating, but not offensively, with brains. I liked her, and promised to read her new novel, though I know that in three pages I shall be hailing the coastguard. Did you read of that pathetic and foolish young lady whose fiancé, swimming in the Serpentine with her, disappeared; she reported to the police, etc. 'I cannot find my boy-friend,' and could not get them to take it seriously, apparently not mentioning that she last saw him in the water. I called on another don, who was closeted with four or five young men to whom he was expounding *The Anglo-Saxon Chronicle*. He and I chatted lightly for a few minutes, while they contemplated me with that derision that one sees on the faces of amiable camels when one throws them buns. I nearly ventured on the Parthian shot as I left: 'Do not fall into the juvenile error of thinking that old gentlemen are as intellectually moribund as they look,' but I refrained. I like Oxford better than Cambridge, though the march of civilization has made a dreadful mess of its appearance in the last hundred years. At both places some of the young men are growing beards, and to my mind and taste a young chin with hair is as indecent as a young skull without it. I had a boy in my house who wore a wig; one evening I visited him when he was about to sleep, and on the pillow was an object like a shell-less egg or a very young horse-chestnut. It looked soft and damp—horrible.

Next week I give the prizes at Shrewsbury, telling them to keep the torch burning and hand it on. I shall speak about choosing a profession, and must say *some*thing fairly new, so you can imagine how grateful I am for your lovely anecdote of the would-be psychiatrist. Absolutely '*ad rem*'. If some of the parents don't like it, they must lump it. The days of prudery are over. Or are they? I expect I shall end by playing safe.

11 June 1957   *Kisdon Lodge, Keld*

Your splendid letter was brought up this steep hill yesterday (Bank Holiday) morning by a charming young couple who had been fagged by the village postmaster. He is also the warden of the youth hostel and so must be obeyed. I am taking your advice so closely to heart that I can scarcely put down two coherent words, so you must blame your advocacy for the ensuing rubbish. When I tell you that I have to-day re-read (after thirty-five years) and thoroughly enjoyed *The Prisoner of Zenda*, you will see how well the medicine is working.

How well, in this book, Anthony Hope got on with the story. There's no padding anywhere. Tomorrow I shall devour *Rupert of Hentzau*. I bought a lot of Oscariana with me, but so far have read only *Both Sides of the Curtain*, an account by Elizabeth Robins, the American Ibsen-actress and novelist, of her arrival in England in 1888, when Oscar was very kind to her. From her book I noted two plums (or anyhow sultanas) for your delectation. (1) When Mrs Kendal put on Ibsen's *Enemy of the People* she sought to soften the blow by introducing as curtain-raiser a recitation of G.R. Sims's *Ostler Joe*. How confused the audience must have been! (2) When Lady Ritchie was asked what Tennyson's reading aloud was like, she said 'melodious thunder'.

Now for your letter. You are hereby forever absolved from struggling with *Finnegans Wake*. When an American professor was sent for review a book called *A Key to F.W.*, he sent it back, saying 'What F.W. needs is not a key but a lock.'

The rigours of the 4th of June were softened by being able to listen to the Test Match in different people's cars. What a day's cricket! Apart from that I saw Jonah and lots of old friends. My elder boy got back from W. Africa the night before (his 21st birthday), so we were all present.

13 June 1957   *Grundisburgh*

I went to the Lit. Soc. yesterday, and sat between Sir Cuthbert and Tim. Sir C. was most affable. He is a dry wine, but very far from flavourless. I enjoy that stern unbending Toryism; his old eye gleamed and smouldered when someone mentioned the *New Statesman*, and I feel pretty sure that if he found it in his house he would eject it with the tongs. By the way, did you see that *disgraceful* apology(?) which the editor made at the end of Birkenhead's letter protesting at his references to his father? Surely even in 1957 journalistic licence doesn't countenance very damaging statements about a distinguished dead statesman's character and actions, and when his son denies them, reaffirms them and adds that the authority for them is incontrovertible but can't be given.

After dinner Tim took Roger and self to White's where we had an excellent crack. Roger had a good Rabelaisian story or two about Queen Victoria, and altogether was in good form. The sales of *Votes for Women* he says are steady but not tremendous. Don't half-a-dozen serial extracts in the Press tend to damp down the subsequent book's sales? I have met several people who said they weren't going to buy or even read Alanbrooke's book after those enormous *Sunday Times* extracts. Peter Fleming took your place at the end of the table. What a particularly pleasant chap he is. And how bad, and at the same time compellingly readable, brother Ian's thrillers are! The pattern of all four that I have read is identical. Bond does not attract me, and that man with brains on ice and pitiless eye who organises the secret service in London seems to be a monument of ineptitude. Everything about Bond and his plans is known long before he arrives anywhere. But I cannot help reading on and there are rich satisfactions, e.g. when Mr Big is crunched by a shark. Very good about food; he always details what any meal consists of. The young women are rather oppressively and monotonously bedworthy, but then of course he isn't writing for septuagenarians.

Coming out of the Garrick we met Dick Stokes and his brother (who, you remember, had the curious and interesting habit of driving his wife about in a small go-cart through the woods, naked). Old Cuthbert greeted his fellow M.P. quite genially; I had quite expected him to hiss like a serpent at the sight of a socialist, but, as he said in the car, S. isn't really a socialist at all.

To-morrow I go to present the prizes at Shrewsbury School and utter the inevitable platitudes, but I shall do a little cutting of the ground from under their feet by beginning with a quote from André Gide: '*Toutes choses sont dites déjà, mais comme personne n'écoute, il faut toujours recommencer.*' I recommend it to you as a very useful opening gambit (not necessarily in French!). It is never easy to know what will click and what will flop, though I don't understand Bob Boothby's surprise at an anecdote he told to a Paisley audience flopping (D. Stokes told me). A recent mayor of P. had had a holiday in Paris. When he returned and someone asked him what he thought of Paris, his reply was: 'I can tell 'ee, mon, f—ing's in its infancy in Paisley.' Nobody smiled and B. Boothby was deeply disconcerted.

(the day on which
Napoleon looked forward to
'une affaire d'un déjeuner.'[1]

I knew there would be one of these insufferable heat-waves when
them above knew I was going to go by train from Ipswich to Shrewsbury and make a speech in a school hall full to the brim with millions
of the freest pores in these islands. However, though hot, it was about
ten degrees cooler than it is today, and fifteen less than it will be
to-morrow, when they know I train, and underground, and bus, and
walk to the heights of Highgate Village to my brother's house. On
Thursday I shall be watching Ramadhin, and Weekes, and Worrell—
and yawning when Trueman bowls, or Bailey bats. (Do you realise
that Trueman walks thirty-five steps from the crease to the end of his
run and that four balls an over the batsman leaves alone?) And then of
course on Friday come the thunder and rain.

Talking of thunder, Charles Tennyson corroborated 'melodious
thunder' for his grandfather's voice—and hinted—only hinted for he
is very loyal—that it must sometimes have been hard not to giggle
at those readings; the old man's 'o's and 'a's were so very hollow and
long-drawn-out. And, still on thunder, you know, of course, Haydon's
superb 'feathered silken thunder' for the sound of the peeresses in
their robes rising when the royal pair entered at their coronation. I
have always thought it a gem of the first water.

How lovely to find you are still fond of *Zenda* and *Hentzau*. I rather
doubt if even now I could read the end of Rudolf R. with entirely
unmisty eyes. Are they still in print?

Your *Hugh W.* is still in the smallest room. My old friend Oliver
Locker-Lampson, who, alas, went off his head, was full of whimsical
ideas; one was to produce a series of books for reading in this place.
They were to be called 'Lampson's Lavatory Literature', and were to
be printed on soft paper with a good many blank pages. I am sure his
amiable ghost would rejoice if his idea was taken up by one of our
leading and more spirited publishers—perhaps one living not a
hundred miles from Soho Square?

[1] i.e. the Battle of Waterloo.

117

By the way how *tremendously* good H.W's little character-sketches of Kipling and Winston are on pp. 296–298—so much so that I cannot help wondering whether—like E.F. Benson—memoirs from his hand wouldn't have easily outlasted his novels. These vignettes are nearly —*if not quite*—in the same class as Carlyle's. And the one of Winston was in 1928, but H.W. saw all the facets of his character that are now common knowledge. It is a brilliant page.

Thank you for that *mot* about *Finnegans W.*, also your letting me off trying to read it again. I can't remember who is the author of the Cloacina ode. Perhaps Gerald Kelly will know when I see him at Lord's. But I fancy he worships rather at the shrine of Priapus than that of the Lady C.

I think I did meet at Shrewsbury about the only famous man you don't know—though I may well be wrong about that. Father Huddleston, who was to talk in the chapel on Sunday. An amiable man. We did not talk about the S.A. colour-problem, but for some reason, obscure at the time, and now irrecoverable, about Sir Ernest Oppenheimer, of whom I know as much as a cow does of a clean shirt. At lunch I sat next to the Chairman, a genial Yorkshireman who was entranced by the story of the two Yorkshiremen watching Y. v. Lancs. One had unexpectedly to go home for an hour—and found his wife in bed with a neighbour. He was much annoyed and showed it to his friend when back at the match. His friend was sympathetic, but added: 'And I can tell 'ee some bad noos too. 'Utton's out' ('U pronounced like 'put on'). And now you will tell me Jelly used to tell that story at Private Business.

Last Sunday my nephew and I had lunch with one millionaire, and tea with another. Both were called Wills. Neither looked nearly as happy as I should if a millionaire. Or should I? Charles tells me they are a good deal fussed about the forthcoming report which will associate tobacco with cancer more definitely than ever before. And of course a generation is growing up many of whom, sensibly, don't begin smoking because they can't afford it.

Two splendid letters from you have been carried up the hill by the farmer in his jeep, and I have loved getting them. 'The first wet day,' I determined, 'shall be devoted to writing to George', but for a fortnight no drop of rain fell, and even now only a sharp shower last (Saturday) evening has broken the drought which is drying up the springs, ruining the farmers' hay, and delighting me. I can't tell you how deeply I am enjoying these enchanted days, which have been broken only (tell Pamela) by two delightful sales in sun-drenched gardens, at which I acquired a number of miscellaneous articles of great charm and beauty. Last night I got Friday's *Times* and the first day's score from Lord's. The second day I shall read of tomorrow evening in lofty detachment.

Since I last wrote I have read (besides *Rupert of Hentzau* and a brace of detective stories) six or seven long books about Oscar Wilde and his friends. The deeper one reads into a subject (particularly a complex one like this) the more interesting it becomes, or so I find. From one book—A.E.W. Mason's account of George Alexander and the St James's Theatre—I extracted this pleasing anecdote for you. The day after the first night of Barrie's play *The Admirable Crichton*, Mason ran into Squire Bancroft:

> I asked, having seen him at the performance, what he thought of the play. He was drying his hands on his towel in the lavatory of his club (? the Garrick) just before luncheon. He dried more slowly and shook his head with melancholy. 'It deals, my dear Mason, with the juxtaposition of the drawing-room and the servants' hall —always to me a very painful subject.'

So glad you enjoyed the Lit. Soc. I do hope you'll be able to get to the July dinner, since after that there is a break for summer holidays. Did I tell you that Peter Fleming is driving to Russia and back on one of these newly-allowed plans? He is to write some articles on the trip for *The Times* and is taking my son Duff as co-driver. I believe they hope to start in a few days' time.

I have a fine collection here of Nelson's sevenpenny series, including the two Anthony Hopes and three Sherlock Holmeses, on which I shall soon descend. I last read them all in 1939–1940, when I could fancy nothing else.

I plan to drive weeping back to London next Sunday (June 30), so write here this week, and to B.F. thereafter. I will resume proper letters directly I stop being all the things you said I was to be—and which I now am—brown, lazy, eupeptic, etc.

27 June 1957   *Grundisburgh*

I enjoyed Lord's. To my mind three days is right for 'a match at cricket'. The wicket was perhaps a bit too lively; several balls left the batsman no option but to duck. One black man seemed to receive one ball from Trueman plumb on the head. If not, how do you explain the hard crisp sound heard all over the ground? But I grant you the batsman was unmoved and didn't even scratch his head. Weekes was good; so was Cowdrey. I passed him and Bailey as they went in on Friday morning. I murmured 'Good luck'. Cowdrey said 'Thank you, sir'; Bailey said nothing. In five balls Bailey was out and in five hours Cowdrey had made 152. The god of cricket likes good manners. The black men are very temperamental; I expected to see Ramadhin cry when he missed literally the easiest catch ever in a Test Match. I much prefer Trueman as a bat to T. as a bowler.

His three sixes off consecutive balls were worth seeing, and never shall I forget the lovely sound of 25,000 people roaring with laughter when Weekes fell head over heels into the crowd and disappeared. Gerald Kelly was in good salacious form. I don't know that I much trust his judgments about people, but he is lively company and on the whole unmalicious. Like old Agate he mostly knows good stuff when he sees it.

For the last two days I have been among the girls—bumbling in and out of classrooms, listening to an anaemic, adenoidal lady with rheumy eyes declaiming the part of Lady Macbeth, watching Miss Biology Jones (this is how the H. Mistress distinguishes her from Miss Cello Jones, but the girls' affectionate name for her is 'Bilgy Rat') keeping sharp watch over the dissection of three crayfish. I took an ignorant but would-be intelligent interest in the three little virgins' work, but shied off just in time, as some little tension in the air told me that my questions were nearing those corporeal regions concerning which the crayfish, that prude of the piscine world, invariably purses his lips. I told one class about the young man after a job at the Lyceum, being tested by Irving and told to declaim a Shakespeare speech; he began 'Is this a *dadger*' etc., and Irving merely rang the bell and said 'Show this bedger out'. I remembered in time that Irving used a different first vowel in 'bedger'! I enjoy the visit greatly, but there are nervous moments—not the least nervous being at prayers where my chair, my hassock, and my little desk—or *prie-dieu*—are all of the lightest and most mobile character, and I remember how easily I get cramp when kneeling and how once I kicked my chair across the aisle.

There is a rich Victorian aura about that Bancroft story. Was he one of those bogus old splendids? I remember his reciting Dickens at Eton in, say, 1898. Very fine, no doubt, but does one become famous by recitation?

That Russian trip for your son and P.F. sounds exciting, if they are allowed to see what they want. I found the snapshot of Krushchef drinking soup in Finland disheartening. He looked so exactly like a pig. Of course soup *is* rather a severe test for anyone, with as many pitfalls to avoid as a golfer or an oarsman. How not to make a noise, or splash, or spill on the waistcoat, and of course if it is '*à la bonne femme*' the stuff is full of *strings*, very toothsome when they get to the mouth, but as hard to shepherd neatly as a flock of sheep. I took the letters of Horace Walpole away with me. Vilely edited. Several letters quite unintelligible if the *dramatis personae* are unknown, and no little parliamentary or literary imbroglio has any light shed on it. When I read that 'old Balmerino's windows have been stopped up because he talked to the populace' my interest is not aroused if I have no idea who B. was or why talking to the populace deserved punishment.[1] The editor was one C.B. Lucas—obviously an impostor.

---

[1] Lord Balmerino was one of the Jacobites imprisoned in the Tower before trial and execution, in 1746.

121

No letter to answer this week, which I *hope* means that you found even more work awaiting you than you had expected, and it had to be tackled at once if you were not to be *spurlos versunken*. But there is always the horrid possibility that you may be laid up, which in St Paul's emphatic but not very lucid words would be 'very tolerable and not to be borne'.[1]

There has been some very repulsive weather here since I wrote to you—by which I mean those cloudless days with the thermometer in the eighties. Like Satan in *P.L.* I often say 'Sun how I hate thy beams', because I have always hated great heat. Even when young an evening party in June could be sheer agony, as I wondered whether damp patches would appear on my stiff shirt-front before the evening was out. I always shirked dances for that reason, though to my taste there were a good many others too. The silver lining to the cloud is that I don't mind the cold and never get one. Though I *feel* it rather more than I did, as the springs run down.

I am being restful at home *pro tem*, but next week I have to speechify about my nephew off to New Zealand for five years, and then face a million exam-papers. One by the way is on *The Knight of the Burning Pestle* which I have just read—*pitiable* rubbish it seemed, but that old bumble-bee A.W. Ward calls it 'highly diverting,' and apparently split his old ribs over a barber being brought to represent the giant Barbarossa. What a lot of *cant* was poured into all writing about the Elizabethan Drama by Lamb and Co. Much, surely, is not worth a moment's attention.

I have just begun Harold Nicolson's *Sainte-Beuve*, who seems, so far, one of those men no one will find any difficulty in disliking rather strongly, but perhaps I may alter this opinion later. The frontispiece is definitely daunting—and has a certain resemblance to another critic I am reading—Edmund Wilson, who slashes dogmatically about. Perhaps he too, like Ste-B., suffers from a constricted urethra.

I am in doubt whether to refer to N.Z. in my speech as 'Pig-island'. The book I read about N.Z. life tells the English visitor he mustn't

[1] George wrote St Paul but must have been thinking of Dogberry in *Much Ado*, III, 3: 'most tolerable and not to be endured'.

mind them calling him a 'pommy' and then he can call N.Z. 'Pig-island' so long as he does it with a smile. I doubt if the risk is worth taking; they might not like my smile. By the way why 'pommy'— and, for the matter of that, why 'limey' which the more bilious Yanks like Vinegar Joe Stilwell still call Englishmen?

The lovelier the holiday, the grimmer the return. My last day on the blessed moors (Saturday) was a happy one. I spent the afternoon (dull and raining) at an auction sale in the Temperance Hall of a neighbouring village, where I secured a gigantic writing-desk, stuffed with drawers and surmounted by a fine cupboard or bookcase, for £1. My sister's car (which I had borrowed for the holiday) luckily has a luggage-rack on its roof, and two village stalwarts lashed the heavier part of the desk to it with rope. My faithful farmer transferred it to his trailer and towed it up the hill-track behind his jeep. Hardly was it in place when the sun poured out hot and strong, and I sat outside the cottage for almost two hours, glorying in the heavenly prospect.

Next day (Sunday) I sadly packed up the cottage and started off in steaming hot sunshine. All went well until, between Wetherby and Doncaster, the fan-belt broke, and the car nearly caught fire. By ringing up an extremely efficient A.A. man in Leeds I managed to get a new fan-belt brought from some garage, but this entailed a wait of one and a half hours. At Doncaster (a loathsome town at best) I ran into a cloudburst—visibility nil and water up to the axles. There-after all the elements took a turn—thick fog, two more distinct cloudbursts, incessant thunder and lightning. Eventually I limped ex-hausted into London just before midnight. My flat was stifling, and from the mountains on my desk it was clear that everyone I had ever heard of had written to me while I was away. My excellent partner Harry Townshend had acknowledged all the letters, saying 'Mr H-D will write to you as soon as he gets back.' This might have been possible if my secretary hadn't been on holiday. Instead I was bur-dened with a pudding-faced 'temporary', who understood no word I said from Monday to Friday. The temperature was in the eighties all week, and ten yards outside my office-window gangs of half-naked men were riveting steel girders incessantly. Never has my hatred of London and publishing been so grim and concentrated.

When I got down here on Friday I found *another* fine letter from you: you've no idea—or perhaps you have—how much I look forward to this weekly treat. Yesterday was so hellish hot that I was incapable of serious effort, though I got through another enormous mass of arrears of correspondence and papers, and all is now up to date. To-day has been much cooler, and I have mowed, and clipped, and picked cherries, and eaten strawberries and raspberries from the garden. I once saw *The Knight of the Burning Pestle* at the Old Vic, with Ralph Richardson in it, and mildly enjoyed it. But then I was very young and a glutton for what I believed was culture. Now I should say that if any play has been produced only twice in three hundred years, there must be some good reason for it. My dictionary says that 'pommy' comes from 'pomegranate', and 'limey' from 'lime-juice'—but why? I must get a better dictionary. What else? Jonah is bringing in the manuscript of his new book next week. It is to be called *Georgian Afternoon*. Nothing is now left for the old pet except perhaps *Elizabethan Goodnight*. Also Diana Cooper is arriving in London to talk about her memoirs. My favourite American writer, Ray Bradbury, turned up last week, and London is stiff with competing American publishers.

No word from Russia, though I daresay you've seen a few brief but quite amusing pieces of Peter's in *The Times*.

Just before I left Yorkshire I read *The Hound of the Baskervilles* with great pleasure: a joy for ever. Forgive this scrappy and disgruntled letter: perhaps by next Sunday I shall be further back in my rut, and better supplied with gossip. Just now I am yearning for the moorland air and the quiet.

11 July 1957   *Grundisburgh*

I can remember so well what getting back to harness was in old days, and how irksome work looked in September, and after all your lot is much worse, for your holiday is much shorter, your work is in

London and I expect the human stresses that you encounter daily are much more tedious than those of any beak, if only because men (and women) are far more detestable on the whole than boys. And of course the heat—so far worse among streets than in the country, coming as it does from walls and pavements as well as sky. Before you started for home I was already thinking of you with deep sympathy, knowing that, unlike me, you couldn't merely wear a shirt and trousers—socks and tie both discarded. But I am sorry to see judges have been doffing their wigs. They cannot realise that, in many of them, *all* the dignity they have resides in the wig, and that without it they are indistinguishable from sanitary inspectors. The great Justice Holmes was the only Yank I know who saw the point of our judicial wig, viz how it raises a probably quite commonplace official from humdrum humanity to an impersonal figure of justice. Even little Darling, bewigged, no longer looked like a mischievous urchin.

Your journey home was a nightmare and your arrival in the great imposthume, as somebody, probably Cobbett, called it—the heat, the din, the new sec, the mountain of letters. Even on my short visits to London, it is the *people* who oppress one's spirits—their quantity, their complexions, their expressions, and you have, further, to deal with them, and must often feel about them as old Carlyle did—and too often his feelings were put down to his dyspeptic grindings, which, as Birrell pointed out, cannot have been all that bad, as he lived to eighty-six.

I have found out about Pommy and Limey from that admirable *Dictionary of Slang* by Eric Partridge, which you are sure to have. Too long to quote and anyway *all* the theories about the origin of both are fearfully silly. This dictionary is a very good bedside book, full of interest and oddities. I had no idea what an enormous vocabulary is devoted to, shall we euphemistically call it, 'the way of a man with a maid' and the relevant apparatus. I don't think Queen Victoria would have been amused.

I look forward to Jonah's book, and indeed to several others from the great firm. A man in the Ipswich club recently was speaking warmly of that book of Herbert Agar's you have just brought out. And it is rare that any book is mentioned in the I.C., so no doubt it is good. H.A. has a very intelligent face. Didn't he marry poor Barbie

Wallace who lost three sons in the war and one after it? They were all in my house and two of them were well above the average.

I am just approaching my hard work of the year—marking exam-papers and subsequently cooking the marks. It is a dreary routine, but at least one does get *some* fun out of what they write on English Literature. Fancy having to mark a thousand Algebra papers—but the silver lining to *their* cloud is that they can mark twelve or fifteen an hour and we only about six for the same pay. The *Art* examiners mark forty-five to fifty per hour, i.e. a glance or two at that number of drawings of a pot—also for the same pay. Justice? Faugh!

P.S. I am enjoying E. Blunden's poems very much. Surely they are the real stuff, their roots deep in English soil, and in each one the experience or the picture, whichever it is, stands out so clean and clear. I don't always follow his thought, but that is to be expected. My taste is for the country poems mainly; the air and even the smell of Suffolk is in many of them, it seems to me. Such a poem as 'The Scythe struck by Lightning' has the depth and richness of a little Rembrandt. (Am I talking fearful nonsense?) 'Hammond' is in that great tradition which insists that cricket is a much bigger thing than a game. What is it? Not exactly an art, though not far off. Can an artist be completely unconscious of what he is doing? Cardus wrote some admirable pages about Woolley, but I am told that W. himself thought them just rubbish. Odd that E.B. should put *Relf* among his heroes. I don't remember that R. had much personality as a cricketer, and *qua* skill was not more than Beta plus. No one ever *wept* while he was batting as they certainly did during a Trumper or Jessop innings.

I am re-reading FitzGerald's letters rapidly. They don't seem to me as good as they once did, or as they are usually supposed to be. Perhaps my taste has coarsened. It is interesting to find how absurdly bad he and Spedding and others found Irving's Hamlet, which C.E. Montague, Agate and Co all said was tremendous. Not very extra-ordinary perhaps. After all, Ruskin said *Aurora Leigh* was the greatest poem in the English language, and Coleridge said neither Gibbon nor Landor could write English, and that Tennyson had no idea of metre.

In an attempt to provide you with a less dreary letter I am reverting to my old plan of beginning on Saturday. Thank goodness Adam
chose to come home rather than go to Lord's, which must have been
pretty miserable. Moreover the motor-mower is still enough of a new
toy to be welcome, and most of the grass has been cut by A. and the
little Linklater boy who has come home with him.

Your excellent letter arrived this morning—with M.B. on G.M.
faithfully returned. Many thanks. It is to be included in the forthcoming new edition of Max's *Mainly on the Air*. How I detest a
practice which compels one to buy another copy of a book one already
had, just for one or two extra pieces. Yesterday afternoon I went to
the Royal Soc. of Lit. to hear S.C. Roberts's excellent lecture on Max,
which was described in to-day's *Times*. It was first-rate and beautifully
delivered: indeed when S.C.R. read extracts in Max's voice the likeness
was too much for at least one lady, who almost burst into tears. The
lecture, S.C.R. told me, is to be included in a collected volume of his
essays during the next few months. Jonah was there, come straight
from Lord's in grey top hat. I am now half-way through the typescript
of his new book, which is delightful, and I think just as good as the
others. I have told him I'll get it out in January. He is now worried
because he has nothing more to write about, except religion, on which
his views are not readily saleable.

Last week was much more bearable than its predecessor—cooler
for one thing, and I suppose I'm growing used again to the hateful
saddle. Edmund Blunden arrived on Wednesday from Siegfried
Sassoon's. I gaily told him, months ago, that he could stay as long as
he liked, and lo he is staying till November! So glad you're enjoying
his poems: they are indeed the real stuff, and I'm glad to say this
volume has had some excellent reviews, notably Betjeman in the
Daily Telegraph and Alan Ross in the *T.L.S.*

Sunday night, 14 July

The death of old Lady Rothenstein (Will's widow) has brought to
light (as I expected) the originals of Oscar's letters to Will, and perhaps
to her. They are coming to me soon. Somehow, before I finish the job,

I must have one more shot at running to earth the *many* O.W. letters which I know are somewhere in America.

Most interesting letter of your son's—an obvious writer in embryo. That *'hypnotically* straight road'—*le mot juste* calling up a picture of a passenger turning slowly into a hen with its beak on a line. And 'knifing' too. Clearly his father's son. The whole letter is very good reading. But Peter's health sounds a little sinister, or aren't the Russian medicos good at diagnosis? So many ailments start in the same way. I once had a boy in my house who got polio. A week later another boy had a temperature and a stiff neck and back and Dr Sprot (an ass) said, in view of the other boy, this 'must be regarded with grave suspicion'. No 2 was whisked home for a fortnight's quarantine, was perfectly well in two days and practically ran amok at home from boredom. I had, by the way, been told by Sprot that there might be a carrier in the house, and asked how we could find out. He replied with a wintry smile that there *was* a way, but he thought it was hardly practicable. I asked what it was. He asked how many people there were in the house. I said sixty-two. He said 'Well you would have to get sixty-two monkeys and inject the blood of the sixty-two people severally into them and one monkey will be paralysed and reveal the carrier.' I thanked him warmly for his helpful suggestion, but thought that as the monkeys could not be supplied under three months, we must regretfully think up something else.

I am back among my exam-papers after the London-New Zealand dinner yesterday, where I had to speechify about my nephew. It was a hot and hearty evening at Goldsmiths' Hall. I was introduced to a score of New Zealanders, who seemed to me immensely amiable and quite indistinguishable—rather as Chinese are, even though some were fat and others were thin. The famous Lord Freyberg was there and was charming about my speech but rather spoilt it by looking quizzically at me and adding 'Donnish, you know'. No doubt it was —the hand becomes subdued to what (for thirty-seven years) it works in, but I then gathered that all he meant was that I had tried to find the right words. And that, he added, was very good for the N.Z. audience, because in N.Z. nobody ever does that. And, you know, it wasn't really all that Max B.-ish. I essayed nothing like his label for Joad—'that mellifluous quodlibetarian'. Anyway it was a very friendly audience. I had some talk with Denzil Batchelor who seemed a pleasant chap. He too spoke and told rather too many cricket stories, not of the best vintage, including one about my uncle Alfred that was wrong in a great many ways—like that meat Johnson and Boswell had on the way to the Hebrides which the Doctor described as ill-killed, ill-hung, ill-cooked and ill-served, and no doubt in due course ill-digested. I sat next to the wife of Judge Aarvold who used to play Rugger brilliantly, and flirted in that shameless way common to the senile. She was very good fun, most amusing (and far from wrong) about the immense tedium of a day at a Test Match.

That sounds a good company at the Lit. Soc. I should like to have met Harold Caccia again. How nice of you—and characteristic—to hand on what I said of old Cuthbert—exactly what dear Dr J. used to advise: 'Sir, it increases benevolence.' And so many love doing the opposite.

My exam-papers are in full spate. I have just dealt with Harpenden, a co-ed school, and as usual the girls are much better than the boys, though one young lady paraphrased old Gaunt's 'this dear dear land' into 'this very expensive land' which is almost too up-to-date; and some of the boys who dimly gathered that the beak had said a 'pelting farm' was a 'paltry' farm, improved it into a 'poultry' farm. On the whole the percentage of candidates who get any good out of studying Shakespeare steadily falls—less speedily than the pound, but still steadily.

We have got to the heavy part of the summer, the foliage has, so to say, a middle-aged spread, and the trees which in May were Apollos are now Farnese Herculeses.

21 July 1957   Bromsden Farm

Many thanks for returning Duff's letter so promptly. Ian Fleming rang up the other day to say that if on his return the boy can write a couple of short articles on his trip to Russia, the *Sunday Times* will print them. I've heard no more from the travellers, and have no idea when they'll be back.

My good resolve of starting my letter to you on Saturday was yesterday broken by my attendance at the Johnson Club dinner at Worcester College. Once again you were sadly missed, and indeed I fancy you would have enjoyed the evening more than most of the Gough Square ones. *Imprimis* the dinner was ample and first-class, secondly there was no paper; only a weakish speech by Harold Williams, welcoming the guests. These included J.C. Masterman (the Provost of Worcester), C.H. Wilkinson (the Vice-ditto), Basil Blackwell the bookseller, the Master of Pembroke (Oxon), and an aged American called Sherburn, who has just published an edition of Pope's letters in five vols—a lifetime's work. I took Simon Nowell-Smith, the ex-librarian of the London Library (who lives near here), and sat between him and Davin, the Assistant Secretary to the Clarendon Press, an aggressive but intelligent and incisive New Zealander. Before and after dinner we talked amiably in the J.C.R., a beautiful room with a barrel-shaped ceiling, from which, they say, Amy Robsart fell to her death.

Last week I had three business lunches—two with American publishers and one with a literary agent. I also took E. Blunden to Lord's on Wednesday, but we saw only an hour's poking and scratching by Richardson and Sheppard on a puddingy wicket before rain put a stop to it. (E.B. went again on Thursday and much enjoyed it. Have you, by the way, ever read his *Cricket Country*? If not I'll send you a copy.) On Wednesday evening I took E.B. to dine with the Day Lewises. It was a gay evening and I told too many stories. On Thursday I gave champagne in my flat to fourteen people, in honour of my American friend Ray Bradbury. They drank seven bottles, and I had a job to get rid of them. By the time I got down here on Friday I was all in. Nevertheless I managed to do a bit of the mowing that evening, and just as well too, since yesterday was too wet by far, and to-day I had time only for about half the rest before thunder, lightning, a cloudburst and hailstones the size of mothballs drove me in to Oscar Wilde. When I have composed another 165 footnotes I shall have brought him to his trials, poor man.

Yesterday a wild deer was sighted near the farm, and this morning the vegetable garden was full of strange footprints, but we haven't yet glimpsed the animal, and I long to do so: they are so graceful and they jump so beautifully. Do you know this poem? I won't tell you who wrote it, for fear of putting you off.

DEER[1]

Shy in their herding dwell the fallow deer.
They are spirits of wild sense. Nobody near
Comes upon their pastures. There a life they live,
Of sufficient beauty, phantom, fugitive,
Treading as in jungles free leopards do,
Printless as evelight, instant as dew.
The great kine are patient, and home-coming sheep
Know our bidding. The fallow deer keep
Delicate and far their counsels wild,
Never to be folded reconciled
To the spoiling hand as the poor flocks are;
Lightfoot, and swift, and unfamiliar,
These you may not hinder, unconfined
Beautiful flocks of the mind.

Good, isn't it? The 'unfamiliar' is part of their charm. I shall never forget the moment when, walking alone on the Wiltshire downs, I came face to face with a fox, and we stood staring at each other for a minute before he withdrew and I lost his bright colour in the grass. Birds' nests with eggs in them produce some of the same wonder and delight. I could easily turn and live with (selected) animals.

Alas, my promised visit to you is fading under the pressure of events, and any moment you will be overwhelmed with grandchildren, and my clock will have to tick a few more million times before its proud owner carries it off. Sometime soon I must spend a couple of days in Dublin, trying to get some sense out of Mrs Yeats, who never answers letters. And Arthur Ransome will soon be offended if I don't spend a day or two with him in rural Lancashire. And Diana Cooper's memoirs (now to be in two volumes) need their spelling, syntax and punctuation seeing to, and authors *will* send me manuscripts, and the

[1] By kind permission of Messrs Sidgwick & Jackson.

riveting outside the office window is loud and continuous—oh well, as Oscar said,

> He who lives more lives than one,
> More deaths than one must die.

I look forward to seeing the younger generation pluming its wings for a flight in the *Sunday Times*. Will he consult Father about grammar and construction? Will infinitives split and participles hang? Humphrey never consulted me about *his* book, and I could have saved him from giving his great-uncles the wrong-coloured beards, and distinctions which they never achieved. Furthermore, though he is always writing articles—for papers even you have probably never heard of—he never, to my knowledge, deliberately learnt anything about style. I cannot think that to have had *Romola* read to him at Sunday Private by Cyril Butterwick helped him much towards the quite lively style which he has. I am pretty sure that what he has got most from is old Shaw's music criticism—by Corno di Bassetto. Do you know of any better model? I always delight in his two vols of *Dramatic Opinions and Essays*, and so, I believe, did Max B. What a bright, sharp, nimble sword the English language was in his hand! And (did I say this last week?) there are, as Serjeant Buzfuz said, critics, 'erect upon two legs and bearing all the outward semblance of men and not of monsters,' who don't think the Inquisitor's speech in *St Joan* superb.

That Johnson Club dinner sounds good fun. I always like Masterman, though I don't know him at all well, and that absurd old C.H. Wilkinson too. Lord Rosebery, when very old, told someone that only the determination to outlive Mary Drew kept him alive, for high among the terrors of death, according to him, was the certainty of being written about by M.D. She couldn't write interestingly for some reason—probably because she had no humour.

I envy you your wild deer—nothing so lovely ever roams the glebes of Suffolk. Who wrote that lovely poem? 'Phantom, fugitive . . . printless as evelight, instant as dew (I was *mouthing* it and wrote, if you please, 'due'!). I like it. But why 'kine' in these days? What is wrong with cows? Though I remember Arthur Benson telling us 'cows' would *not* do in poetry. That, however, was in 1899. And you remember Dr J. protested against the vulgarity of 'blanket' and 'knife' in *Macbeth*. I wonder why you don't tell me the author's name. Is he a *bête noire*? I once had a similar meeting with a fox to yours—a red-letter moment. I still recollect the piercing intelligence of his eye—all curiosity and vigilance and a general air of being equal to any occasion. I bet Chaunticleer would never have outwitted him as the Nonnes Preeste recorded, and as half the school population of England have been writing about this week—damn them! I am about half-way through my oakum-picking, but the worst is yet to come—mere essay-answers on five different books, and to separate the wheat from the chaff is a really infernal job. These exams are full of surprises. Can you tell me why the papers on *The Devil's Disciple* are mostly v. bad, while those on *The Riddle of the Sands* are mostly v. good? Because I can't. No outstanding howler so far, but I like 'yhact' for 'yacht,' and there are some good names—Grut, Seex, Allbless, Gbow, Jaglorn, Jellinek, Pedgrift, nicely sweetened yesterday by Flowerdew and Lillies.

Your visit, alas! but I know how pressed you are. We will *somehow* get the clock up to London in the coming months, probably when they put the railway fares up. My brother-in-law (Ld Leconfield) meets any grumbling about inflation with what *he* calls the comforting thought that the value of money has *always* depreciated since William the Conquerer (when a pig cost threepence).

27 July 1957   *Bromsden Farm*

You won't get much tonight, for I am full of sleep after a long bout of gardening. The Russian travellers are due home on Monday; Eton breaks up on Wednesday; and soon the house will be stuffed with untidy, large, noisy but charming children. If you look at *Cricket Country* again you will find two oblique references to me. Somewhere, in a forgotten place of safety, I have an excellent photograph of E.B. and myself coming down the pavilion steps to open the innings in 1935 or thereabouts.

So glad you liked the Fallow Deer poem. It is by Drinkwater, and I thought his name might possibly put you off. He wrote other good poems, but made himself a joke and a nuisance, and is now, I fancy, scarcely read. I knew him 1930-32, since Peggy Ashcroft had been in the original production of his play *Bird in Hand*, but I offended him (he was very touchy) and we met no more.

Sunday night, 28 July

Just now, as I was addressing an envelope to you, I thought how astonishing it is that by scrawling a few marks on a piece of paper I can get it delivered to you in Suffolk the day after it's posted. We take everything for granted nowadays, and complain if the miracle doesn't always work properly. Perhaps a long day of mowing has made me thus wonder.

My Canadian friend George Whalley (didn't you meet him?) came to tea with his wife and three children, otherwise a peaceful day, and now Tchaikovsky's Fifth Symphony is delighting me from a little box as I scribble rubbish to you. Miracles never cease.

Last week was oppressively hot in London, and I had a lot to do. On Monday Jonah and Evy gave a dinner-party of eight people in a private room at the Travellers' Club. The Duke of Wellington, Hamish Hamilton, Lady Harlech, Muriel Gore and Jonah's daughter Lavinia were the other guests. Very agreeable, but just now I have so much editorial work waiting at home that I begin to fret soon after the coffee is brought in. I particularly liked Lady Harlech—I expect you know her, elder sister of Salisbury and David Cecil.

On Tuesday I couldn't avoid a cocktail party on the third floor (walk up) in Harley Street. It was so hot and airless that I could soon feel sweat dripping down me. I talked to A.P.H., Gerald Barry and others, drank two champagne cocktails, and dashed on in pouring rain to the Garrick, where I gave dinner to Blunden and his wife. Wednesday was quieter, but Thursday left me breathless. In the morning I went with Diana Cooper to the Crypt of St Paul's to choose a place for Duff's memorial tablet. We were taken round by the Clerk of the Works (who would keep showing us where the bombs fell—and indeed I can't understand how the building stood it) and the accredited architect, Lord Mottistone, a very agreeable chap of about my age. (He is the son of Jack Seely and I remembered how once at the Beefsteak (or perhaps the Other Club) someone accused Duff of being the worst Secretary of State for War in our history. Duff answered: 'How dare you say that, with Jack Seely sitting at the table?') We had the Crypt to ourselves, and since in the Cathedral over our heads two bishops were being lengthily enthroned by the A B of C, there was much fine singing coming down to us. I'd never before been in the Crypt and was much moved by it all—the majesty of Nelson's sepulchre, the massive ugliness of Wellington's. 'You've no idea,' said the Clerk of Works, 'how difficult it is to fit in the hot water pipes among all these graves.' Mottistone would love to move forward the altar in St Faith's Chapel, 'but,' pointing to a splendid tombstone on the floor, 'Bishop Creighton's in the way.' We chose quite a good place for Duff, round the corner from Nelson, and I dashed back to make polite conversation to a Dutchman who markets our books in Holland. After lunch I had to make a tiny speech at the A.G.M. of the London Library, which was attended by maybe a hundred members. The only other speakers were T.S.E. and Harold Nicolson. That evening I dined with Sam Behrman and the Jepsons. On Friday morning I went to the Tate, and checked the texts of Oscar's surviving letters to Rothenstein. It was worth the effort, since I found the printed versions full of misreadings, and a new letter as well. Idiotically I left my umbrella behind, and the small metal tag they gave me in exchange won't keep much of me dry. Tomorrow the circus starts again. *Ora pro nobis.*

1 August 1957   *Grundisburgh*

Your life is simply Masefield's *Odtaa*[1]. Ceaseless activity! The very opposite pole to mine—eight hours a day for the last three weeks, I agree, but all of them in my chair. Let me say magnificently—all *my* activities are those of the spirit, though possibly you may think that is putting rumination and mild meditation and day-dream rather high! My first bout of drudgery nears its end. The last lap was tedious—young men and maidens to the number of two hundred pouring out

[1] One Damn Thing After Another.

135

not what they thought but what they had been told to pretend they thought about Falstaff and Wordsworth and Coleridge and Browning and Tennyson and Boswell and Johnson. Some of it was very dreary. The girls are the worst infliction because they have imbibed *all* the right things to say and their regurgitations are relentlessly copious. They know all their five books by heart, and have that disgusting habit of quoting twelve lines to prove a point where two would be ample. And I can *never* pass a quotation without verifying it and sometimes they take a long time to find. (Do you know that in my three-vol Wordsworth the Tintern Abbey poem is among the contents simply as 'Lines'. Isn't that frightfully silly?) The best (or worst) thing so far is a perfectly sound and knowledgeable reference to the 'bona roba', Jane Nightwork,[1] infinitely spoilt in one way, and infinitely improved in another, by her being called 'Florence Nightingale'.

I agree with you about the daily miracles—the post etc (I hope you ask 'has the *post* come' and not the 'mail'?). Wireless and TV still seem to me *sheer* magic. And though doctors don't go in much for wonder, I imagine the human body and its workings are the same. We too listened to Tchaikovsky. Very rich. I suppose the Leavises of the music-world have long put him on the scrap-heap—but who cares a rap about them? I literally *am* that figure of everybody's fun who knows nothing about music but does know what he likes. The truth is that *he* isn't absurd, but the remark is.

Mima Harlech is delightful and always was—also her sister, the lovely Mowcher. What *do* these Cecil nicknames mean—Fish and Linky *inter alia*?

Did you hear Winston last night? Very old. The words petered out at times and he often misread a word and corrected it. Why did he have to make sure of getting the great Coke right? Surely one of the names everyone knows.

I like your uncle Duff's retort about Jack Seely. I never met him but my Uncle Alfred didn't like him—'a bumptious fellow,' and indeed I heard someone else say he was the most conceited man in the world. But I believe he *was* very brave and that should count for something, as Bishop Gore said of Bishop Ingram's being a good man,

[1] See *Henry IV*, Part Two, III, 2.

after they had all been pouring contempt on his theology and utterances in general. I have never been into St Paul's crypt; it sounds very impressive. Is Donne there—a very tremendous man. 'If some King of the earth have so large an extent of dominion . . .'. Do you know that sermon? But I expect you have your favourites among them. I am not clever enough for much of his poetry, but, golly, he could write prose —as Housman said, a much more difficult job.

4 August 1957   *Bromsden Farm*

I imagine that this date means nothing to our children, but although I was only six in 1914 it tolls for me every year the death of the Golden Age, while September 3, which affected my life much more, passes almost unnoticed. I envy you and all those who had some grown-up years before the deluge, for the true *douceur de vivre* will not come again in our time.

It is said that Jack Seely recommended his soldier-servant for the V.C. saying: 'He's as brave as a lion: he goes everywhere I go.'

Yes, I do know that Donne sermon, and that particular sentence is in my commonplace book. Many of his poems are wonderful, even if one doesn't fully understand them. Try declaiming in the night-watches:

> At the round earth's imagined corners, blow
> Your trumpets, Angels, and arise, arise
> From death, you numberless infinities
> Of souls, and to your scattered bodies go.

Pull out all the stops, and the mice will marvel in the wainscot.

My two elder children have gone to Wales for the week-end, so we have only Adam with us. He missed a Distinction in Trials by thirty-five marks, but seems unmoved. Yesterday I got a note from Birley to say that Eton has awarded my elder boy Duff a 'Miss Goodall Bursary' of £100 a year for his three years at Oxford. It's most generous and will be an enormous help.

Last week I once again lost my precious little engagement-diary, on which my pell-mell life depends. For thirty-six hours I was helpless, unable to remember anything—and then a blessed taxi-driver brought it back. I rewarded him with 10/-, feeling that it should be £10.

On Monday I gave lunch to a friend from the country, signed some cheques at the London Library (a one-man meeting of the Finance Committee), visited Lady Emily Lutyens, who is very frail and thin but full of life and delight in her book's good reviews. That evening I dined with the Ray Bradburys and another friend at the Mirabelle restaurant in Curzon Street, which is probably the most expensive in London. Admittedly we had a very good dinner, with two bottles of reasonable wine, but the bill for the four of us came to £16!! Even our American hosts were a little shaken. How can *anyone* afford such prices out of to-day's incomes? Clearly it's impossible, and indeed most of the other customers looked as though they depended on expense accounts. I felt quite guilty for the next day or two.

Monday night, 5 August

This morning, before I was up, Comfort and Adam set out for a rag regatta at Wargrave, from which they didn't return till 7 p.m. This left me happily marooned for the day, but it also delayed this letter's departure till tomorrow. I divided the day placidly between Oscar and the garden, eradicating a large area of nettles under the walnut tree, and getting very hot even in its shade. All farmers were supposed to plant a walnut near their farmyard to keep off the flies. I now begin to think it was efficacious because all the flies in the neighbourhood are attracted to it, rather than repelled by it.

The rest of last week was comparatively calm, but the hideous and incessant clangour of the builders outside my window (the permanent closing of which makes the room suffocating) prompts me to spend as little time in the office as possible. On Thursday, for instance, I spent almost half the day in the Reading Room of the B.M., looking up things for my Oscar notes among the stuffy rustle of all those black clergymen and other *habitués*. Once in a way I enjoy such a diversion. If I could concentrate solely on Oscar for a month I could polish off the whole huge job: as it is, moving by fits and starts, heaven knows when I shall finish. Most of my considerable collection of reference books is in Soho Square and too heavy to bring down, so at week-ends I have to concentrate on what I can do here. This evening I have succumbed to a fierce *furor notandi* (if there is such a phrase) and have solved (or skirted) a few nasty cruxes (or cruces?). I've just read Evelyn Waugh's new book[1]. Short though it is, it should be shorter, but much of it is interesting, and it's straight fact lightly disguised as fiction. Have also read Stevenson's letters to Charles Baxter, and that old but still amusing skit, *The Green Carnation*. Also a rotten biography of Lord Alfred Douglas, not to mention sundry MSS and proofs. Are you going away? Or just resisting the invasions of grandchildren? Fleming has written three *Times* 'turn-over' articles on the Russian trip. They should appear this week.

7 August 1957   *Grundisburgh*

Another good instalment of your diary. How right you are about pre-Aug. 4 1914. I can of course remember it very well, and equally of course that we didn't in the least realise at the time that it *was* a golden age. In fact I am pretty sure that the real golden age was before the Boer War. At the time of the Diamond Jubilee there literally wasn't a cloud in the sky, whereas from 1902 onwards there were continuous though not loud rumblings about the German menace— and a good many strikes too. I remember an evening at Hagley when Leo Maxse shook us all to the core telling us all he *knew* about German plans, and how pleased he was after hearing that the Kaiser and Bülow had foamed with rage over one issue of the *National Review* and said that such a man as the editor oughtn't to be allowed to live. He also reported that the most encouraging news from Germany was that sodomy was about to be, not abolished, but legalised, as that must mean decadence pretty quick. How nice it would be if everything was as simple as that!

Apropos of the *National Review*, is it in that organ that the Lord Altrincham has been attacking the Queen and her entourage? I haven't seen it and, like James Forsyte, nobody ever tells me anything. In fact it becomes increasingly clear that if (a) you have no television, and (b) you never read the *Express* or *Mirror*, very soon you are cut off from all knowledge of what is going on. As I have often said before,

[1] *The Ordeal of Gilbert Pinfold.*

there is a great deal to be said for being seventy. Probably there always was, at least after 1897. I suppose *you* have never handled a golden sovereign? A beautiful coin! It rang with a note like the song of a bird, as Homer says the string of Ulysses's bow did when he twanged it. And what a lot of things it bought—including a *ton and a half* of coke. But that way madness lies. Carlyle—that very great and much underrated writer—declared that three hundred years of trouble were needed for the human spirit to purge and rebuild itself after the first blast from heaven, i.e. the French Revolution. So we're not far past the middle of that. I think that dyspeptic old genius—who, with Ruskin, really *was* made unhappy by the awful gap between rich and poor a century ago—would not have been noticeably blither now. Of course you know his Johnson essay—surely one of the noblest things ever written. But how Victorian are these naive enthusiasms!

Next week I go to Cambridge for a week. If the spirit continues to move you (this refers to the week after next) please send the results to me at the University Arms Hotel, St Andrew's Street, as we shan't finish before Thursday or Friday week.

I like your Seely story, but—well I prefer the A.J.B. attitude, re-calling something that happened 'When I was Prime Minister, or something of that sort', or the Duke of Wellington. Wasn't it Tennyson who said a French hero's answer to the ass who said he was delighted to have shown the way to 'the great Duke' would have been '*Oui; on m'appelle le grand*'. That type of modesty is strictly English, I suppose. Foreigners from Tamburlaine onwards have never had it.

How good that you too spotted (when?) that great Donne sermon —'damped and benumbed, wintered and frozen, smothered and stupefied' (but, my dear, we mustn't admire *beauty of language* now-adays; that is hopelessly *vieux jeu*). Some criminal stole my volume of Donne's prose and I suppose now it is out of print. I must wander down the Charing Cross Road again soon.

I have just embarked on Aldington's biographical sketch of D.H. Lawrence and, after fifty pages, dislike both men about equally. It is a library book, but much greater strength of mind than I possess would have been necessary to prevent my twice writing 'ass!' in the margin. The Ipswich Library books are full of pencilled comments. The one I like best was on a volume of H. James's short stories. One reader had written 'Tripe', and another had prefixed 'Worse than.' *Sic transit!*

Congratulations on the Goodford Bursary. Do you remember Miss Goodford? It was impressive to see every day in chapel the daughter of the last headmaster but five (or are *you* right in calling it Goodall? If so, who in thunder *was* Miss Goodall?). Miss Goodford and her brother, both blind, used to watch cricket on Agar's by *ear*—just as Wilfred Rhodes does now—not, I am glad to hear, at all sorry for himself.

Your Mirabelle dinner gives me goose-flesh. I remember seeing old Agate at the Ivy doling out paper after lunching me and a Baconian solicitor from Birmingham, whom J.A. mocked at unceasingly. But I did not feel particularly compunctious, as it was *his* double brandies and cigars which inflated the figures. The weekly advertisements in the *Tatler* seem to show there is still plenty of money about. Is it all stock exchange profits, or is everybody living on capital?

11 August 1957   *Bromsden Farm*

I don't think you need waste any time on either the *National Review* (now a paltry rag) or Lord Altrincham. I only wish the Queen or the Duke of E. could hit back!

Your instructions about my writing to Cambridge are, alas, not wholly clear. After much thought I have decided that this letter should go to Grundisburgh and next week's to Cambridge: I hope that's right.

Why will you persist in reading books by the loathsome and fifth-rate Richard Aldington? You never enjoy them, and there's so much else. Rather the egregious Leavis any day.

The din in Soho Square is likely to continue for months: 'hammer-ing' is altogether too gentle a term for the combination of circular saw, cement-mixer, and metallic crashing—sometimes one can't hear a word in the room. They start before 7 a.m. and go on for at least twelve hours.

The H.M. certainly wrote Miss Good*all*; blessings on her, how-ever she spelt her name.

Fleming has driven to Scotland for the Twelfth. What did you think of his *Times* articles? My Duff is now struggling to cover the same ground without repeating what P.F. has said. He (Duff) has taken some first-rate colour-photographs, and he is trying to persuade the *Illustrated London News* to buy a page or two of them.

Last week was both shorter and quieter than usual. The silly season must now mercifully be upon us. One day I went book-hunting with E. Blunden to our old haunt, the barrows in the Farringdon Road. There are only half as many as there were twenty years ago, but we struck a sixpenny day and came back happily laden. In my time I have picked up wonderful bargains, and a large part of my library came from there.

In the past twenty-four hours I have read two detective stories and reviewed eight, besides adding a few Oscar footnotes to the pile. *Punch* have proved extremely co-operative, giving me an exact list (with dates) of all Ada Leverson's contributions. This has enabled me to date several letters and explain otherwise obscure references. I must confess that there are times when the sheer weight of work still to be done on the Wilde letters fills me with the gloomiest apprehension, but I love the job and must just plug on, doing as much as I can each day.

Next Tuesday I have been summoned to lunch with the Editor of *The Times*[1] in the Ritz Grill! Why? You shall have a full report next week. I've only met him twice, once at a dinner-party and once in the Athenaeum. We shall see.

If I go to Rapallo to see E. Beerbohm, it may be easiest to go next week: perhaps I shall spend my fiftieth birthday by 'the bluest and beautifullest of seas'. If my mission there is successful, I shall have *another* book of letters (Max's to Reggie Turner) to edit alongside Oscar. And at any moment the manuscript of Diana Cooper's memoirs will appear. How much can one do in a day? You've no idea how often I envy you your summer-house and your leisure. The latter is a blessing which youth squanders carelessly, and in the modern world it largely disappears until one reaches 'that unhoped serene that men call age'. So you see how enviable you are!

[1] Sir William Haley.

What a detestable month August can be! Today the garden is carpeted with thunderbolts, so to speak, and the thunder has that explosive suddenness and violence which led that lunatic (who ought to have been instantly set free) to exclaim 'God has shot himself'. If at lunch-time I hadn't run like Jesse Owens from summer-house to kitchen I should have been wet to the skin. Augusts in the nineties were not like that. 'The sunbrown harvest men with August weary' is right off the bullseye in mid-twentieth century.

Your interpretation of my slightly half-witted directions was perfectly correct. I could not get out of my head that I was going to Cambridge on Monday when it was really Wednesday, i.e. tomorrow. *Next* Tuesday I shall be at the University Arms Hotel, surrounded by Americans.

I have finished Aldington on Lawrence. You are surprised at my reading anything by the man who in a competition for the post of Europe's prize sh-t would surely win hands down. Well, I will tell you why I do so. I can hardly read ten consecutive pages of D.H.L. without being invaded by boredom raging like toothache. But apart from so many people saying so, I am sure he is a genius—and in descriptive bits he can touch almost any height. And you know, one of the chief dangers of senectitude is a contented nestling in tastes and opinions formed many years ago, and of necessity steadily narrowing, so I quite often have shots at writers like D.H.L. and—dare I confess it?—Jane Austen!—to both of whom I am on the way to being allergic. And besides that I find getting angry (not with living people) is rather a tonic. And again—I often used to tell boys about Tolstoy deciding that Shakespeare was absurd, and the universal admiration of him merely showed that the world was mad, and while you and I (I said to them) read one book half through and decide the author is bad, he formed his opinion after reading all Shakespeare *seven* times, and had a right to his opinion.

But this is all very boring. And one opinion I shall never change, i.e. that whatever D.H.L. was as a writer, as a man, a member of the human family, he was as near impossible as anyone could be—a dreadful compound of hatred and malice and arrogance and deliberate wrong-headedness. As for Aldington—but why should I take coals to Newcastle? You have got him docketed all right.

Goodall is no doubt the name—Provost a hundred and more years ago, one of those bland, learned, virtuous dignitaries who resisted any change of any kind, and in whose time that 'Long Chamber'[1] flourished at the memory of which, according to Strachey, 'aged warriors and statesmen would turn pale'. What a clever family you have. I shall keep an eye on the *I.L.N.* My five offspring were never within sight of a prize or a scholarship, though I fancy *theirs* may be. To date I have thirteen grandchildren, and rumour says that within a year I sha'l have sixteen. My daughters have no misgivings about the future of civilisation—in marked contrast to their father. Their view no doubt is the more praiseworthy one.

Peter Fleming's articles were very good reading, and had what I always think is a most enviable trait, viz making the reader think the author must be a very nice man. I gather from John Raymond and Co. that 'charm' is about the most damnable literary quality there is— 'the logical and deathly end-product of the mandarin tradition' is his amiable reference to David Cecil's latest essays. What *is* the 'mandarin tradition'? It seems to me to be the pronouncements by the widely-read critics of the last generation on books they enjoyed and why they enjoyed them. Why all this rage? Half these angry young men, I suspect, in praising each other's stuff, are whistling to keep their spirits up.

What are they doing in Soho Square with all that hellish din? It would drive me mad. Don't, please, be driven mad—or wilt under Wilde. Remember that more than once Boswell seriously thought of abandoning the life of J., the burden of it being so great. I am taking the latest vol. of his journal to Cambridge. The reviews of it are very variable. Some, no doubt, detect traces of that deleterious element, charm. It is amusing to think what Macaulay could have added to his abuse of B. if he had known as much as we do of his character.

---

[1] The dormitory for junior boys in College at Eton.

This evening, contrary to my principles and practice, I attended a local cocktail party, at which I consumed two tumblers of what must have been very nearly neat whisky, so if this letter is illegible or incoherent, you must forget and forgive.

This dull grey wet weather I find most depressing. Will Italy be hot and sunny? I shall soon know, for on Tuesday morning I set out in great comfort on the Rome Express, first-class with sleeper at the firm's expense, and should reach Rapallo at 8.30 a.m. on Wednesday. Write this week c/o Lady Beerbohm, Villino Chiaro, Rapallo. I shall probably stay three or four days and then come home via Cagnes-sur-mer, near Nice, where some friends have taken a villa. Altogether I don't expect to be away more than ten or twelve days. This is my first visit to Italy, and I speak no word of the language.

Your fear of senectitude and hardening of the literary arteries seems to me morbid. Never did I know anyone less likely to congeal. Therefore I see no need to mortify yourself with Aldington, Leavis and company. I have always found *Don Quixote* unreadable, but there's plenty else to wear out my eyesight. If you haven't even begun to ossify (mentally) at seventy-four, you never will, and I should, if I were you, read for pleasure only. What cheek—it must be the whisky!

My son's efforts to market his Russian experiences have so far aborted: have you read Peter's article in the current *Spectator*?

The din in Soho Square is unabated. Building houses of steel and reinforced concrete is a grim and cacophonous business.

My lunch with the editor of *The Times* (in the Ritz Grill) was most enjoyable. He definitely *is* Oliver Edwards,[1] and his whole interest, outside his job, lies in books and reading. We gossiped hard about books and writers, and with the minimum of encouragement he told me the (most interesting) story of his life. I should say he has almost a genius for organising and running large institutions. I told him a bit about the Wilde letters, and within forty-eight hours he had had the files of *The Times* combed and the date of publication of the first volume of the *Yellow Book* established. There's nothing like harnessing the

[1] The name under which Sir William Haley contributed literary articles to *The Times*.

stars in their courses to work for one! In his letter he said he 'couldn't say how much he had enjoyed our lunch'. I answered ditto, and he is to lunch with me when I get back.

That afternoon E.B. and I drove out to Bushey to look at the books of a friend of his, recently deceased. E. was told he could take what he liked, but was too modest to comply, though with my assistance we pretty well filled up the car. On Thursday I dined with the Jepsons and worked on Max's letters till 12.30.

I look forward to the long train-journey with its excellent meals and time for reading. I am taking my bathing things and a panama hat. I haven't glimpsed the Mediterranean for something like twenty-five years—perhaps I shall never come back!

22 August 1957   *Cambridge*

I have had rather a sweaty week here, dealing with a million scripts, and staying in a hotel which has to be heated up for an army of Yankees. And there has been some species of scout jamboree which fills the dining-room with hairy-kneed, shiny-faced, wholly grown-up black men in shorts. Generally speaking rule 1 for shorts is that the wearer must be young, white, and well-shaped.

We have run up against some very loose and inefficient examiners —mostly women—whose marks have to be considerably doctored, and that delays us a good deal. However we get our own back by writing acid little reports on the bad examiners, and hope that they will be sacked before next year. The most depressing part of the whole business is the conviction that examination on set English books ought never to have been instituted. More than half the candidates merely retail what they have been told they ought to think. But this is all very shoppy. Let it cease.

But now you are sun-and surf-bathing without—I hope—a care in the world. Why don't you call on P. Lubbock at Lerici? He would love it. Tell him I urged you to. Be careful. Remember Shelley[1]; and tell me *all* about it next week.

---

[1] Shelley was drowned off the coast near Lerici.

I am starting this in the train on a blazing hot day at Ventimiglia on the Franco-Italian frontier. If, as I expect, you wrote to Rapallo, I haven't yet got your letter, for reasons which will speedily become apparent.

The first part of my journey passed off beautifully—a smooth Channel crossing, a happy chance meeting on the boat with Cecil Day Lewis and his wife (on their way to an Hellenic Cruise), two smashing meals on the Rome Express, and a fairly good night in my exclusive sleeper. When I detrained at Rapallo at 8.30 a.m. on a hot sunny morning I was surprised not to see Elisabeth B. on the platform. Nothing daunted I found a taxi and by means of almost the only two Italian words I knew (*Villino Chiaro*) managed to get there—only to find that Elisabeth was *away*! Some hideous misunderstanding, still not fully explained. The little Italian maid was most sympathetic, and knew a few words of French, but she had no idea when E. was coming back, the taxi-driver was asking for his fare, and it seemed to me the only thing to do was to push on to Cagnes-sur-mer, where I knew there was room for me, though my friends weren't expecting me for several days. So I left a note for E., giving her the Cagnes telephone number, and told the bewildered cabman '*Stazione*'.

Here my woeful lack of Italian was a great handicap. A request for a ticket to Nice threw the booking clerk into a frenzy of words, so I pacified him by asking for one to Genoa. Armed with this I sat on my suitcase on Rapallo station for one and a half hours, during which I chummed up with two Welsh girls and a female physiologist from New York City, none of whom spoke much more Italian than I did. Eventually I reached Genoa, where the main station is bigger and more modern than you'd believe. Lugging my three bags down corridors and up flights of stairs I finally found a ticket-clerk who spoke some English, and from him bought a ticket to Nice. There were then four blistering hours to fill in, so I left my luggage in the right place (found by tackling a policeman and saying '*Baggagio*' in a hopeless voice), had some coffee in a café and explored the city a little. It's enormous, with huge modern appartment blocks jostling the most squalid and picturesque of slums. But it was too hot to walk far, and soon everything shut for a long siesta. At the university bookshop I bought a little English-Italian phrasebook, just in time to learn that the Italian for lavatory is *ritirata*. Then I had a moderate lunch in a restaurant, some more coffee in another café, and at 3.20 literally *fought* my way on to the train. (Now this one has started again, so farewell legibility!) It was on its way from Rome to Barcelona and was already stuffed to bursting. For three and a half hours I sat on my suitcase in a crowded corridor (now we have stopped at Bordighera), reading a life of Oscar Wilde in French, while the temperature soared into the nineties. Eventually, three-quarters of an hour late, we got to Nice at 8.15 p.m., and the second taxi I tried agreed to drive me the eight miles to Cagnes. I had sent my friends a telegram from Genoa, but it took seven hours to arrive. (Now we're off again). The Cagnes villa is charming, built into the ramparts of the old walled city on a hill, in sight of the sea. (An Italian train official has just come in and made a long speech, of which I understood only one word—*Biglietto* (ticket). I smiled at him sweetly and he went away.)

On Thursday and Saturday I had heavenly bathes, but on Friday torrential rain fell all day. (Now we have stopped at San Remo, which would be unspeakable without the deep blueness of sea and sky.) On Friday night Elisabeth rang up in great distress over the misunderstanding and begged me to go back. I arranged to do so yesterday (Sunday), but on Saturday night I was seized with violent pains and diarrhoea, couldn't face the journey in such a condition, so put it off till to-day. I am recovered but feeble, and am eschewing the restaurant car in favour of a packet of petit-beurre biscuits. This train (bound for Rome) is due at Rapallo at 4.30—or so I gather, since no-one ever knows such things for certain, and I dare say I'll doss down in the Eternal City yet! I'll write more this evening. Too shaky now. R.

Tuesday, 27 August 1957   *Villino Chiaro, Rapallo*

My arrivals at Rapallo are clearly ill-fated. Yesterday I got there at 4—but once again no Elisabeth. I waited for a quarter of an hour, and then engaged the same taxi-driver as last week. When we got here, there was no one here either: the driver clearly thought me an idiot with a recurrent obsession and was unwilling to leave me. I persuaded him to go, well tipped, and soon afterwards E. arrived. Of course she had been told the train arrived at 4.20.

The whole place is exquisite: the little *villino* (all on one floor) right on the road: above it a huge wide terrace, with a tiny work-room in the middle of it: above again and behind, the *casetta*, a three-storied guest-house, an old peasant's house, with the disused Roman road behind. Everywhere Max's books and drawings, all exactly as they were. The garden is full of figs and grapes and oranges and olives. I am sleeping in the *casetta* where Max recorded his broadcasts. E. has all the records and last night played me the George Moore one. She is spoiling me with wonderful food and loving care. The only snag to the whole place is the road, on which endless vehicles of all calibres crash, roar and screech past. Doubtless one soon gets used to it. Below the road the blue Mediterranean stretches away, and at night the lights of Santa Margharita shine gaily across the bay. You can imagine with what joy and excitement I examine all the books, and the drawings in them, and all the other treasures. I shall go back to Cagnes tomorrow (my fiftieth birthday) and home a few days later. Send your next letter to Soho Square, since I probably shan't be at Bromsden till the week-end after next. I'll write again from wherever I am next Sunday, with the latest news of my journeyings on the Côte d'Azur. I did some Wilde work in the train yesterday, and here so much is germane. How I long for Max himself to be here, knowing all the answers to the questions that need so much research.

1 September 1957   *Grundisburgh*

What hideous adventures you record—with every appearance of cheerfulness. It must have been an immensely tedious experience, as it always is when modern organisation breaks down. One can't really doss down by the roadside as e.g. in Chaucer's day. All foreigners are immensely stupid in such circumstances. There must be *someone* in Rapallo who could talk English and put you on the right road; is there no British Consul there? The phrase-books leave out all that one wants. Percy Lubbock used to wonder how Max could stand the noise and nearness of that road—which I suppose was a little country lane when he first settled there. Anyway noise soon becomes tolerable, especially if incessant.

I read John Sparrow's review with great interest. He is severe on Watson, and I suppose that is all right *unless* that queer streak *was* in A.E. Housman, and I always understood—not knowing anything about it—that the 'homo' side of him was a matter of general acceptance. In which case all the cross pooh-poohing of attempts to grapple with and elucidate it are rather off the point and also rather unfair. I still think a lot of Watson's book is devilish interesting, whatever they say. And A.E.H. is one of those who somehow invite odd comment—some of it contemptuous, some patronising, some silly—e.g. John Wain, who says A.E.H. failed in Greats on purpose! It serves the old curmudgeon right really. No one has a right to be so arrogant and inhuman. But no one also has a right to say, as one ass did recently, that H. was less of a poet than Manilius ('Once in the wind of morning . . .' etc. Match me that in Manilius!). Critics are odd. Do you remember Walter Raleigh writing 'A wiser man than Macaulay, James Boswell'? Just trailing his coat, of course, for some reason.

I think I have had enough of Boswell *pro tem*. His absurdity is unvarying, and the unvarying grows tedious. And did anyone ever have venereal disease so often—and ultimately so luckily, for he was always cured. And the mystery of why so many people liked him and no one ever told him he was a B.F. Perhaps they did and he didn't mind. The Doctor of course did, but B. was full of family pride and surely wouldn't have taken it from anyone else.

Pamela and I went last week to *Look Back in Anger* in Ipswich. I wish you would tell me why it has had such success. I gather it is regarded as tremendously original, but surely a young man ranting away at the world and its conventions and absence of 'enthusiasm' etc. is about as old as anything can be—only another form of Byronism. We found the young man a good deal of a bore, but no doubt that is exactly what he would have hoped we should. They say the dialogue is very fine. Well, it is well enough, and never 'literary' etc. But isn't all that sprinkling of 'bloody's' and 'bitches' merely another form of pretentiousness? I am quite prepared for you to say I am quite wrong and out-of-date, and that it is first-rate stuff, etc. But when I remember the good Shaws and Galsworthys, it seems to me that we got more for our money, and also got *somewhere* by the play's end.

Monday, 2 September 1957 *Villa Lucie*
Cagnes-sur-mer
Alpes Maritimes

I meant to write to you yesterday, but in this lotus-land it is indeed always afternoon and later than one thinks. It is now 9.30 a.m. and I am sitting, dressed in shirt and shorts, on a vine-covered terrace on a hillside looking across to a very blue sea. Later today I will send you a postcard showing the position of this house below the battlements of the little mediaeval town, whose crooked winding streets (and open drains) draw in great numbers of sightseers. Luckily cars cannot get as far as this house—the street is too narrow.

My two days at Rapallo were idyllic. Perfect weather and such cosseting as you wouldn't believe: Max's last years must have been blissful. We ate all our meals (except dinner) on a little terrace covered with ripening grapes: Max called it the Vining Room: and on my birthday Elisabeth greeted me with a large silver tray on which she had arranged fifty flowers in a garland surrounding the figures 50 in scarlet geranium-petals. It looked quite lovely and I was much touched. She gave me several books that had belonged to Max, including one with a superb drawing in it (which I will show you). The whole place is saturated with Max's personality—he lived there for forty-five years, with gaps during the wars.

Eventually I spent another seven hours chugging back to Nice with the typescript of Oscar's prison-letters on my lap.

Sure enough there had been a muddle about my return ticket, and since I felt quite ready for a few idle days I was delighted to discover that I couldn't get a sleeper till next Saturday (the 7th), arriving London Sunday (8th).

My friends here have hired a tiny Renault, in which each morning I drive them to the beach—three miles away—for prolonged bathing and sunning. It's so long since I swam in the Mediterranean that I had forgotten how warm and clear and buoyant it is: one can keep afloat without movement. Most days I bathe again in the evening, after a considerable siesta. There are many books in the house, mostly French, German and Tauchnitz, including some Maughams, which I am re-reading with pleasure—*The Narrow Corner* (novel), *The Casuarina Tree* and *First Person Singular* (stories). Readability (extreme) is his great asset, for much of the prose is slipshod and many of the stories marred by a tiresome superiority and know-all cocksureness. I have also bought, and am enormously enjoying, Maurois's latest biography *Les Trois Dumas*. There isn't in fact much (all too little) about the mulatto general of Napoleon who sired the novelist, but *his* story is astonishing, and I have still to reach the *fils*, of *La Dame aux Camélias*. Maurois's French is easy to read, and the book exactly suits my mood. Occasionally I summon up a picture of the mounting piles of letters on my office desk, as a delicious antithesis to this remote and peaceful eyrie, where the postman brings me nothing—though we generally get *The Times* the same afternoon. I am sunburnt, mosquito-bitten and infinitely relaxed. I could always take a month or two of this sort of thing each year.

At Rapallo it was the greatest fun looking through Max's books, with their manifold inscriptions, marginalia, drawings, and (best of all) his touching-up of illustrations, often so skilfully done as to be almost invisible, but always exactly to the point. I should love to spend a week or two there, for I had time only to scratch the surface.

8 September 1957   *Grundisburgh*

Welcome home and all that! Reading not between the lines so much as the lines themselves, you have enjoyed your trip greatly in spite of those malicious logs dropped in your path by Fortune, who simply has no idea of what is cricket and what is not. And I hope you have got all the Max stuff you wanted. No, of course you can't have, but I am sure we may look forward to some very toothsome dishes from your *cuisine*. Do you communicate at all with David Cecil who is writing the life, or are you both driving on different lines? I hear of him from time to time from his and my old pupil John Bayley who has just published a formidable book called *The Romantic Survival*—the sort of book that always makes *me* feel thoroughly humiliated, because it is equally clear that the writer knows exactly what he means, and that I don't. And you too, I have no doubt, with such a book before you, resemble Pope's politician after coffee and 'see through all things with your half-shut eyes'. But when I meet a sentence like 'It is an inflexible application of the romantic egotism that the poet's universe must be purely his own' I know what the words say but seldom what they quite mean. You, as a Yeats expert, will perhaps be interested to read the W.B.Y. chapter. Bayley is a delightful chap who manages to be indubitably highbrow but nothing at all of a prig. His wife is Iris Murdoch whose brow is practically out of sight in the empyrean. I met her in his rooms at New College. A woman in college-rooms in my day would have meant a major explosion. So perhaps Tuppy H. wasn't entirely right in his complaint that *every* change was for the worse. The prurience of the Victorians was tremendous. They were convinced that for a girl to drive in a hansom with a man could end in nothing but rape. Their salacious imaginations, as you see, easily out-soared the facts of space and the exigencies of posture.

I wish I had known George Wyndham (Pamela's uncle) though John Bailey used to say that with all that charm and conversational gifts etc. you never got to know him any better, and after a delightful evening's talk on Monday, he might easily not recognise you on Friday. Anyhow charm to-day is *out*—practically a word of abuse. And if it often was bogus, well plenty of what has replaced it is bogus too, just as the Hemingway toughness is really just as sentimental as Kipling's strong silent subalterns.

To-morrow we have a governors' meeting at Woodbridge School and the chief item on the agenda is the HM's temerarious action in sacking the son of the Governor of Reading Gaol, and the Governor, who is 'strong upon the Regulations Act' like his predecessor, maintains that this action is agin 'em. Judging from the correspondence the HM has blundered into that major house- and head-master's error of putting on to paper things which he knows about the boy but couldn't prove; and of course if you want to burst any paternal blood-vessel, all you have to do is to imply that a boy of seventeen who spends forty-five minutes with a perfectly respectable girl and so is late for lock-up and climbs into the house is a criminal past reclaim.

But it is quite possible that the HM has more on his side than appears.

Since Sunday is my proper day for writing to you, and this train is at the moment stationary in the Gare du Nord, Paris, here goes!

I left the Riviera last night after a final week of heavenly weather—clear blue skies and warm waveless sea. Yesterday, my last day, was the loveliest of all, and I spent most of it in the water. The night before I dined out on a terrace looking across to the sea on which a full moon was reflected. This morning, after a goodish night in a sleeper, I woke to a blood-red sunrise, since when steady rain has fallen. Neither I nor my companion has hat, coat or umbrella, so what should have been an agreeable stroll through Sunday morning Paris (the train stops here for two hours) turned into a rush into a café opposite the station, buying the English papers *en route*, and a speedy return to the warm dry train. Last night's dinner was superb, and I have high hopes of lunch, which is due half an hour after we start again. My holiday, not having been arranged to last more than a few days, turned out to be the most restful and delicious for years—no mail, almost no work (though I've done a bit to Oscar and to Diana Cooper's MS), any amount of swimming and idleness and sleep. What horrors shall I find waiting for me in Soho Square this evening? However frightful, they will, I hope, be tempered by at least one letter from you. (Write to Bromsden this week. I shall be there on Friday evening.) I'm still reading and enjoying Maurois's book about the Dumas family, and you must certainly read it when it's translated, as it assuredly will be. Their lives (the Ds') are exactly like an exaggerated mixture of their works.

5 p.m. Mid-Channel

The lunch was so excellent and so large that the rest of the journey to Calais passed in a pleasurable coma. This boat is full to the scuppers, and we are lucky to have seats in the bar, and a sailor engaged to get us places in the train.

I can't remember how much I told you about Cagnes. It lies between Nice and Cannes, about three miles inland. Most of the streets are luckily impracticable for cars, and many are worn and very steep steps. The drainage system (if such it can be called) is truly mediaeval, and each narrow passage is bordered by two malodorous and flowing streams. A derelict cottage labelled CASA VERDE has had its appellation deftly changed by some wag to read CASA MERDE. Our villa was relatively unsmelly, and nicely placed on the hillside with three terraces and a garden of its own.

I think I shall finish this at Soho Square tonight and post it to-morrow, so as to surprise you on Tuesday morning. This bar is swarming with people buying cheap cigarettes.

Monday afternoon   *Soho Square*
Alas for good resolutions. The train from Dover was unaccountably more than an hour late, and by the time I had got here and unpacked, I was ready for bed. To-day has been fully occupied in simply *reading*— not even answering—the huge pile of letters which has accumulated in three weeks. Your two were the highlights, and I will answer them properly next Sunday. I also found a number of birthday presents waiting for me, including three bottles of champagne from an author(!) and a fine cigar-case from the office staff. The trouble, I can see, will be to keep it filled.

September 13 (Friday!) 1957   *Grundisburgh*

Your picture of Cagnes is delightfully vivid. 'Casa Merde' gave me a good grin. I suppose the inhabitants are as impervious to smells as everyone must have been before Jonas Hanway was born (I never quite remember whether it was the W.C. or the umbrella that he invented, but I am in the summer-house, my reference-books are forty yards and more away over open country, and a thick prohibitive rain is falling). It is odd that the age when all such things were hideously primitive and obtrusive was the age of the Olivias and Violas, and Walter Scott's immensely refined heroines, whereas *now* it is the *ritiratas* which are refined and the ladies who are coarse, so they tell me. (How *proud* some of the young ones are when they utter words which would have made their grandmothers faint—like prep. school boys over their first 'damn'!)

I am now reading, believe it or not, *The Pilgrim's Progress*, not exactly for fun, but I have to set a paper on it for next year—only two questions of the essay type, but it is fatal not to know something about a book set, and I have not read it for half-a-century. A plebiscite at Columbia University placed it *top* of the list of 'the most boring classics,' which I find hopeful, as nobody supposes that Columbia University can be anything but plumb wrong about anything. Wasn't Dulles an alumnus? Still, I must admit that after forty pages or so, I did have the best night's sleep I have had *in years* (American!). I should hate to find myself on the same side as Dulles.

It is time we met again and had a long crack, feet on fender (there are no fenders in Suffolk). A monstrous suggestion to make to an overworked publisher—or would be if I didn't know you have that engaging and impressive trait of M.R. James, i.e. however busy he was, he was always ready for a talk.

15 September 1957   *Bromsden Farm*

No letter from you yesterday, to my sorrow. It's sure to arrive tomorrow after I've left, and I shall find it on Friday evening. Here, as in London, I found vast arrears of bills and letters, but in both places I am now pretty well up to date, except for unread MSS, which I feel increasingly disinclined to tackle. No word has been heard from Duff since he set out for Germany nearly a fortnight ago, to take some photographs for a retired Major living in Cornwall. Duff answered an advertisement of his in *The Times*, and I fear the expedition may cost a pretty penny, since D. apparently failed to get either an advance payment or anything in writing from the gallant gentleman. Comfort is beginning to worry at the lack of news, but I tell her that we should surely have heard if he was in trouble. Meanwhile, after all, the *Sunday Times* show signs of printing his article on Russia next Sunday. They also asked if they might print some of my introduction to the G.M. letters: naturally I agreed: so next Sunday's issue may prove to be the Hart-Davis Benefit Number. On the other hand it may not.

Last week was mainly taken up with full mopping-up operations, but was brightened by the enclosed letter,[1] which my natural boastfulness prompts me to send you: please send it back for my archives. Of course I accepted, with a mixture of pride and trepidation. It's an appalling baby to have to hold just now, but if I can cope with it I can cope with anything. And there's still a hope that the rest of the committee (the impish R. Fulford *et cie*) may revolt.

You and I, who agree so often about all literary matters, differ only in this: I take all precautionary steps to avoid reading Leavis and Aldington or witnessing such plays as *Look Back in Anger*, whereas you positively seek them out. This peculiarity of yours I take to be, not so much masochism, as some ridiculous idea that if you don't attempt all this nonsense you will quickly be out of the swim and on the shelf. I assure you, dear George, that there was never an unlikelier candidate for the shelf than you, with your ready sympathy and unresting interest in life and letters. Please let this idea sink in, and stop torturing yourself with these dreary excursions.

While I was away, Peter hit on an idea for his next book—an account of the siege of the foreign Legations in Peking during the Boxer rebellion of 1900, together with the story of the relief expedition etc. I encouraged the plan, which please keep for the moment under your hat.

Your praise of the Autumn List is particularly welcome, since the travellers complain that almost all the books in it are totally unsaleable except in the West End of London. Do they think I cater for Asia Minor?

I think that in some way Alfred Douglas was a cousin of George Wyndham, and must therefore have been related to Pamela, though perhaps, let us hope, only by marriage. Did I tell you I got three new Wilde letters from America last week? Quite good ones too.

I knew Ronnie Knox slightly during my short time at Oxford. He was then R.C. Chaplain to the University, and I remember a bare beautiful room in the Old Palace containing the minimum of furniture

[1] From Harold Nicolson, asking me to succeed him as Chairman of the London Library Committee.

and a barrel of beer. Of him I remember little, save that he was friendly and unalarming. When I, or perhaps someone else, asked him if he knew the egregious ex-priest Montague Summers (then living in Oxford), R.A.K. said that Summers lived with a little boy and a huge dog. Plenty of people had seen Summers and the boy, and Summers and the dog, and the boy and the dog, but nobody had ever seen all three of them together. Which I much enjoyed.

I have just finished the Maurois book on the Dumas family, which I loved. Edmund B. has taken his family to Belgium for a fortnight, so for the moment I mercifully have the flat to myself. Even the dearest guests can become a burden if there isn't much space, and one is constantly busy already.

20 September 1957   *Grundisburgh*

I hope you have heard from your son now. I hate gaps of that kind, and get a good deal of chaff from my family (wife included). It is in the blood. My father to his last day was convinced in the teeth of all experience that a telegram always announced a disaster, and naturally was a little peeved when, as often as not, it contained a s.o.s. for money from one of his sons. The optimism of the young is superb. *I* should be quite sure that the retired Cornish major is an impostor. I shall search the *S.T.* next Sunday.

I love your blunt refusal to see anything remotely laudable in my senile endeavours not to be left 'with the rear and the slaves'. But I can't help it. So many silly old men—contemporaries of mine—stick firmly, and, what is worse, complacently, in the mud of their ancient tastes and prejudices, all 'sealed of the tribe' e.g. of Sir A. Munnings. You will be derisively amused to hear that for the last two nights my evening book has been Colin Wilson's *Outsider* and my *bed*-book Trollope's *Prime Minister* which I hadn't read—a diet as it were of caviare and sago. And I find the sago far the more toothsome. Frankly I can't really see what *The Outsider* is all about, and my acquaintance with the young man's mentors—Sartre, Roquentin, Meursault, Krebs and Co is of the flimsiest possible. Household names to you I expect? Colin Wilson gives the impression of having read everything, but I gather from some of the reviews that, like the River Finn in my garden, the depth is not as great as it looks.

I revelled in the George Moore letters and wished they had gone on longer. I wonder what hers were like. Why have I got the feeling from his letters that I shouldn't have liked her very much—whereas one can't help admiring and liking Lady Emily L.? The picture of Lady C. in the Twenties gives her a pretty *hard* look.

I say, Rupert, the London Library! Have you as it is *any* spare five minutes in the week—and at this moment when the poor old institution is under fire from those marble-hearted fiends of the Inland Revenue. I beg you to *delegate* shamelessly from among your vast acquaintance. Lawyers no doubt are already active. Couldn't that admirable Somervell help? It couldn't surely take much to upset that sickening ass who said that the L.L. was a sanctum for the well-to-do, as it didn't bring Shakespeare to the costermongers. I have never belonged, as I never lived in London, but my grandfather was one of Carlyle's first associates in it. I once met old Hagberg Wright, who struck me as the rudest man I had ever seen—till I met his brother Almroth who easily dead-heated. But I have no doubt H.W. did fine work for the Library. How I do hate the recurrent evidences of a general trend to diminish, pare away, destroy all standards save those of the damned 'common man'. The last decades have given him confidence, and in any controversy his voice rings out loud and bold like that of faithful Chapman. I smell the same trend in your travellers' complaint about your list. At the same time it is very odd that pretentious stuff like Colin Wilson's should at once find a huge and hungry public. What *do* they think they get out of it? Anyway thank God for R.H-D and Co and all their works.

I have just finished reading 150 papers from Barbados on *Northanger Abbey*. Not very good—but I gave high marks to the candidate (I think a girl!) who, describing J.A's Bath, wrote 'They kept their balls in the Pump Room.' 'Held' of course would have done all right, but idiom is a little fragile in Barbados.

Here is a tiny and not very interesting mystery for you. Watson—following several others—says that Moses Jackson was a rowing and running blue at Oxford. Well, he wasn't. No Jackson of any sort ever rowed for Oxford. There was a hurdler S.F. Jackson (also of John's) in

March 1877. But Moses didn't go up till the autumn of that year, so it could not be he. I don't think this discovery throws a light of very startling novelty onto the relations of Moses and A.E.H., but the latter hated inaccuracy of any sort, and after all would spend half a morning crossing a 't' in Manilius, and no sane man can really say *that* is very important.

I met the Lord Woolton at dinner last week. A genial old boy, with a pleasant but intermittent little Lancashire burr. My cousin Oliver can mimic it to the life. He (Oliver) also told me that Winston never could resist ragging old Woolton, who (like a sensible man) never said much in the Cabinet. W., who knew his knowledge, say of Egypt, was not extensive, would say, if E. was on the tapis, 'Well, gentlemen, I thank you for your opinions; but I feel that in order to be sure that we have a wide and balanced view of the matter, we should like to hear what Lord Woolton thinks about it.' Mischievous old urchin!

22 September 1957   *Bromsden Farm*

Today has been hot and sunny, and once again the ever-growing grass has taken all my time. With us this autumn has brought more mists than mellow fruitfulness: not a single apple, pear, plum or damson (after last year's plenty), and only half-a-dozen shamefaced quinces to harvest. Have you any fruit?

Did not Sir John Harington invent the W.C.? See Strachey's admirable *Portraits in Miniature*. If so, perhaps Jonas Hanway was responsible for the umbrella. God bless them both!

A wise old Dublin lady, I was told last week, says that when she was young, people's class was a constant subject of discussion (Is he a gentleman? etc.), while their sex-lives were never mentioned. Now every sexual peculiarity is hotly debated, while the subject's U-ness or otherwise is rapidly becoming tabu.

At long last we have heard from Duff in Germany—a glum letter full of the boredom of driving two thousand miles alone and camping out in weather too dull for the photography which is the excuse for all this gallivanting. Anyhow he seems all right, and should be home this week—I hope perhaps in time for a dinner on Wednesday at the

160

Whitefriars Club, over which I am presiding, and after which P. Fleming is to talk on his trip to Russia.

If you seriously think that only a nightly tussle with Colin Wilson's pretentious rot can prevent your sharing the tastes and outlook of that foul-mouthed old Philistine Munnings, I suppose I can only leave you to your unnecessary mortification. After one glance through *The Outsider* I decided it was both unreadable and not worth reading. You'd better buck up: his next book appears tomorrow!

So glad you enjoyed the Moore letters. Wasn't Harold N's review in today's *Observer* fine. I agree with every word of it, except perhaps the 'usual astringency and taste'.[1] There have also been excellent notices in the *Daily Telegraph* and *T.L.S.* (the latter written by Joe Hone, Moore's biographer). As you doubtless saw, the *Sunday Times* (which is now too heavy to lift) printed a good chunk of my introduction (for which they promise twenty-five guineas), and postponed Duff's Russian piece on the grounds that father and son together would sink one issue.

Last week my secretary disappeared with flu, the Asian variety for all I know, and this delayed and complicated everything. On Wednesday I reluctantly agreed to dine with my father at the St James's Club—reluctantly because such evenings are generally a waste of silence and complaint. This one didn't begin too well, since we drank our sherry with a retired Civil Servant, who was slumped incoherently in a chair with a big glass. Just before we were due to go up to dinner your cousin Oliver arrived, at his most amusing, and dined with us gaily. My father perked up considerably, ordered grouse and champagne, and laughed heartily at O's many good jokes and stories. Of the retired Civil Servant O. said: 'He has been fighting a losing battle with Haig & Haig for years.' He mimicked Winston brilliantly and was altogether delightful. (As I daresay you know, his son Anthony is a partner in my father's stockbroking firm.)

Next day I lunched with Roger at Boodle's. He was very *affairé*, carrying piles of half-answered letters about with him, but very charming. We talked of the London Library, the Lit. Soc. and so on. At three I left him in Piccadilly, still carrying a mass of paper, on his way to a very necessary haircut. He won't be back from abroad in time

1 Referring to my editing.

for the Lit. Soc. dinner. By all means let us have a preliminary crack. Will you come to Soho Square about six? I shall just have had (that afternoon) my first London Library committee meeting in or near the chair, so you may find me wild-eyed and wondering.

I haven't added a footnote to Oscar for *weeks*, and shall soon begin to feel overwhelmed by the work outstanding there if I don't get a move on. But how and when? I am reading proofs and manuscripts like mad already—now in the midst of Druon's next historical novel, *The Royal Succession*, which needs a certain amount doing to its translation before it can go to the printers. And soon Diana Cooper will turn up, expecting me to have transformed her MS., and I haven't—oh dear! Already newspapers and magazines are bidding high for the serial rights, but there won't be any book to serialise if I don't invent some free time to do it in.

26 *September 1957*   *Grundisburgh*

I think I told you how much I enjoyed the George Moore book, and I am glad to see the reviews—all that I have seen—noticed the great care and fullness of your notes as well as the really beautiful 'get-up' of the book. Do these things get rewarded in this world as surely as they will be in the next? I have noticed a tendency (not apropos of *this* book) to that line which invariably gets one of my many goats, the line briefly of 'Who is interested in George Moore now?' Am I right in feeling in these letters a slight but definite and recurrent touch of the *pathetic* about the old man? There are of course many glimpses of his naughtiness, but all the sting has gone out of his malice. I wonder why he had such a strong admiration of Edward VIII, and so firm a conviction that he had only to go to Ireland and there would be no more 'troubles'. I suspect that he was like many other men, great in some way or other, of one of whom it was said that he was right about everything except politics.

I hasten to tell you that we too have no fruit—hardly an apple, no plums, and our pears are playing their annual joke of falling off the trees while still as hard as bullets. Damson and quinces we never did have any truck with—*one* fig appeared and was solemnly presented to me. No law is more invariable than that a dry April and May means a wet August and September. Yesterday we had twenty-four hours' rain, but that typhoon or hurricane was *entirely* out of breath by the time it came here, and in sober fact:

> Each chimney's vapour, like a thin grey rod,
> Mounting aloft through miles of quietness,
> Pillars the skies of God.[1]

The weather pundit was quite sheepish about it on the air, as they had so confidently promised a rousing gale for all of us.

Of course you are right. I had quite forgotten Strachey's excellent paper. Hanway gave us the umbrella—and was stoned in the streets when he first produced it. And your old lady was quite right about class and sex. It is well worth remembering that Mrs Gladstone whispered in Gladstone's ear that she was about to have a baby. He was thunderstruck—and would have been still more so if he had known it was going to be Mary Drew—really rather a dreadful woman —scheming, bossy, conceited, humourless.

I am glad you have news of Duff. I shall keep an eye open for his article. I am quite sure it will be more readable than most of that portentous paper. How right you are on Colin Wilson. Unreadable. But *how* did he make everyone read him? You, as a publisher, must have an inkling. I haven't. Some of the reviewers surely rather lost their heads. As an antidote I read in bed Trollope's *Prime Minister*— about 940 pages—with great satisfaction for the best of all reasons. *You want to know what is going to happen.* Full of faulty art and psychology and all that, no doubt, but immensely readable—and what else matters?

I am glad cousin Oliver was in good form; he is very good value on such occasions. You didn't, by the way, say anything of my thrilling bit of research over Housman's friend Jackson. Can it be that you didn't think it thrilling? Incredible.

---

[1] From 'Dusk' by A. E. (George Russell).

I'm sorry I failed to applaud your detective work: well done, my dear Jackson! The author has had such a pasting in the press that I scarcely like to report such a thumping inaccuracy to him. The only ways in which good editing and production get any reward in this world are (a) by creating, through good reviews, that intangible (which is said to be an asset until you try to cash in on it) called 'goodwill,' and (b) by tempting authors to try and get their books similarly handled. When new writers turn up out of the blue I always ask them why they've come to *me*, and they nearly always say it's because the books look so nice. Nevertheless, shoddily produced best-sellers butter more parsnips!

Duff turned up exhausted at 10.30 last night. He had left Düsseldorf at 5.30 in the morning and driven three hundred miles before trans-shipping the car (a friend's) to Dover. With the resilience of youth he seems quite recovered today, except for a heavy cold in the head. I only hope he doesn't give it to Comfort, for she always takes *weeks* to shake one off. When I was young I caught cold almost weekly, but now I haven't had one for seven years. Let's hope I don't boast too soon. Duff's trip has cost him (or rather *us*) £65, and my hopes of recovering any substantial part of this from the Major in Cornwall are slender. Adam went cheerfully back to Eton on Tuesday, and we are daily expecting the usual letter asking for a collection of heterogeneous and unpackable objects to be posted immediately—a squash-racquet, a pair of roller skates and a pocket microscope.

I have *no* inkling of why Colin Wilson's rot suddenly broke loose, and certainly nobody was more surprised than his publisher, who had expected a miniscule sale and perhaps some *succès d'estime*. I daresay some of the bright boys will be gunning for C.W.'s next book. I have never read *The Prime Minister*, or indeed much of Trollope's mountainous *oeuvre*: I am keeping it until I am as unbuttoned as he is, but oh, when will that happy day arrive? I have just read a 400-page manuscript first novel about a rape in the suburbs of Philadelphia, and the awful thing is that it's very well done. As you say, no narrative is any good unless you want to know what's going to happen. That's why *Marius the Epicurean* and the later George Moore novels are no good: one couldn't, as they say, care less what is coming.

Last Wednesday I took the chair at a dinner of the Whitefriars Club (a dimmish sub-Fleet-Street affair) and Peter spoke about his trip to Russia. He is far from a polished speaker, but he answered questions well, and I think they all enjoyed it. The room in the Cock Tavern, Fleet Street, was hellish hot. The gossip is that P.F. is to be offered the editorship of *Punch*: there's probably no truth in it, and I doubt whether he'd take it on.

One day I had a drink with darling old Lady Emily Lutyens. At eighty-three she is frail but full of humour and interest in everything. She told me her fan-mail was keeping her busy, and she is conducting an immense correspondence with a passionate admirer in Karachi. She is thoroughly enjoying her old age, which makes it always fun to be with her. I only wish she could write another book, but I fear she has no more material.

For the first time since 1939 Peter has reared some pheasants—four hundred and fifty survived the hatching, they say—and now our garden is like a fashion parade of cock pheasants in fine plumage and all unconscious of their approaching doom. My Uncle Duff always preferred autumn to the other seasons, but I can't agree with him. Give me the cuckoo and the bursting buds of promise. I hate vests and sweaters and overcoats and fogs and cold. To cheer myself up I have bought Gordon Craig's memoirs, though I haven't yet had time even to begin the book. It should have lots of peripheral Wilde information in it. Craig's father, E.W. Godwin, decorated Oscar's house in Chelsea, and there are a number of letters to him. Last week I got hold of a water-colour painted by Oscar when he was twenty-two—a landscape, or rather seascape, in the West of Ireland. It might have been painted by any of our aunts, but his signature on the mount lends it a factitious interest. I'm having it photographed. Every day in the office I write up to a dozen letters about Oscar, asking for letters, information and so on, so, while my footnotes linger, my Wilde file bulges more and more.

Your son must be amassing a lot of valuable experience—much more than he would have in my day—a bit of silver lining to the clouds of this century. I do hope that plethoric *Sunday Times* will open one of its thousand columns for him and so pay for it that, contemplating your depleted bank account, you may say with Ulysses 'though much is taken much abides'.

Meanwhile I further risk your derision by telling you I am reading a book of L--v-s's. It is a form of masochism—a word of which I know the spelling, but not the pronunciation and am by no means secure of the meaning. Anyway I am indulging that odd human propensity to bite on an aching tooth. But I hasten to add, I am also humbly and admiringly reading Verlaine and shall probably interlard my conversation next Tuesday (I am rather George Moorean about putting the right figure to the day of the week) with French aphorisms, e.g. (though not from Verlaine) '*La deluge n'a pas réussi; il reste un homme*', which I happened upon recently. It suits my misanthropic mood, which is invariably strong at the time of party conferences. But I am (at last!) going to take the hint given by your invariable silence on such topics, and say nothing about politics, knowing as good Johnsonians should,

> How small, of all that human hearts endure,
> That part which laws or kings can cause or cure.[1]

Not that the second line passes any more sweetly into the ear than Browning's 'Irks care the cropful bird' etc.

Is editing *Punch* much catch? I doubt it nowadays. My daughter and other of the young praise it, but there are a humiliating number of jokes in it that defeat me—mostly the captionless pictures—and when explained the joke puts no strain on my ribs. ('Old, Master Shallow'!) Is there still a plump head waiter at the Cock? And did you have lark pie or am I confusing it with the Cheshire Cheese? And shall you be at the Johnson Club on Oct. 17? Because I shall.

I agree with you about autumn—a sad month October, all its beauty rich with decay, the dead leaves, the shortening, ever more

[1] Johnson, 'Lines added to Goldsmith's *Traveller*'.

slanting sunshine—no, I can't understand liking out of doors as in the spring. When the day is shut out one's spirits rise, but no thanks to the season. How grim the next five months must have been in, say, William the Conqueror's time, and how much he must have welcomed 'the simple bird that thinks two notes a song'.

6 October 1957   *Bromsden Farm*

If I (fond, impious thought) were a psychiatrist, I should doubtless feel certain that, for all your protestations, you have for some time been sub-consciously shying away from our meeting on Tuesday. First you repeatedly referred to its date as the 9th; then, when I pointed this out, you ended your letter of last Thursday with a reference to 'Tuesday week'! It is on *this very next Tuesday* that in fact I shall expect you at Soho Square. It's possible that E. Blunden may be there: I don't yet know his movements: but you will like him anyhow.

I daresay that if you succeeded in fighting your way through the forty pages of to-day's *Sunday Times* you came on my Duff's long-awaited article: not at all bad, I thought, and they seem pleased with it. The boy is delighted, and this early success will certainly strengthen his determination to be a journalist. He goes up to Oxford (Worcester) next Thursday, but I have a feeling that three years there will seem too long to him: we shall see. Adam has got flu at Eton—one of seventeen in his tutor's—but doesn't sound too bad. My daughter got leave from her rich employers in Upper New York State and spent last week-end most enjoyably with the Caccias in the Embassy at Washington. She was particularly impressed by the multitude of servants—a circumstance unknown to most young people of to-day. Which reminds me that in my childhood Sir Lionel Phillips, a South African millionaire friend of my father's, had *seventy* gardeners at his house in Hampshire. Somewhere I have a snapshot of myself, aged two, sitting on the lawn there, beside Robbie Ross.

Meanwhile I am correcting the proofs of Jonah's new book, *Georgian Afternoon*. This is the third time that I have read most of it, and I'm enjoying it as much as ever: there is a good case to be made for its being the best of the three, if one can compare them at all: certainly it has much more *variety* than either of its predecessors: I shall await your verdict eagerly.

Have you ever tried to burn substantial lavender-bushes? Yesterday we uprooted some ten-year-olds which had grown too big, but the splendid bonfire we made of them keeps going out. A preliminary crackle and flame soon turn to smoke and fizzle: I shall have to try again next Saturday.

Alas, I can't manage the Johnson Club on the 17th. I hate to miss you, but the paper doesn't promise to be a rib-tickler.

Despite what I wrote in my last letter, I have read enough Trollope to know for certain that you are right about him, and that one day I shall enjoy his whole panorama to the full.

I gather that the somewhat totalitarian election at the London Library has passed off with some show of unanimity (one name only put forward: approve or else . . .). Last week I was accosted on the stairs by Esmond de Beer. He said he was delighted I was the new chairman, though he would have preferred Veronica Wedgwood. Naturally I agreed heartily.

Last week I was visited by an old Oxford friend (hitherto penniless) who told me he had just inherited £900 a year from his uncle. 'Hadn't he any children?' I asked. 'He had one daughter,' said my friend, 'but she was electrocuted by an electric iron at Beersheba.' He went on to tell me that this girl was a dipsomaniac who married a commercial traveller in whisky, and together they emigrated to Israel. Ironically enough, the only job the husband could get was in charge of the waterworks at Sodom! They saved his salary, and every three weeks went up into Jerusalem for a blind. Which only goes to show that truth is stranger . . . it's an ill wind . . . etc. Would you believe it?

9 October 1957   *67 Chelsea Square*
                                                              S.W.3

There is something faintly but decidedly absurd about this, but as you know very well, there is about a great many of the things that are worth doing. And I just want to show those foolish persons who think that I can have nothing particular to say to you to-day, are wholly without understanding. It may be in the blood.

I was particularly pleased to meet Edmund Blunden again. One gets in his company the same—what shall I call it?—easeful satisfaction that one used to get from Monty James. It comes—doesn't it? —when great kindliness of heart accompanies great distinction of mind. I remember M.R.J's cordial listening to a story which I knew he knew, and on another occasion to a man making assertions about the history of some cathedral which were so wrong that they *had* to be corrected, but how gently and beautifully M.R.J. did it. And now *I* am telling *you* about impressions E.B. made on me which you can't possibly want to hear. (As for my chuckle-headed messages to you about the Lit. Soc. date, 'Old, Master Shallow' is the only defence. I kept on confusing it with another gathering *next* Wednesday, though all the time it was securely in my book.) How unfailingly enjoyable these Lit. Soc. evenings are—the only fly in the amber being that so much excellent talk with A. and B. means that one can't have the same with C. and D. Harold N. was delightful, as was John Sparrow. I am not sure you ought not to have put me next to old Dunsany instead of shouldering all the burden yourself, but of course you would do that.

And the evening ended in the glow of Peter's kindness in taking me to this very door. He and Bernard F. insisted on waiting till they had actually seen the door open to my key—rather as debutantes were escorted home in Edwardian days with 100% protection of body and soul. Their belief that I am hardly to be trusted to look after myself in London is as benevolently obvious as it is justified. Cyril Alington once told me that in his study one morning he twice heard the same remark outside. It was 'Thank you; I think now I can manage for myself.' One was made by his father *aetat* 88, the other by his youngest son *aetat* 3. Both were being helped down the stairs.

I delight in your exact and generous appreciation of E.B., and I need hardly tell you that your feelings were warmly reciprocated. So glad Peter and Bernard saw you home so carefully: you're most precious and valuable to us all, you know: and you'd be surprised at the number of Lit. Soc. members who have referred to you as a fine acquisition. I do hope we succeed in getting Jonah in: he would love it so. I'm afraid Tommy thinks him a bore, and maybe others do too, but he's a pet, and *literary* as well, which is more than some of the members and candidates are.

E.B. is not in the Lit. Soc. because he lives (alas) in Hong Kong and is very shy of gatherings. H. Nicolson would, I fear, be vastly bored by the Johnson Club—but then aren't we all? Nevertheless it's surely a *good thing*.

On Wednesday I went to the opening of a new bookshop in the City at 11 a.m.—lots of authors and publishers, with champagne flowing. Then I lunched at the Ivy with Neville Cardus. He was as sympathetic and amusing as ever, but he is now so deaf that one has to shout, and since he whispers conversation is a bit of a strain. Then to a meeting of the Royal Literary Fund. Thursday was even busier. Two long sessions with Jonah, going through his proofs and persuading him not to write 'in the case of' all the time; lunch at the Travellers' with Allen Lane, the head of Penguin Books; a visit from a leading American librarian; drinks with Nancy Cunard; after which I had to preside at a dinner of my old club the Society of Bookmen because their new chairman had flu. After all that I was almost too exhausted to sleep.

Yesterday I took time off from the garden for writing and reading—the whole of an engaging gossipy book about Barrie in the theatre, 100 pages of Matthew Arnold's letters (humour was not his strength), a charming new book called *Tea with Walter de la Mare*,[1] a chunk of Gordon Craig's reminiscences, and part of a detective story. To-day has been digging and a huge bonfire. I much enjoyed the profile of Humphrey, but could have done with more about his father.

[1] By Russell Brain.

Well, if one must be likened to something in the vegetable kingdom, I suppose an oak-tree is about the top specimen.[1] At all events
no one could ever describe a pumpkin, however giant, as 'branch-
charmed by the earnest stars'.[2] I wonder who does those 'profiles'; I
thought this one was definitely good—well-written, and perfectly
accurate in its facts—which, I suppose, they have the sense to get
from the victim?

And of course it immensely pleases me too to hear that the Lit. Soc.
does not disapprove of your last candidate. All men love praise. Some
pretend they don't. They lie—though of course there is that superb
double-barrelled snub which the world's leading curmudgeon
(Housman) spat at the scholars who commended him: 'You should
be free to praise me if you did not praise each other'. Apropos of whom,
I have just been reading John Wain's *Preliminary Essays*. A pretty good
young man, isn't he? A few coat-trailing sillinesses but, as Johnson
said of some woman, he has 'a bottom of good sense,' and his brilliant
flashes are neither too many nor self-conscious. And, in its way, I have
never read a more brilliant bit of comparative criticism than his
demonstration of the superiority of Wordsworth's 'Lucy' to a Housman poem on a similar theme. Do read it and tell me if you agree with
me that it is frightfully good.

I do hope Jonah's candidature will go through. I too have heard
him called a bore, but always referring to him as he was thirty or forty
years ago. He isn't the first Balliol scholar to have been called that,
and as I used to take pleasure in telling my pupils, the young are very
often much greater bores than the old. Anyway I am blowed if Jonah
is a bore now. Those two books could not have been written by a
bore.

I didn't know E.B. lived in Hong Kong, but suspected he might
dislike gatherings—like Henry James when John Bailey asked him if
he would be Chairman of the English Assocn. Do, for your own
pleasure, look up his letter (P. Lubbock's 2 vol Edition. Vol. II p. 279).

[1] George had been so described in the *Sunday Times* profile of his son Humphrey.
[2] Keats, 'Hyperion'.

He was having that painful bout of shingles at the time, and couldn't use a pen; he apologises for having to reply 'as I can and not at all as I would,' and then dictates a perfectly beautiful letter of courtesy, and humour, and understanding, and masterly English—the finest flower of civilisation, you might say. I once told Percy that this letter was my favourite; he agreed about its excellence.

But probably all this is perfectly familiar to you. When is your James-Wells correspondence coming out? It should be of the greatest interest—the contact of two first-rate minds at absolute odds about art and life and everything else. It is difficult to understand V. Woolf's inability to see anything good in H.J's writing, or so she said to Lytton S. By the way J. Wain is refreshing about L.S's impertinence in deriding Clough—a much better man than himself. That is of course the (probably, in the end) fatal flaw in Strachey, viz that through his not having any basis of principle or belief, his satire often gives an effect of *tittering*. Don't you feel he is always showing his superiority both to his subject and to hoi polloi? But of course one must face the fact that Max B. greatly admired his writing, and there wasn't much M.B. didn't see through.

Poor luck yesterday. In the bus to Ipswich I noticed a small child of extravagant plainness, its face, like that of Sulla in Plutarch, resembling 'a dish of mulberries sprinkled with flour'. I was recalling that lovely remark of Groucho Marx when someone said he hated to see a small boy crossing the street, 'I hate him anyvay.' This child sensed my feelings and retaliated suddenly by being sick—only just missing me, but in such cases a miss is as good etc. Shortly after the bus ran, rather wildly but with a good deal of splintering of glass, into a tree. Later on, after I had got out, I heard that a lady's shopping basket, into which she had thrown her cigarette, had caught fire. It must, in fact, have been the very opposite of 'The Celestial Omnibus'.

19 October 1957   *Bromsden Farm*

Raking and burning leaves today made me think of Laurence Binyon's fine poem, 'The Burning of the Leaves', written in his old age. Do you know it? If I could find my copy I'd write it out for you, and for my own pleasure, but so far it eludes me. I love bonfires, don't you? Everything about them is most satisfactory.

Just now I took down *Ego 8* (*your* one), opened it at the page where a G.I. describes Bedford as 'a cemetery with traffic-lights,' and read on happily. Surely these volumes will survive—or is our pleasure in them bound up with our knowledge of most of the people and events?

Did you hear that Eisenhower lost interest in the satellite as soon as he found it wasn't pitted like a golfball?

The London Library occupies much of what I must call my thought. Did I tell you that what it needs is an *additional* £12,500 a year? Last week I had an idea so simple that it can scarcely succeed: namely, that if I can persuade the English publishers to *give* their new books to the Library, instead of selling them as now, the Library will at once be £3500 a year better off. I feel fairly confident of cajoling *most* of the publishers. Then I plan to raise £100,000 in cash, which would bring in another £3500 a year. That would leave us £5500 short—which would be more than covered by an increase of two guineas in the subscription (there are 4000 paying members). As a first attack on the £100,000 I have applied to the Pilgrim Trust, which luckily meets in November. If they would give us a substantial sum in annual instalments, we might even get off paying rates, since one of the reasons for the failure of our first appeal was our inability to prove that we are supported 'wholly or in part by annual voluntary contributions'. I'm sure my only hope of persuading the publishers is to beard each important one in his office—about forty of them! There's a certain irony in trying to collect all this money when I'm at my wits' end to pay my sons' fees at Eton and Oxford. I hope all this doesn't bore you. Please keep it all to yourself. Do you know any rich people who might contribute? Now I must go to bed. Last night I slept uninterruptedly for ten hours, and I'm hoping for much the same tonight. Then, after more raking and burning, I'll return to the charge.

Sunday evening, 20 October

Another nine hours' sleep left me feeling quite limp this morning—there's nothing like prolonged rest for relaxing one to the point of total immobility—but a further bout of raking and bonfire has set me up.

I fear the James–Wells correspondence, when it appears early next year, may disappoint you: what there is is good stuff, with James coming out on top after the row, but so few letters (especially of Wells's) have survived that the book is scrappy and rather unsatisfying.

Surely the great thing about Lytton Strachey was his style and literary artistry: I'm sure that's what Max so much enjoyed. But as a historian, or critic of anything after the eighteenth century, he is worthless, I should say. The only thing is to enjoy his books as purely literary essays, and give them pretty good marks.

Last week I dined out three nights running—with a publisher and party at the Garrick, with the Ransomes at Putney (an hour's journey each way), and with the Jepsons in Bayswater—all agreeable but exhausting. Next Friday I am nipping up to Yorkshire for two days on the moors, and to shut up the cottage for the winter. So write to Soho Square and I'll send you a line from my hilltop, which I have never before seen in October. My heart leaps up at the thought. Oh for several months there! Then I should surely get something on to paper. As it is, I can hardly keep pace with the chores and engagements, so that Oscar is neglected, and that mass of miscellaneous information about his life and times, with which an editor's head *must* be brimming, grows dull and gets forgotten, and will have to be painfully regained. I know it was silly to take on so big a job amid my bustling life, but it's exactly the sort of job I like, and can do, best. Soon perhaps I'll be able to break the back of it. Unfortunately my tidy mind is worried by tasks unfinished. You mustn't mind my pouring out all this tiresome nonsense to you: there must be, alas, much rough to very little smooth. I do hope you'll be at the November Lit. Soc. I can't face Dunsany without my oak-tree!

23 October 1957   *Grundisburgh*

This should catch you before your northern trip. How pleased old Agate would have been at one perceptive reader spotting the permanent value of the *Egos*. They are everlastingly readable and full of little plums like the one you quote on Bedford. It always seems very odd to me that he should have so much admired Arnold Bennett's *Journals* and modestly hoped that the *Egos* might be *almost* as good. The A.B.'s are full of entries like 'Long and interesting talk with F. Swinnerton,' and little or nothing more.

I forget whether you knew A. Bennett. A good man, I always think, with all his limitations and blind spots. You knew, of course, that it was G.M's *A Mummer's Wife* ('squalor and sordidness turned into poetry') that showed A.B. what could be done with the Potteries. (Some day you can produce *one* of your anthologies 'Things told me by G.W.L. which I knew already'. Only less damning than the one M.R.J. *could* have compiled 'Stories told to me by A. B. and C. which I had originally told them'.)

Bonfires, *yes*, superb; the smell, the noise, the spectacle. One of the human tests surely—i.e. a man who does *not* love them must, in some way or another, be a poor creature. And what a sense of humour they have, viz just when the smoke is thickest and one is poking and prodding, the wind suddenly and momentarily changes and one retreats rapidly, but not rapidly enough, choking, eyes smarting, smut-bestrewn (which sounds like a line of Hopkins), a figure of fun. I don't know the Binyon poem; please send a copy when found. I ask brazenly, because I know that you, like me, frankly enjoy copying out something you really like. But wait a moment. You won't have any time, with the L.L. now on your back. How typical it all is—you personally bearding one publisher after another—suave and tireless and resourceful. The result, I suppose, of having a profile rather like Wellington's, and an energy entirely like Napoleon's. The £100,000 ought to be exactly the sort of thing to appeal to a rich American. But perhaps they are all buttoning their pockets against a slump. A jumpy lot to be leaders of the modern world. I wish I knew some rich people. The richest man in Suffolk is Sir C. Fison, and if only the L.L. dealt in chemical manure rather than in books, hopes might be bright. Shall I attempt with him a bold flight of fancy or analogy on the lines of books being manure for the mind? At the moment Ipswich is all bye-electing, and the air is thick with platitude, recrimination and mendacity, none of which, they tell me, changes a single vote, though Hailsham's oratory was the most popular. What rot it all is!

Sleep! Yes, but I suppose *in the end* all those hours are restful? I have long outgrown all that stuff about eight hours and beauty sleep, etc. and hug the recollection of Horder's dictum that many people sleep much too much. Though I grant you a post-prandial snooze is not eschewed as rigorously as it might be.

I agree with you, *toto animo*, about Strachey. His style is perfect joy, and it is only when one has come across a fairer and kindlier handling of one of his victims that one is resentful of his tittering, however mellifluous. And with all his admiration, Max said some pretty sharp things about Bloomsbury—though mainly about those sillies who crabbed 'beauty' and intelligibility.

Did you look up the James letter to J. Bailey? I should hate to think you were too busy to enjoy its rich savours. Don't you like that positively granite refusal to compromise the tiniest jot of artistic principle that underlies all the honey and flowers so lavishly poured out by the most courteous of men? Of course he and H.G.W. were not talking the same language. But what an artist H.G.W. *might* have been—'"Wasn't it them Greeks as used to be so clever?" "*Used* to be," said the young man with dark scorn.' Was ever so much sociology packed into so few words?

I shall be at the November Lit. Soc. Put me next to Dunsany. One must earn one's keep.

P.S. Can you imagine Mrs Sidney Webb ever enjoying a bonfire? Or Mrs Humphry Ward? H.J. would have, so long as he didn't have to build it.

27 October 1957   *Yorkshire*

I entirely agree about Arnold Bennett's journals, though our disappointment may be partly due to the prudish timidity of their editor, old Newman Flower. According to Hugh Walpole, N.F. was so appalled by much of what he found in the journals that he published only brief extracts, and those the safest. Perhaps we shall one day be given the whole works. I did know A.B. slightly, and liked him—most people did.

I still haven't run that Binyon poem to earth, but shall hope to copy it out for you next Sunday. Knowing exactly where ninety-nine out of every hundred of my large collection of books are, I am entirely baffled when one goes astray—and this is only a pamphlet. I dare say that the bonfire H.J. enjoyed most was the one at Lamb House, to which he consigned the great mass of the letters he had received from everybody (it scarcely bears thinking of), retaining only a few choice exhibits. He seemed to think that this indiscriminate holocaust would also destroy all the letters *he* had written to everybody, but naturally they had all been kept; my friend Leon Edel has already examined more than seven thousand, and still they come.

Last week began with a dinner-party, in (of all places) the Artillery Mansions Hotel, of three booksellers and five publishers, to discuss privately the troubles of the trade. I need hardly tell you that, though some agreed on the diagnosis, no two could begin to find a remedy acceptable to both.

On Tuesday evening I had sausage-rolls, cakes and coffee at the Royal Photographic Society, among a mass of hideous and unknown persons, whose skill with a camera has, I hope, compensated them for other things. Thus refreshed we all trooped upstairs to a lecture by Alvin Langdon Coburn. Does the name ring any bell? He is an American of seventy-five, who came to England in 1905 and has lived here ever since. He was a remarkable pioneer of photography—being an artist who happened to use a camera rather than a photographer trying to take artistic pictures. A great hero-worshipper, he managed to photograph most of the leading writers, artists, musicians, etc. from 1905 to 1912, and published the results in two remarkable books, *Men of Mark* and *More Men of Mark*. I'll show them to you on your next visit. In 1907–8 Henry James asked him to take special photographs for frontispieces to the big New York Edition of H.J.'s works, which he did. It was through this that, perhaps eight years ago, I got in touch with him, and we then published a new edition of Stevenson's *Edinburgh* with Coburn's photographs. (Have you seen that book? If not I'd love to send you a copy.) Anyhow I got quite fond of the old boy, and long ago promised to attend this lecture, which was to celebrate his fifty-year-old membership of the R.P.S. What I didn't know till I met him among the sausage-rolls was that his wife had died ten days before, after fourteen weeks of great pain, during which he nursed her alone in their little house in North Wales. She died on the forty-fifth anniversary of their wedding. He told me about it quite simply, and said that his faith was sustaining him. Incidentally he is a terrifically big bug in Freemasonry. The lecture was dullish, but in the circumstances rather touching. Afterwards I escaped fairly soon.

On Wednesday I attended, as Vyvyan Holland's guest, a dinner of the Saintsbury Club in the Vintners' Hall. A long succession of most potable wines, Laver was in the chair, and Douglas Woodruff made an admirable speech about Saintsbury, wine and letters. It seemed unprepared, and gave the effect of a fine artist improvising on the piano.

On Thursday afternoon I attended a conference in the Chambers of the London Library's leading Counsel—none other than Mr Geoffrey Lawrence Q.C., the saviour of Dr Adams! He is a small neat man, with a quiet, well-modulated, exact voice, and (it seemed to me) unusual clarity of mind. We discussed our coming appeal before the Lands Tribunal (probably in January) and I rather enjoyed it.

After all this (and entertaining E.B. in the flat in the intervals) you will realise with what joy and relief I drove off at dawn on Friday and got here at lunchtime. Since then the weather has steadily worsened, and the wind on this hilltop almost blows one over. But I have a roaring fire and an Aladdin lamp, and would like to stay here for months.

31 October 1957   *Grundisburgh*

What disservice these mealy mouths do us all! Like the premature Alanbrooke reminiscences, an emasculated Bennett *Journal* merely stops, or at best postpones, the full and (probably immensely) interesting publication of the whole lot. You will see, but I shall not, the full story of the abdication as told by Baldwin. I forget where it is deposited, but it will not be published till all concerned are dead. An idle biographer too can queer the pitch; I remember how cross old Agate was about O. Elton's inadequate life of C.E. Montague, which, he said, merely prevented a good life being written, and gave no good picture of C.E.M. I was pleased to see from various reviews that

R.H-D's outstanding merits as an editor are getting general recognition. And there will soon be a third string to your bow, as the Lord Leconfield, who frequents the London Library, speaks very highly of the new chairman.

Yes, how horrible to think of that bonfire of letters at Lamb House —almost as bad as the destruction of Byron's memoirs. Why do men do these things? Because any amount of stuff in the letters to H.J. must have been vastly interesting and not in the least personal to him.

Coburn? No, the name rings no bell. Cameron is the only name I associate with photography—apart from Lewis Carroll photographing small girls naked, John Everard doing ditto to larger girls, and so acting with horrible appropriateness up to his name (to show how far we have travelled from the days of Q. Victoria, let me tell you it was a young lady who told me this fourth-form ribaldry). I look forward to seeing *Men of Mark* and Stevenson's *Edinburgh*. I like to think of you among the sausage-rolls. They ought to be much better than they are; the pastry is always too dry, and the sausage lacking in flavour. Someone should start a revival—a golf-club perhaps could become famous for its sausage-rolls—like Westward Ho for its curry, Rye for its buttered eggs, and somewhere I forget for its potted shrimps (Lytham-St Anne's?).

The only lack in your letters is that you don't *always* specify the fare at your dinners and lunches. This should always be done—as, indeed, you once stated, and are the only man I know beside myself who knows exactly what old Heythorp had for his Last Supper. (And there are thin-witted, pince-nezed, flute-voiced men with Adam's apples bobbing up and down like the glass ball in Victorian lemonade-bottles, who presume to look down on Galsworthy!)

You will be contemptuous or cross, or both, when I tell you I have just read John Osborne's *The Entertainer*. My dear Rupert, I feel (almost) scared—like Douglas Jerrold in convalescence, reading *Sordello* and terrified that, though physically mending, his mind had gone; he handed the book to a visiting friend, and when he saw him completely baffled, ejaculated 'Thank God' and sank back into refreshing sleep. *The E.* is utter, hopeless, outrageous rubbish, and yet T.C. Worsley in the *N.S.* uses words about it like 'brilliant', 'dazzling', 'gripping', 'masterly' etc. My only hope is that it looks and sounds quite different on the stage. In the study it is puerile. I suppose the enormous increase in the numbers of those who *can* read accounts for the popularity of so much rubbish; discrimination is still to come. They tell me the young flock to concerts, and Humphrey is always infuriated by the wild applause of every item, good bad and indifferent. Quite different somehow from what is meant by a catholic taste—like old Saintsbury's who saw the good in Paul de Kock as well as in Milton. Not that he liked everything. I seem to remember his always having a down on Byron, but it was the B. of *Childe H.* and not of '*Donny Jonny*', as B. called it himself.

You didn't, I suppose, ask G. Lawrence about Dr Adams. I once asked the late Mr Justice Lewis about Greenwood, and he said it was quite certain Greenwood poisoned his wife (he was a junior for the prosecution) but got off because his daughter swore she had drunk from the relevant bottle of Burgundy. She disliked her father but wasn't going to have him hanged. I must go to another trial; I always enjoy them. Not a murder perhaps, though I have seen one or two very decent murderers in court—and one in Whitechapel, pointed out by Dick Sheppard, to whom he had confessed. He was never caught, and according to D.S. was a very good fellow. I like to listen to judges, especially the sort of judge whom somebody once described as 'belonging to the great traditional line of judges. He was slow, he was courteous, he was wrong.' (Quoted by J. Agate, who added 'the exact opposite of me, who am rapid, rude, and right.')

P.S. Poor old Dunsany. It gave me quite a turn. Not that he need be pitied.

3 November 1957   *Bromsden Farm*

More bonfire-work yesterday, but last night's heavy rain extinguished everything. Rain fell almost incessantly during my week-end on the moors, but I was warm and cosy and busy and blissfully cut off from the telephone and other intrusions. Never on any account disclose my Yorkshire address to anyone, particularly not to dear Roger:

if he discovered how comparatively near it is to him he wouldn't rest until he had disturbed my solitude in the friendliest way. I *still* can't find the Binyon poem, but it's worth waiting for. It was one of the only two poems my dear old Egyptologist uncle-by-marriage Walter Crum ever copied out. The other consisted of this extract:

> The solemn peaks but to the stars are known,
> But to the stars, and the cold lunar beams;
> Alone the sun arises, and alone
> Spring the great streams.[1]

Friday was E.B.'s sixty-first birthday, and I invited some twenty of his family and admirers to a buffet lunch at Soho Square (sausage-rolls and all). It went with a swing and I'm sure pleased him. By the way, I've just discovered that he would dearly love to be a member of the M.C.C. Is there anything we can do, any string we can pull, to get him in? He plans to return finally to England in 1961, when he will be sixty-five. His cricket writings, in prose and verse, are, as you know, first-rate, and his knowledge and love of the game you have witnessed. Please give the matter your careful attention.

I see that all my efforts to wean you from deliberate mortification of the wits have failed: *The Entertainer* indeed! What a misnomer! All seem agreed that only Olivier's virtuosity keeps the play on, and I can see that he welcomed a change to shine in something so far from his normal playground. When I was a student at the Old Vic, the performances of Shakespeare alternated with those of Opera. Every night the stage-door was besieged by lunatic girls with autograph books. One night, as I was signing my quite unknown and worthless name, I asked the girl whether she came to the Opera too. 'Oh, yes.' 'What's the Opera company like?' I asked. 'Oh', said she, 'just like the Shakespeare company: it doesn't matter whether they're good or bad; we clap them just the same.' Such, I fear, is the mentality of much of the great new reading public which universal 'education' has brought forth.

By the way, I see that a new book (possibly the last) by one of my favourite living authors has just appeared: *Last Tales* by Isak Dinesen: order it from your library at once. And then her two earlier volumes,

[1] From 'In Utrumque Paratus' by Matthew Arnold.

181

Seven Gothic Tales and *Winter's Tales*. Sometimes she writes under her own name, Baroness Blixen. She is an elderly Dane, reputed to take drugs—but a smashing good writer. My Uncle Duff thought that one of the stories in *Winter's Tales*, 'The Young Man with the Carnation', or words to that effect, was one of the best short stories ever written. She certainly makes most modern practitioners look pretty thin. I hope you don't know her books already: it will be such fun for you coming to them fresh.

Poor old Dunsany: I bet he's boring the wings off the angels with disquisitions on rock-salt and the semi-colon. I now feel rather smugly satisfied at having endured his last Lit. Soc. appearance (and incidentally touched him for a pound which he had owed me for more than a year). We now have *three* vacancies, and so far *seven* candidates. This time last year I was interested only in your candidature: this year it's chiefly Jonah I'm concerned about: Dunsany was all for him, but perhaps the younger members won't be.

Last week produced *six* new Oscar letters, one of them twenty-two pages long, though he didn't get as much on his pages as we do on ours. My son Duff lectured on Russia (with coloured slides) to the Literary Society at Eton on Friday and thinks it was a great success. Yesterday he shot with Peter, who was taking time off from his mother's humiliating litigation. How silly can people be? There are surely many more enjoyable ways of spending large sums of money.[1]

THE BURNING OF THE LEAVES
by Laurence Binyon[2]

Now is the time for the burning of the leaves.
They go to the fire; the nostril pricks with smoke
Wandering slowly into a weeping mist.
Brittle and blotched, ragged and rotten sheaves!
A flame seizes the smouldering ruin and bites
On stubborn stalks that crackle as they resist.

[1] Mrs Fleming, aged seventy-three, was being sued by the Parsee Marchioness of Winchester for, among other things, the 'enticement' of the ninety-three-year-old Marquess.

[2] By kind permission of Mrs Nicolette Gray.

The last hollyhock's fallen tower is dust;
All the spices of June are a bitter reek,
All the extravagant riches spent and mean.
All burns! The reddest rose is a ghost;
Sparks whirl up, to expire in the mist: the wild
Fingers of fire are making corruption clean.

Now is the time for stripping the spirit bare,
Time for the burning of days ended and done,
Idle solace of things that have gone before:
Rootless hope and fruitless desire are there;
Let them go to the fire, with never a look behind.
The world that was ours is a world that is ours no more.

They will come again, the leaf and the flower, to arise
From squalor of rottenness into the old splendour,
And magical scents to a wondering memory bring;
The same glory, to shine upon different eyes.
Earth cares for her own ruins, naught for ours.
Nothing is certain, only the certain spring.

7 November 1957   *Grundisburgh*

First of all, will you and your lady dine with us on *Thursday Nov. 21
at 67 Chelsea Square*? It is the house of Alexander and Mrs Hood (my
daughter) who have lent it to us for a day or two while they are in
New York. If that day is impossible what about Tuesday the 19th?
Not *quite* so good as the 21st but very, very far from bad. I have an
inkling that Mrs R. does not come to London during your working
week, and if I am right, will you yourself come? *Moreover*, we shall
have your clock with us, and you could take it to S. Square with you
after the dinner (long after). It all seems *to me* a good plan, but (like
the late Field-Marshal Robertson) you may 'think different'. Let me
have a p.c. with 'Oh well, yes, I suppose so' or 'Good God, no!' on it;
you won't be writing a letter this week-end as we meet on Tuesday.
Is the ritual of my calling on you before the Lit. Soc. intolerable?

Because that is what I should love to do. But it may well be that if I didn't you would be doing some important and profitable business.

I like the Binyon poem *very* much. It has all the smell and the noise and the spectacle of *the* bonfire (do you remember how cross Wordsworth was when someone referred to his writing a poem to *a* daisy instead of *the*?). And the reflections which rise therefrom. There is a grim note in the last two lines, for it is hard sometimes to believe that the mess *homo sapiens* is making of his affairs may not some day soon be found irreparable. Even so spring will return—like 'the august, inhospitable, inhuman stars, glittering magnificently unperturbed'. I imagine even Khrusch will take some time before annexing those stars which are over two million light-years away.

The other favourite of your Egyptologist uncle was also one of Charles Fisher's (killed at Jutland 1916). The very last time I heard the stanza declaimed—or even mentioned—was in 1912 on the top of Glaramara—'Thin, thin the pleasant human noises grow' . . . Old Mat laid them dead sometimes, though at others—! What do you, what can anyone, say about:

> Look ah! what genius—Art, Science, Wit,
> Soldiers like Caesar, Statesmen like Pitt;
> Sculptors like Phidias, Raphaels in shoals,
> Poets like Shakespeare—beautiful souls![1]

I mean, isn't that the writing of a complete and incurable *ASS*? By the way, another tiny fragment Charles Fisher was fond of was from old Daddy:

> So have I, not unmoved in mind,
> Seen birds of tempest-loving kind
> Thus beating up against the wind.[2]

Where did I read recently (Humphry House?) a strong commendation of at least three stanzas in a very old favourite of mine, the hideously

[1] Matthew Arnold, from 'Bacchanalia: or The New Age'.
[2] Wordsworth, 'To a Highland Girl'.

named 'Extempore Effusion on the death of James Hogg'?[1] Granted that

> On which with thee, O Crabbe forth-looking,
> I gazed from Hampstead's breezy Heath . . .

is lacking in thrill, what about 'The rapt One' . . . etc., and 'Like clouds' . . . ? What does E.B. think of them? He gave me the impression the other day of knowing practically all the poets have written. Of course he ought to be a member of the M.C.C. and I have written this very day to Harry Altham (the Treasurer) to find out if there are any ways and means. I am not immensely optimistic, as they are pretty rigid about their rules and regulations, and the austere shade of Lord Harris still broods morosely over the Committee Room. Some years ago there was an attempt to get Cardus in; I did what I could, but to no avail. But N.C. would, I suppose, be found by many much less likeable than E.B. Another difficulty is that many excellent cricketers are practically illiterate, and have no realisation of the obvious truth that it is the poetry of and in the game which keeps it alive. Tom Richardson had as little poetry in him as Achilles, but the sight of him bowling in 1896, or rather the mere thought of it, set N.C. writing stuff with the glow and quality of

> Stand in the trench, Achilles,
> Flame-capped, and shout for me.[2]

Isak Dinesen. I must confess that she is to me what the Holy Ghost was to the Corinthians. Why have I never heard of her? I shall order her stories at once.

[1] Nor has the rolling year twice measured,
From sign to sign, its steadfast course,
Since every mortal power of Coleridge
Was frozen at its marvellous source;

The rapt One, of the godlike forehead,
The heaven-eyed creature sleeps in earth:
And Lamb, the frolic and the gentle,
Has vanished from his lonely hearth.

Like clouds that rake the mountain-summits,
Or waves that own no curbing hand,
How fast has brother followed brother,
From sunshine to the sunless land!

[2] By Patrick Shaw-Stewart (killed in action 1917).

I do hope Jonah gets in. Apart from him, you must tell me on Tuesday how to vote. Old Dunsany had a striking career, and I suppose was, in his prime, a considerable man. So was Herbert Spencer, but that didn't prevent Carlyle describing him as the greatest ass in Europe, and in the American class as a bore.

How frightfully tiresome that law-suit must be for Peter. I never met his mother, but his father was one of the best of my Eton friends. What a caddish business cross-examining is, but I suppose it is all part of the game, and both judge and jury discount it. Asquith was a balanced and kindly man, but an old lawyer-friend told me he was a brutal cross-examiner—shouted, if you please, at the witness, which is hard to believe. Old Russell, of course, was a mere bully at the job, which I should have thought his skill made unnecessary. How heartening to remember the slightly squiffy subaltern who met his recriminations at the club after the subaltern had bogged his whist-hand: 'All right, all right, old cock! But remember ye're not in yer bally old police-court now!' Very salutary for the Lord Chief Justice of England.

I have been re-reading some of those delightful essays of G.M. Young which you gave me. How tragic that he should have collapsed. Writers of real quality are rare. His picture of old Gladstone is masterly. What a pity the 'noble old foghorn' was before the days of wireless and gramophone. Nobody believes in spell-binding who didn't see or hear the spell-binder. Tell a young man about W.E.G. or about Chatham and 'Sugar'[1], and he laughs with the implication that it wouldn't have impressed *him*.

Note I. Don't bother to write unless you can't come or face seeing me at 6.30 on Tuesday. I will assume you can if I don't hear.

Note II. Did you know geese are very fond of music? They flock into the corner of their pen when my wireless is on. They were clearly indignant at Schubert's symphony being unfinished.

Note III. How thin and slick and *indistinguishable* many of Haydn's symphonies are! Didn't he write too many?

[1] Alderman Beckford, when opposing the tax on sugar, had been interrupted by laughter. Pitt the Elder followed him and began his speech 'Sugar, Mr Speaker'. A hoarse laugh. 'Sugar, Mr Speaker', thundered Pitt. In the dead silence that followed, 'Sugar, Mr Speaker' he whispered in his most dulcet tones. 'Who will laugh at sugar now?'

Let us have a standing arrangement that on Lit. Soc. nights you will come to Soho Square at *six*, or as soon after as suits you. Press and pull every bell: they have just been mended and we must keep them in practice. I'd love to dine with you in Chelsea Square, but alas Comfort cannot get to London: her teaching keeps her tied here all term-time, and some child or children in the holidays. So may I come alone? Tuesday 19th would suit me much better than the Thursday, if you can manage it. Tell me this Tuesday. All this and the clock too!

E.B. (who may be present at S.S. on Tuesday) does indeed know almost all English poetry by heart, and not only the greatest. He is a firm Wordsworthian—and so am I. Inspired by your references I have just re-read the 'Extempore Effusion': those three stanzas are superb. Many other great poets have written as many bad poems as W.W. (Tennyson for one), but has any other managed to hide away tremendous lines and stanzas in mediocre poems? What about:

> My former thoughts return'd: the fear that kills;
> The hope that is unwilling to be fed;
> Cold, pain, and labour, and all fleshly ills;
> And mighty Poets in their misery dead.

And then back to that egregious old leech-gatherer. Did the old gaffer realise that these matchless lines were any better than the lame verses that surround them? I doubt it. I have never known a poet or writer who had any idea which was their best work: each poem or other work is inextricably bound up with the mood and circumstances of its creation.

I fear your championing of E.B. will make no impression on the dragons of the M.C.C., but it's angelic of you to try. It was I who asked you years ago to try and get Cardus in. His deafness doesn't seem to stop his hearing music, only other people's conversation.

I so agree about Haydn and his symphonies. As Sarah Bernhardt said, when asked by a reporter what she thought of the ten commandments, 'Zey are too many.' I can't tell one from another and am bored by all.

Sunday morning, 10 November 1957

More bonfire this morning with Adam, home for Long Leave, very tall, pale, long-haired and with a sniffling cold, but charming as ever. He wants to specialise, God help us, in Science! Duff has got flu at Oxford, but is confident of turning out next Saturday for Coleridge's Old Boys v. the Field.

Last Monday I was Stephen Potter's guest at a dinner at the Athenaeum, at which he spoke on English and American Humour. Menu enclosed: it tasted slightly better than it sounds, and was helped by a decent bottle of claret each. If you and I had been set down to invent a list of A. members, respectable, even distinguished, but deadly dull, we should scarcely have improved on the enclosed list. My other neighbour was an agreeable retired Treasury official with a deaf-aid (they all looked like that) called Sir Frank Nixon. During the speech he passed me a note asking me to a party, but I politely refused.

On Thursday I dined with the Haleys at their flat in Ashley Gardens—very richly furnished. At dinner I sat next to an immensely forthcoming neighbour of yours—Lady Albemarle. She spoke of you as a recluse, and I see your point. According to *Who's Who* she seems to run everything. Lord A. was there, also Hartley Shawcross and wife: she very attractive, but he rather supercilious. Also Joseph Harsch and wife: he an ace American radio-commentator. Good stuffed veal, and first-class cold chestnut pudding. The H's are teetotal but the wine was good and ample. Sir William talked about the B.B.C. and *The Times*, of which next day's first edition arrived at 10 p.m.

14 November 1957   *Grundisburgh*

That was again a wonderfully pleasant evening, and the appearance and demeanour of Sir Cuthbert were positively *chirpy*—there is no other word for it. I cannot help feeling that for the general friendly atmosphere the Secretary must be largely responsible. (Apropos of Sir C. my father always maintained that after a certain age many old men were rather *pleased* by the deaths of their contemporaries, if not great friends. Dunsany? Hush!) I was glad to meet E. Link later again;

his discourse was full of flavour. He has sent one of his boys to Eton and another to Winchester, after long and shrewd consideration of their respective characters. It all sounded very sensible; though the Ancient of Days' impish propensity for upsetting human plans may send all agley.

I thought poor Peter F. seemed in rather low spirits and no wonder. I have a feeling his mother may come in for some harsh treatment, or at least comment, by the judge Devlin. According to my brother-in-law, old Winchester is and always was a horrible man—though anyone remotely 'enticeable' at ninety must compel some respect. M.R.J. loved to tell how some old King's don over a century ago had to give up his Fellowship when they found out he was married. Well he was only, so to speak, married in the sight of God, and was reported by a friend as saying '. . . and let me tell you, sir, that it's a damned lugubrious thing to be turned out of one's fellowship for fornication at the age of eighty-four.'

In your last letter you commented on what poor critics poets are of their own poetry. I would add 'and often of anyone's'. Are you familiar with *The Oxford Book of Modern Verse* chosen by Yeats? I don't know it well and in fact rather left it when I found his *wicked* omissions —including some of the best of his own early stuff. And what of Auden's *insufferable* comments on Tennyson, which so infuriated D. MacCarthy, and good Dame Sitwell's contempt for Emily Brontë's 'Cold in the Earth', which actually led to Q, in his senility, omitting it from the new *Oxford E.V.* (though I *believe* he left in 'Meet we no angels, Pansie?'—but I may be wrong). What does surprise me is how many of FitzG's alterations to Omar are *not* improvements, because his palate, though eclectic, was a fine one. And am I right in thinking Henry James's re-writings were often unfortunate?

I have not yet heard from H.S. Altham about E.B. and the M.C.C. Of course there should be a possible entry for such people; it needn't be any larger or easier than the secret way into the Capitol (was it?); but you must know how sticky these old foundations are. (A pupil of mine was almost relegated to outer darkness once because, at the age of about twenty-five, he played a round at St Andrew's in sand-shoes.)

I never go to London without finding all those *faces* deeply depressing. 'Zey are too many.' A trainload in the rush-hour—silent, hurrying, mud-faced, wrapped either in private worries or in the evening-paper, but not *interested* in either, not really alive in any full sense—don't they devitalise you? My brother-in-law says if you live in London you don't notice them. I suppose they all have got to that point and so look as they do: Suffolk faces are often hideous, but they *are* faces: these aren't.

Give my regards to E.B. I never meet him without feeling a better, nicer, wiser man. I don't say even then that I am particularly good, nice, or wise, but, well, my uncle once heard a preacher enlarging on the miracle in the valley of Hinnom, and describing how when God breathed upon the skeletons they were 'elevated to the condition of corpses'. Consider me as having reached the corpse stage.

N.B. Dinner Nov. 26 (Tuesday) 8 p.m., don't 'dress', 67 Chelsea Square. Agenda: (1) to eat drink and be merry (2) to tire sun with talking (3) to add to the public stock of harmless pleasure (4) to meet Sir Terence and Lady Nugent (5) to meet Lord Leconfield (6) to take home cottage pendulum clock and till further notice to hear in every tick of it a message of affection and goodwill from your host and hostess.[1]

17 November 1957   *Bromsden Farm*

I'm sure you're right about Cuthbert, and that the death of a contemporary, better still of a junior, is the breath of life to him. Did you realise that Eric L. was far from sober when he arrived? Not that liquor makes him tiresome—only loud, vehement and repetitive. I think I told you his eldest daughter had lain unconscious for seven weeks after a road accident. Clearly E's arrival in London was the signal for tension to be released in alcohol. After leaving the Garrick he collected some friends from the Savile and spent most of the rest of the night in some frightful nightclub. Next morning he woke when the bar opened, spent three hours over lunch, and arrived at Soho Square at 4 p.m. very merry indeed. Somehow I propelled him to some nearby

[1] I still (1979) do.

binders, where by means of astonishing will-power he managed to make a creditable shot at signing sixty copies of a limited edition of his new book. With great difficulty I found a taxi and sent him back to the Savile. Next morning he turned up, very sick and sorry, but bearing a letter from his wife to say that the child had at last spoken, and there was hope that her brain wasn't affected. You can work out the moral of this story if you're clever enough.

Yeats's *Oxford Book* cannot be taken seriously, except as a gloss on W.B.Y. Great writers are almost the worst critics, being egoists and usually interested only in their own work.

I entirely agree about the London street faces, and try not to look at them more than I must. Certainly a pretty girl stands out like a good deed in a naughty world.

Since I saw you I have been to lunch in the inner sanctum of *The Times*. Bidden by Lord Astor of Hever to a 'small intimate party', I found myself one of twenty-two men, including the Archbishop of York (who, as Bishop of Durham, so tenderly supported the Queen through her coronation). I was between old Mr John Walter (whose ancestors founded the paper and used to live in that very house). He is eighty-four and almost stone-deaf, so that was, as they say, tough sledding. On my other side was dear Laurence Irving, who made up for Walter. Food and drink were good and plentiful. The other guests were mostly directors of the paper and big business executives—all very unexpected, inexplicable, novel and amusing. Haley was of the party, but I scarcely got a word with him.

Yesterday Duff came over from Oxford and went on to Eton, where he played the Field game for F.J.R.C's old boys against the School (who won 5-0). At the same time Comfort disguised herself in black face and gipsy clothes to tell fortunes at the village fête. This left me happily alone, and at last I got back on to my Oscar Wilde treadmill. It took me some time to *get* back after so long an interval, for to do this sort of writing properly one must be steeped in the period and all its details. Often a neat footnote seems to have put paid to some event or individual, but then it or he crops up again and must be cross-referenced. Don't imagine I don't like it all, but it's hellish difficult to fit into the maelstrom of my ordinary life. E.B. leaves for Hong Kong at the end of the month—sorry to go, I fear.

I am greatly looking forward to the 26th, and only hope I shall end up in a fit state to carry proudly home my precious clock.

I have just read the latest novel of a man whom I consider one of the best living novelists—R.C. Hutchinson: have you read anything of his? If not, try this one: it is called *March the Ninth*, and though not his best is still jolly good. If you like it, then try *Shining Scabbard, One Light Burning,* and *The Unforgotten Prisoner.* He is an Englishman of roughly my age, and all his best books are about some European country to which he has never been: apparently his imagination has to be kindled by being far-flung. His long novel of the Russian Revolution, *Testament*, is astonishingly good, and he always writes beautifully. Here's another treat in store for you!

20 November 1957   *Grundisburgh*

That is an epic passage about E. Linklater. I had not realised the situation at the L.S. but merely noticed that he had plenty to say and that it was worth listening to. I am glad his daughter mends, but I see now he has just lost his father (or mother was it?). I expect, like most Scots, he is pretty good about the bludgeonings of fate. The Savile sounds a more convivial spot than it was forty years ago when I was a member, and some older man described it—I am sure unjustly—as 'the home of seedy prigs'. I didn't—being a very shy young man—much like its custom of a communal dining-table, and you took your chance about your neighbour. I lunched there only once and found myself next to Ray Lankester who talked of nothing, as far as I remember, but the criminal folly of the club management in having no fires just because the month was August. I had vaguely hoped I might go home with some valuable light thrown on the next world. Doesn't Max B. write somewhere of the importance of *not* meeting great men in the flesh? And what about Charlotte Brontë's horror on seeing Thackeray munching and enjoying potatoes! And many surely must have had a shock to see how dirty Tennyson's hands were.

I have a pleasant little malicious triumph coming next Saturday when the Revisers and Setters of English Literature papers in the

G.C.E. meet. The Revisers comment on our papers and, as you might expect, often, in our opinion, pick holes which aren't there. The Chief Reviser has objected to a judgment on Keats in a paper set by me, and an explanation of a Shakespeare phrase. Well the judgment is that of Bridges and the explanation taken word for word from a note of C.H. Herford, both of whom, I imagine, knew what they were talking about every bit as well as this amiable old bumble-bee.

I suspect I am steadily becoming more curmudgeonly and narrow in this matter. There are five Dickens novels I love, but last week I re-read (after half a century) *Bleak House* and am now in *The O.C. Shop*, and I find his obvious and admitted defects outweighing the genius; and as for the humour—well now, do *you* go chuckling about Soho Square whenever you think of Mrs Jellyby, and Mrs Pardiggle, and Messrs Chadband and Turveydrop, and Mrs Jarley and Dick Swiveller? B. Darwin does, I am sure—just as *I* do about Pecksniff and Mrs Gamp and the Wellers and Mrs Nickleby etc. Why is this? Why do I, in my bones, *know M. Chuzzlewit* (for all Macaulay called it 'dull and frivolous') to be *leagues* ahead of *Bleak H.*? Why do I love reading about Mr Squeers and don't a bit want to go on reading about Quilp? These are questions 'spirit-searching, light-abandoned', as one of the literary ladies said to Martin C.—and the worst is still to come, for little Nell is still alive.

P.S. What does G.M. Young mean by 'the ribbon-development' of George Moore's English? I am always coming across these brilliancies and so often failing to see that their point is all that sharp. On the other hand, almost everything G.K.C. says of Mr Pickwick gets me, so to speak, where it tickles. E.g. on that old suggestion that the idea of Mr P. was really Seymour's: 'To claim to have originated an idea of Dickens is like claiming to have contributed a glass of water to Niagara', and his play on the idea of Mr P. always being 'taken in'. Isn't his book on Dickens of quite extraordinary merit? It always seems so to me.

Please give E.B. my warm regard to take back to Hong-Kong *if you think he would like to have it.* Such things do fail sometimes. One of the least attractive episodes of old Gladstone's career was after his last Cabinet had said good-bye to him, practically all of them in tears.

He himself wasn't, and used to refer to them as 'that blubbering Cabinet'. I sometimes wonder whether George Meredith was right in saying W.E.G. was a man of marvellous aptitudes but not a great man. But who told me recently of A.J.B. in a company who were all telling of the most frightening moments in their lives? Battle, and fire and flood, crag and torrent, etc cropped up again and again. A.J.B. knew nothing of any of these, but merely recorded Mr G. looking at him in the House, *and his eyes widened*. But that brings me to La Rochefoucauld: 'Why have we memory sufficient to retain the minutest circumstances . . . and yet not enough to remember how often we have related them to the same person?' I have a suspicion that I heard the A.J.B. story with/from you.

24 November 1957   *Bromsden Farm*

Stay me with flagons, comfort me with apples! A glance at the enclosed will show you what I mean—but more of that later. I've always understood that it was *Frank Harris* who, on being taken to the Savile Club at a time when the conversation and the cellar were famous, said: 'The worst thing about this club of faded prigs is that you can't get a decent glass of wine.' ('faded' is better than 'seedy', don't you think?) I expect you know that the S.C.'s present premises in Brook Street were formerly the home of 'Lulu' Harcourt. When Max was asked how he would describe the *décor*, he said: '*Lulu Quinze*'. And I'm certain I've already told you of J.B. Priestley's superb remark, 'The *Savage* Club is the place where dirty stories go when they die.'

It's so long since I had time to read Dickens that I'm in no position to debate with you. The last I read was, funnily enough, *Bleak House*, about five years ago, and I loved it. All the same, *Martin Chuzzlewit* is my favourite too: when shall I have time to enjoy it again? By the way, if you haven't read Humphry House's book *The Dickens World*, do get it from the library.

The best description of George Moore's later prose compared it to one of the large French rivers—wide, placid, seemingly endless, no current, occasional felicities on the bank, shallow, and *just* moving.

This applies to *The Brook Kerith, Héloise, Aphrodite in Aulis,* etc. I suppose that by 'ribbon-development' G.M.Y. meant to indicate an endless projection without apparent plan or meaning, as opposed to a single building designed compactly as a work of art—but I agree that it isn't a wholly happy phrase. You have never before told me that story of A.J.B. and W.E.G. So there!

Last week was gruelling. Those two dinners alone, on consecutive nights, almost laid me out. Food and drink were on both occasions first rate. Lionel Fraser (although a teetotaller and non-smoker) was a perfect host, and it was amusing for once to mingle with all the riches of E.C.4.

The Trinity Hall evening was cosier, beginning at the High Table in their lovely little hall, and ending in the Combination Room with a horseshoe table and a little railway for the decanters. I was lucky to sit between the only two representatives of the humanities, my host Graham Storey and Brooke Crutchley, the Printer to the Cambridge University Press. Later, when we were scattered among the Professor of Metallurgy and other such terrors, conversation became tougher. When at last I got to bed at 12.45, my hostess's hot water bottle had filled my bed with water. Luckily I know her very well and she was still up to produce a complete new set of bedding. (The same thing once happened to me in the icy house of the Geoffrey Keyneses. I daren't wake them, and spent the rest of the night in my underclothes, bath-towel and goodness knows what.)

On Friday I lunched with Cecil Beaton at his exquisite house in Pelham Place (butler and all). The other guests were Nancy Cunard, Mrs Ian Fleming and W. Somerset Maugham, older and more lizard-like than ever. His stammer is as bad as ever, and he now clicks his fingers with annoyance when he can't get the word out, which adds to the confusion. When he came in, Cecil said: 'Willie, you look so sweet I shall kiss you'—which he did. The food was again delicious, but I am getting surfeited—comfort me with apples.

Yes, that *was* an evening! It is odd and pleasant to commend one's own provender, but really we were all guests together enjoying the hospitality of Alexander and Diana from overseas via Janek and his admirable wife, who beam all over when told what we and the others thought of the little banquet.

The Reviser who found fault with C.H. Herford's explanation of a Shakespeare phrase climbed gracefully down—or at least as gracefully as is within the power of a seventeen-stone man with a broken hip-joint. But he stuck to it that a dictum of Garrod's about Keats was devoid of meaning—almost seeming to regard it as on the same level as the Frenchman's rendering of 'Bacchus and his pards', i.e. '*B. et ses compagnons*'. He had apparently learnt English via the mining stories of Bret Harte. By the way in last week's *Spectator* the man Amis described 'St Agnes' Eve' as that 'sugary, erotic extravaganza'. It is not really much good setting up as a judge of poetry if *all* your five senses are blunted. (More or less apropos, I often remember one of the sisters in *Quality Street* in charge, mildly, of some school; she hated teaching Algebra 'where you always have to be proving that x is equal to y, and you know all the time that it isn't'. I love that kind of touch in Barrie—e.g. his telling of the first time he saw Plum bat, when he made 1, 'but in the second innings wasn't so successful.')

That may well have been Frank Harris at the Savile (of course I should have realised that you would know it!). 'Faded' *is* better than 'seedy'. I have never really had a London club. *You* wouldn't regard my present one, the Royal Empire Society, as anything but an omnium-gatherum of hearty and earnest bores, who used to quote Kipling, and like to listen to addresses about Ghana and then refresh themselves with egg salad and blancmange. But it is very cheap and has quite good arm-chairs and is v. near Charing X.

You *hadn't* told me J.B.P's remark about the Savage Club. I like it. I am drifting through Hesketh Pearson's *Dickens* and steadily sharing your opinion of it. Surely to say that Sam Weller is as abysmally *un*funny as Touchstone is a foolish trailing of the coat. How tremendously important *tone* is in all writing: isn't it that mainly which makes one hate or love the man behind the pen? E.g. Max B.—but

I believe there *are* those who don't like that courteously twinkling eye. I think I confessed to you once that I *couldn't read The Brook Kerith*, and God saw to it that I never should, because my copy was burnt in the Hagley fire. But it did go on and on, and I never got used to the absence of any typographical help. I do hope that idiotic fancy for having no capital letters will never take root; perhaps it *has* died out? Wasn't it e.e. cummings who started it?

I am glad you enjoyed Cambridge. I always find dons very friendly folk, and they nearly always talk very good sense unless you run up against some conscientious eccentric like Provost Sheppard. It seems to me one of the odder anfractuosities of the human mind to want to kiss old Maugham, but one never knows. Surely the expression on his face must have been ultra–Graham-Sutherlandish—especially as there looks to be every chance that he may well not realise his ambition of leaving the record sum ever made by a writer, with Agatha Christie in the very centre of the big money. That hot water-bottle *contretemps* is very disheartening. Twice it happened to me long after everyone was in bed. A doubled bath-towel under and another above the sheet is effective unless the leak has really soaked the mattress, but apprehensions of rheumatic fever, pneumonia and paralysis don't permit a very refreshing slumber.

Bishop Henson couldn't bear his Dean, Welldon, and once at Eton when odd old sayings were being discussed (e.g. 'right as a trivet', what *is* a trivet etc) when asked if he had ever seen pigs in clover, answered 'Well, no, not exactly—though I have seen the Dean of Durham in bed'. You would have enjoyed his company.

Sunday, 1 December 1957   *36 Soho Square*

I had scarcely packed E.B. off to the Orient on Thursday when I was bowled over by my first cold in *seven years*, but so virulent a one that it seemed to contain all the malice of those seven defeated winters. I staggered to bed that evening, and stayed there, half-blind, half-dotty, every tube awash, all Friday and most of yesterday. This caused me to miss (1) St Andrew's Day (2) my week-end in the country (3) your letter. All the more fun next week-end!

To-day I am up in a feeble sort of way, and tomorrow shall totter down to my overcrowded desk. I daresay I was generally overtired, and this enforced rest badly needed, but you won't, I fear, get much of a letter to-day.

I am madly in love with my clock, now installed in the little hall here, and doubt whether I shall ever move it: you will be able to inspect it on the 10th, before the Lit. Soc.

That *was* a superb evening in Chelsea Square—and what heavenly food! Thank goodness my cold didn't come on me a few days earlier. Today, in the fitful and to me unaccustomed way of convalescents, I have been reading alternately Harold Nicolson's *Journey to Java* (delightful), Gordon Craig's excellent memoirs which I never finished, Priestley's *Thoughts in the Wilderness*, the newly-published original four-act version of *The Importance of Being Earnest*, a detective story, the new Isak Dinesen, and Tony Powell's latest—enjoying them all by turns and then switching. But in truth I have no energy yet, for reading, writing or aught but delicious drowsing.

4 December 1957   *Grundisburgh*

Apropos of that evening at 67 C.S. it is quite possible that we shall again have another week, as A.H. and my daughter are insistent that that admirable cook *enjoys* dinner-parties, the simple fact being that she is an artist, and to have nobody in the house is like depriving a painter of his brushes. Well, I give you fair warning, *you* will always be among the guests. Old Anne Talbot was immensely pleased with her company at table and in taxi!

I have Harold N's *Journey to Java* on my list, also J.B.P. (what a lot of people he seems to irritate ('No, sir, what made your head ache was the sense I put into it!'). I bought and read for the journey a very wretched detective story by Philip Macdonald called *X v Rex*. The murderer who has done in innumerable policemen is *first* mentioned two pages from the end and is without point or substance. Surely P.M. used to be good (*The Rasp* etc). Is the new Agatha any good? Like Haydn, she has written too much. I am glad to be told by the Penguin 'blurb' that she enjoys her food (does Ngaio Marsh hate the stuff?) and plenty of it must be at her command, but she ought to stop now and think upon her latter end.

Flushed with the satisfaction of having compiled fifty Oscar footnotes this week-end, I sit down late to answer your two fine letters. Despite Agatha Christie's phenomenal success of late in the theatre, I fear she won't leave a quarter of old W.S.M.'s haul. He made a great deal of his money in America (where the rewards are greater) and has mostly lived in France, paying no income tax of any kind.

I'm happy to say that last week's avalanche has subsided into a faint catarrhal trickle. The clock continues to charm me, and, as you proudly boasted, it keeps perfect time. Did you abandon the strike because you didn't want it or because the expert said it was past repair? If the former I feel inclined to try and get it into action.

So sorry you won't be at the Lit. Soc., to which I shall come hot-foot (or perhaps coldfoot) from the University rugger match. Tomorrow I go to see the Queen Mother present the second Duff Cooper Memorial Prize to Lawrence Durrell for his book *Bitter Lemons*, which I haven't read. On Wednesday I have to go out to luncheon, cocktails and dinner. On Thursday I take the chair again at the London Library—and so it rackets on.

Philip Macdonald *was* good and *is* bad. The new Agatha C. is no more than Beta plus. I am well back in the swing of the editing now, and only wish I had more time for it.

Last Thursday I was taken to the first night of the Stratford *Tempest* at Drury Lane. Gielgud spoke beautifully, as always, and Caliban wasn't bad, but except for the flashes of poetry it's a boring play, and I found my eyes closing more than once. In the audience I saw my former wife Peggy, looking very young and beautiful. Thank God I no longer have any ties with that intolerable profession the Theatre!

The Oxford term ended yesterday, and this morning I drove over to fetch Duff home. His kit filled our large station-wagon to the roof.

I don't think he did much work during the term and only hope he'll do some in the vac.

Have you been listening to George Kennan's Reith Lectures on the wireless? I've heard the best part of three of them and have been much impressed by his modesty, grasp, and general good sense. Duff has been to some lectures of his in Oxford—nothing to do with his Greats, but clearly the most interesting ones in Oxford—and thought them excellent. Peter Fleming says his (G.K.'s) book on the Russian Revolution is first-class.

The other day, thinking of you, I took down *Earlham* from the shelf and read its opening chapters in bed, delighted to find their spell as potent as ever. It is surely a lasting piece of literature: when I've finished it again I shall write to P. Lubbock. You've no idea how I envy your being able to read exactly what you feel like *when* you feel like it (exam-papers permitting). The lack of such freedom is my chief objection to my own life, though I daresay forbidden fruit tastes all the more delicious for being forbidden when one *does* get a chance at it.

12 December 1957   *Grundisburgh*

Good news *qua* both cold and clock. I won't swear it (yes I will, because P. has just come in and is sure that) no one has ever looked at or wound up the strike as she never cares for it; but of course there it is, governed by the second weight, and if it needs a little doctoring, any good clock man can do it. Our friend in Ipswich says the mechanism is a very simple affair—compared e.g. with one of those gold, butter-smooth watches of about the size and thickness of a shilling bit. It gives me a feeling of nice fat satisfaction that the clock at last has come home.

When we were at 67 Chelsea Sq. I found a dozen Maughams on the shelf and read a lot of the plays and stories. Very efficient, very read-able, but—well there is a vacuity somewhere, moral and spiritual very likely. (But on the whole one should try not to talk like a bishop!) You must be my Goethe and put your finger on the spot. The bishops on the whole did better than the rest of their lordships in the homo-sexual debate. Odd that nobody pointed out what seems to me the real flaw in the law, i.e. that it can't be enforced (two consenting adults being normally pretty good at covering their tracks), and so practically any detection is keyhole work, undertaken with blackmail of some kind in view. That wise man, old Warre, was always very emphatic that to make a rule you can't enforce is not only futile but damaging.

The Rugger match was what we used to call 'suction pie' for the ebullient Cantabs. I am no Rugger fan, though I played the game for two terms at Cambridge, but I have always known how comparatively easy it is for a strong lot of forwards *on the day* to muck up a brilliant lot of backs. If they played five matches C. would win four. But yesterday was the fifth. I suppose you bellowed with Oxonian glee at the close, and hurled your cushion into the arena? The first O. and C. match I ever saw, I sat next to R.S. Kindersley, a staid old colleague of rigid respectability. But he had been a great player (in Vassall's team), and as a fast close match proceeded, the blood rose to his head, and, ignoring the sensibilities of the many parsons and occasional ladies within earshot, he endeavoured to nip in the bud any bit of brilliance by a Cambridge player with the simple stentorian advice: 'Poot him on his arrrrse!' There are too many women in the crowd nowadays. Tuppy used to complain of this in a penetrating voice, pointing out that most of them were in hopes of seeing a player deprived of his shorts. But these are deep Freudian waters.

What did you think of L. Durrell? His Cyprus book was good, if a bit over-written. The speeches sound to have been rather good. The critics were very enthusiastic about Gielgud's Prospero. I am immensely amused at your finding the play boring, because, to read at any rate, all the plays have always seemed to me bad *as plays*— though over and over again the poetry simply knocks one endways. But the action, the plot, the whys and wherefores are so often supremely absurd. One dislikes agreeing with D.H. Lawrence, but can't always help it. Surely

> When I read Shakespeare I am struck with wonder
> That such trivial people should muse and thunder
> In such lovely language

hits the bullseye?

Really the serious questions we have to set about the behaviour of Orsino and Olivia, and Bassanio and Portia, when it is hardly ever quite rational. But when they speak, you just don't mind *what* they do. I have just finished a lot of G.C.E. *Richard II* papers. Nearly all very bad. A leading scholar from Clayesmore brightened my morning by calling Bushy Blushy, and Bagot Bandot, but on the whole I think they have sent me the sweepings of the asylums. One boy, describing Richard's death, says that 'when he refused to eat his dinner, there was a bit of a mix-up, and when it was over he was found to be dead'.

Has Duff *got* to work at Oxford? Because if he is reading masses that he likes on his own, and seeing a good lot of intelligent people, and talking till 3 a.m., that is of course what the University was for, in old days, for any number of young men. But in these days—any way my views on education are subversive and immoral—almost George Mooreish. One thing I know, and that is that there is much to be said for being seventy-five if the education and 'culture' of the future is what Hogben and Co want it to be.

I don't listen to the wireless as our reception is so bad, but I have read every word of Kennan's lectures, and devilish good I thought them. But do you fundamentally see *any* hope? The thing that sticks in *my* gorge—and incidentally in that of Arthur Bryant—is 'Why are the Russians set on building a thousand submarines—more than twice as many as the rest of the world put together? And if and when the hydrogen bomb is abolished what are they going to do with these submarines?' Who *is* Kennan? Because his English for lucidity, point, and balance is in the same class as Hensley Henson's or Hal Fisher's or Inge's. Entirely different and every bit as good (and why the hell, Dr L. and Co., may we not enjoy *both*?) is of course *Earlham*. I am delighted with what you say of it, and *mind you write to P.L.* He would love it, I know. Will you, by the way, do something which I do about six times a year, and that is read *aloud* the last scene in *Earlham*. Your voice will get husky (as mine does—and also did M.R. James's and Hugh Walpole's) and I am sure you will arrive at exactly the conviction that I do, i.e. that with all its deep emotion there is not the smallest touch of the precious—sentiment if you like but no sentimentality. But what a lot of people don't know how to read! Tuppy, oddly, was one, but he always did everything much too fast. You can't read P.L. as if he was Phillips Oppenheim, and after all let us face the fact that most readers resemble Jock Dent's Tommy in an *Ego* who, after a glass of vintage claret, called for a 'pint of wallop'.

I have just finished my *Twelfth Night* papers. I was pleased to find the following answers to the Q. 'What is a pedant?'—a clown, a criminal, a chap who kept order in church, a salesman, an ornament for the ear, a yellow pole with ribbons, a tramp, a kind of dog. Some of them are not so very wide of the mark. And I have one gem for you. 'Viola couldn't have married Olivia as she was a girl, and not, as Olivia thought, a boy eunuch.' What a pity E. Blunden is in China.

We are coming to Eton on Saturday week for ten days or so and should immensely like to lunch with you again. I believe both Sundays are bespoken, but otherwise the day that suits you suits us. I want to get again the 'aura' of that book-lined study of yours.

15 December 1957   *Bromsden Farm*

First, and most important, Comfort suggests Saturday, 28 December (Holy Innocents' Day!) for your promised luncheon visit. Does that suit? Send me your Eton address and I'll write there next Sunday, reminding you of the exact way here.

Now to your letter. I imagine that Willie Maugham's money will go to his daughter Liza, his only child, now married to John Hope and living a mile or two from here. But the old villain is quite capable of leaving a wayward and capricious will, and since he seems quite likely to outlive us all, we may never know. I have known him, rather more off than on, for twenty-six years, but I dare say 'acquaintance' is nearer the mark than 'friend'.

The rugger match was without exception the most *exciting* I have ever seen in more than twenty years, and what more can one ask? The crowd is usually generous to what seems to be the under-dog, and when Oxford got the ball five times from the first five scrums, and clearly had Cambridge confused and disorganised, few believed it could last. Then Oxford scored their well-deserved try (a score of 9–0 at half-time wouldn't have seemed unfair), and hung on to this frail lead for the rest of the game. Their tackling was *superb*—never seen better—and tension rose when Cambridge several times got within feet of the Oxford line. The last ten minutes were excruciating, and then I did indeed lend my voice to the mighty roar that echoed round Twickenham. I do wish you could have seen the game: you'd have been thrilled.

The Duff Cooper prize-giving went off beautifully on Monday. The room was looking lovelier than last year, with a silver Christmas tree above the parade of champagne-bottles, and the number of people (eighty to ninety) made less of a crush than last year's hundred and twenty. The Q.M. looked quite lovely in silver: her beauty and immediately irresistible charm are amazing. I explained the simple drill to her, and she was wide-eyed as a little girl who had never done such a thing before. After Durrell had been presented to her and they had taken up their positions, she whispered to him: 'I'm terrified. Are you?' which did much to calm his palpable fright. David Cecil made a tip-top speech, brief, poetical and entirely to the point. Then the Q.M. gave Durrell the prize and said some charming words about Duff, at which Diana's lovely eyes filled with tears. Then Durrell briefly said thank-you, and the ceremony was over. Champagne was briskly circulated, and the Q.M. talked to many, I think rather enjoying the informality.

Kennan has mostly been what the Americans call a 'career diplomat' and was U.S. Ambassador in Moscow until the Russians turned him out. One is so accustomed to U.S. ambassadors being millionaire business men that Kennan's choice of words and serene commonsense make him a peak in such company. This evening I forbade myself to listen to his final lecture, so as to write to you instead. Although you miss a few good things by not being able to listen to the radio, you also miss temptation to waste hours on twaddle. I seldom switch on except for music, which I find an agreeable background to footnote-writing. And if it takes one's fancy one can stop work and listen for a bit.

I have obeyed your orders and read aloud to myself the closing scene of *Earlham*: it is indeed most moving, without one false note. I shall write to P.L. when I have re-read all.

On Wednesday, after a cocktail party in South Kensington, I tooled out to Putney to dine with the Arthur Ransomes. On Thursday I presided at the London Library committee and delivered an interminable report on what had been done since the last meeting. Most of the members of the committee who were still sentient expressed their approval, particularly R. Mortimer. Altogether I spoke for more than an hour, and as the meeting broke up Rose Macaulay burst in, looking like a wall-painting of a mummy, and said: 'Am I late? Do tell me all that has been said.' I was too exhausted to comply, and I fear she thought me churlish. The old pet is really quite useless on committees now, bless her.

19 December 1957   *Grundisburgh*

We will do the *28th* with great pleasure. I remember we turn left at the top of that long incline after leaving the Long Mile, but am rather vague after that—and snow will be falling, and darkness will cover the earth, and gross darkness the people. And I have always been one of those whose instinct for missing the way is unfailing. Pamela is better when by herself, but I invariably muddle her. So in the more derogatory sense the Holy Innocents' Day is the right one for us to be groping our way to you in darkest Oxfordshire.

Your vignette of the Rugger Match makes my mouth water. But you know I still have a strong childish strain in me, and will confess to you that though, now, I rather wish I had gone to Oxford, I still *hate* seeing Cambridge beaten, especially when they are expected to win. I should like to have seen you yelling *à la* Kindersley. Twickenham is the only place where the clock manifestly takes sides. If one's side is clinging to a tiny and precarious lead, the minute-hand, to my certain knowledge, flatly refuses to move. I bet you noticed that last week.

That Duff C. ceremony as described by you must have been lovely. I always thought the Q.M. quite charming on the three occasions on which I met her. Once when she visited Eton the senior beaks were presented to the King and Queen. H.K. Marsden was next to me. He had taught Maths to the K. at Osborne (or Dartmouth?). The Queen graciously told him that the King remembered him and mentioned it to her. All she got was the menacing reply: 'Then he must have been talking during the service' (which they had attended) and of course the old dervish forgot to add 'Ma'am'.

Jan Crace's[1] target at the moment is *Macbeth* in modern dress. All that modern dress stunt always seems the wildest rubbish to me. When all the behaviour and speech in the play are archaic and of their time, doesn't modern dress merely distract one's attention or make for laughter? Does Duncan wear a Homburg hat and spats as Edward VII did on a visit? And what *is* the right twentieth-century fashionable dress for a witch? And do you or do you not find it intolerably incongruous that a contemporary field-marshal should soliloquise about sleep knitting up the ravelled sleave of care? Enough.

Your power of work is really terrifying. An *hour's* speech at the L. Library! And how many hours went to its making? My processes are—to compare small with great—like those Housman said were his when he had to compose an address or inscription (in English: Latin he claimed was quite easy)—one day spent staring at a blank page and longing for death; a second one jotting down phrases and crossing them out, feeling rather sick—and so on. But in his case no one would guess at the hideous history behind the majestic pageant of his prose.

Why is there no *Earlham* in modern prose anthologies? Perhaps there is. I don't really know any. I *knew* you would react as you did to the last pages. Bless you!

22 December 1957   *Bromsden Farm*

Delighted you can both come on Saturday. We shall expect you, in your oldest clothes, about 12.45. I enclose a brief résumé of the route.

Not only did the Twickenham clock dally at the end of that match, but the referee dallied still longer.

Shakespeare in modern dress is rubbish. Its advocates pretend that the process enables the audience to appreciate the words without being distracted by fancy dress, but in fact the effect is exactly contrary. When I had my viva at Balliol in 1926 I was questioned about the

[1] Eton master.

modern-dress *Hamlet*, which was then a novelty and clearly tickled the dons. My answers were so vague that I wonder they ever let me into the beastly college at all.

When I said 'an hour's speech' at the London Library I didn't mean a set oration. In fact I just sat at the head of the table and talked for an hour from a half-sheet of notes, which hadn't taken long to jot down. So, you see, I unconsciously dramatised and heightened a very ordinary task into something that sounded admirable. (It's true that one of the committee wrote to me next day: 'Thank God we've got a chairman at last,' but truly I hadn't much to surpass.)

I was much saddened by the death of Michael Sadleir. He was always very sweet and generous to me (as to most people) and I shall miss him. In fact I fancy he was ready to go. After a recent operation on his tongue (which must have been for cancer, though they never said so) he began to fail. They then said he was suffering from anaemia and gave him blood-transfusions, which probably killed him, for he died of a thrombosis. I went to his memorial service at Windsor on Friday: there would have been many more people if they had held it in London. John Carter drove me down there.

Last week wasn't too bad: one huge hideous cocktail party at the Hultons', one delicious dinner-party at the Jepsons', a mass of Christmas shopping and other nonsense. Tomorrow I return to London till Tuesday evening, and then five days peacefully here, with your much-looked-forward-to visit in the midst. Both the boys will be here, unless they're out shooting.

Today I read solidly from breakfast to supper—the papers, a grim French novel (which I may publish in translation) and a long manuscript, so I don't feel very fresh or bright. Glad to see Harold Nicolson picked the George Moore letters as one of the best books of the year, and only hope his words will sell a few more copies. So far only a thousand have been, as they say, 'shifted'.

No word from E.B. I fear the lecture tour in India on his way back to Hong Kong must have exhausted him. I go on sending him an airmail letter each Sunday. What on earth do you do about Christmas presents for all your descendants? Or does Pamela cope with them all? I have *nine* godchildren, ranging in age from twenty-seven to six months, and their needs baffle me afresh each year. What a nuisance the whole thing is—except that it brings you within driving distance. Now I must go to bed. A happy Christmas to you all. See you on Saturday.

This pleasurable habit has proved too much for me, so I propose to steal a march on you with this brief note. Your visit, I scarcely need say, was as usual pure pleasure, and I only hope Pamela's cold wasn't accentuated by it. Your hat has been recovered at the Brunners', and tomorrow Comfort will retrieve it and post it to Grundisburgh. Going hatless in Cambridge you will be mistaken for an undergraduate or an emancipated don, but I hope you won't catch cold thereby.

After tea yesterday I took C and A to the local cinema, where we saw a good but well-nigh interminable programme (more than three and a half hours), which included a spirited rendering of *Robbery Under Arms*—a book which I have never read and now feel absolved from attempting.

Looking through Emerson for an elusive quotation, I came on this excellent analysis of literary reputation. I expect you know it, but never mind:

> There is no luck in literary reputation. They who make up the final verdict upon every book are not the partial and noisy readers of the hour when it appears; but a court as of angels, a public not to be bribed, not to be entreated, and not to be overawed, decides upon every man's title to fame. Only those books come down which deserve to last. All the gilt edges and vellum and morocco, all the presentation-copies to all the libraries, will not preserve a book in circulation beyond its intrinsic date. It must go with all Walpole's Royal and Noble Authors to its fate. Blackmore, Kotzebue, or Pollok, may endure for a night, but Moses and Homer stand forever.

Isn't that splendid? Old Edward Garnett used to put the same sentiments into shorter space—'Everything finds its own level in the end'—

but I am charmed by Emerson's rhythms. I shall read more of him.

Peter looked in to-day and bewailed missing you. He is writing—or thinking of writing—a Strix piece about nicknames, and would like to rifle your store: perhaps he can wait till January 14.

This afternoon I did a modicum of gardening, but the wind was keen and I soon returned gratefully to the fireside. These five days, for all their solid meals, seem to have passed in a twinkling, and I have not done all I hoped to do—work, I mean. I shall think of you sorting out the Revisers, and hope that by Sunday I shall have some amusing items to recount. Meanwhile a happy new year, with many meetings.

31 December 1957   *Royal Hotel*
                                                          Cambridge

How *very* good of you to be so prompt about my wretched hat, and I hope Sir Felix took the episode kindly. I have in fact a *cap*, luckily, which is more convenient in a small car, so I am not, when I emerge, the sport of every wind. But my career as Mr Pooter continues. This morning I was rather sharply diverted from the ladies' lavatory which I was trying to enter, having not seen the notice, and this is a hotel we have not been at before. Food and bed quite good, but the tables in the dining-room are too close together, and apparently anyone sits anywhere, so while I was waiting for a colleague, the place at my table was filled by a stranger, whose nurse some thirty years ago had omitted to impress on him that porridge should be eaten silently.

Yesterday I dined in Trinity and my neighbour was a Russian mathematician with very little English. It is apparently a Russian habit to swallow or soften the final consonants of a word—an awkward habit I thought, when he asked me to pass the toa, and was slow to grasp that he must mean toast, and not toad or toes. N.B. If and when you dine at Trinity, the Madeira should not be missed.

Pamela thoroughly enjoyed that visit. Neither of us could believe that it was 4 before we left. *Robbery Under Arms* was my favourite book over sixty years ago, and I am furious at having forgotten the name of Captain Starlight's horse. As good a horse as I ever came across, though

I was fond of what H.G. Wells called 'that soundly Anglican' horse Black Beauty and wept inconsolably when he/she died.

That is fine Emerson—an oddly under-rated writer *me judice*. Perhaps there is too much bread to the butter. Do you remember his description of genius, 'that stellar and undiminishable something'. As near as anyone ever went I think? Old Samuel of course had the same belief in the judgment of the public (when given time) as opposed to that of the intelligentsia, and 'Few things are more risible than literary fashions' hits a nail neatly and finally. Among my colleagues are nice sensible Oxonians who do not draw a very attractive picture of Bowra, A.J.P. Taylor, Rowse, Trevor-Roper or, in fact, any of the louder Oxford voices. I liked Bowra at that Johnson luncheon, but they say he now indulges relentlessly in monologue, which of course does not go down well in a community where all want to do the same. Rum places, universities. Gow told me that Housman attended *one* lecture of Jowett's, but when the great man mis-pronounced one Greek word he attended no more. Nevertheless B.J. was a better man than A.E.H. The conversation of both was largely composed of usually unnecessary and uncalled-for snubs, but J. was much less conceited and thin-skinned and morose.

THE TRUE SON OF VIRTUE[1]

by George Lyttelton

On the walls of the dining-room at Hagley before the calamitous fire of 1925 was displayed the whole gallery of ancestral Lyttelton portraits. There was the great legal light of Edward IV's reign, swollen to Falstaffian proportions by his preposterous robes, with the bad lord on one side of him and the mad lord on the other, and directly opposite the portrait of him who was pointed out to us children as the good lord. It was only a head and shoulders, so there was no opportunity of judging, later on, how far Horace Walpole was right in saying he had the figure of a spectre, or, according to another writer, that every limb was a blemish, every movement a disgrace. Doctor Johnson's adjective for his face, 'meagre', was perfectly just. The large curved nose gave it a distinct likeness to the Duke of Wellington's, without the strength, or the 'air of cold command', but the head was well enough poised, and by no means, as Chesterfield described it, 'hanging upon one or other of his shoulders as if it had received the first stroke upon a block'. A mild, remote, colourless figure he seemed to us, markedly inferior in interest to his handsome scamp of a son. Why, and how, we asked, was he the good lord? Was he always in church? Was he a missionary?—these being our simple criteria of goodness. No, came the answer, no, he was not a missionary, he was a statesman and a poet—and a very good man. Later we discovered that he was not a very good statesman nor a very good poet; and as to being a good man, well there seemed to be several who didn't think so, who in fact spoke and wrote of him, not with the passing irritation of the Athenian voter towards Aristides, but in words edged with genuine dislike and contempt.

Horace Walpole clearly thought him a solemn ass and derided both

[1] Delivered at a luncheon of the Johnson Club at Brown's Hotel, Dover Street, on 15 April 1953.

his wits and character, regarding them as overrated by a coterie, Mrs Montagu and her maenads, as he called them. Horace's anti-Lyttelton feelings seem at first sight proved by a letter in which he wrote that the sight of the river at Oxford gave him particular pleasure from remembering that two Lytteltons had been drowned in it; but as the letter was written to Richard Lyttelton, it is, so to speak, a dig in the ribs and not a stab in the back. Still, a good deal of the fun he pokes at Lyttelton has an acid flavour—and something more. A man need not be called double-faced for expressing to an author a different opinion about his book from what he gives to a third person when the author isn't there, but it is hard to acquit Walpole of this charge, unless he had his tongue in his cheek when he told Lyttelton that his *History of Henry II* was a book not to skim but to learn by heart, and that his style would fix and preserve the language. To another he writes 'How dull one may be if one will but take enough pains for six or seven and twenty years'. (Of Lyttelton's conversation 'I have heard him discuss points of midwifery with the solemnity of a Solon' and 'Sir George'—as he was then—'came here to expectorate with me as he called it'.)

Another to whom Lyttelton appeared far from good was Smollett, but he may be discounted, partly because his temper was always on the boil, partly because Lyttelton, to whom he had sent his tragedy, responded kindly but tardily by advising him to devote himself to comedy—and which of the *genus irritabile* would forgive that? Lyttelton did in fact put in a good word with Garrick for Smollett's play, but Smollett may not have known that, as, in the words of his biographer, 'the play never struggled on to the stage'. Even so his savage burlesque of Lyttelton's 'Monody on the Death of his Wife' seems well below the belt even for a literary feud. But later Smollett did make some amends, and perhaps it was only in his rages that he was what Handel called him, 'ein tam fool'.

But why is Doctor Johnson's Life of Lyttelton so grumpy and sour? All kinds of explanation have been given, but most of them do not hold much water. Lyttelton was a Whig, but so was Burke, and who has praised Burke more nobly than Johnson? Lyttelton, when young, wrote pastorals, but escaped, as did Pope, with a mild growl or two. Lyttelton was religious, and wrote a treatise on Saint Paul which

Johnson actually praises, saying 'infidelity has never been able to fabricate a specious reply to it'. I doubt myself whether infidelity has ever tried very hard to do so, for its main theme is that Saint Paul was entirely sincere, which I never heard of anyone doubting. Then again, though Lyttelton had learning, it was too bookish for Johnson's approval. 'That man sat down to write a book to tell the world what the world all his life had been telling him.' (But that cap fits many a literary head a good deal more closely than 'poor Lyttelton's'.)

For the grounds of Johnson's personal antipathy to Lyttelton we have mainly to explore the realm of fancy, or, what is often much the same thing, the recollections of Mrs Thrale. She says that Johnson told her how he and Lyttelton had been rivals for the affections of Miss Hill Boothby, and that she could see from his Life how he still resented her preference of 'that fellow Lyttelton'. Her tale bristles with improbabilities, as Croker showed, and, though the old Johnson never minded laughing at the young Johnson, does not somehow ring true. The same lively lady tells us of Johnson's visit to Hagley, when he stayed with William Lyttelton after the good lord's death. 'He was enraged', she writes, 'at artificial ruins and temporary cascades, so that I wonder at his leaving his opinion of them dubious. Besides he hated the Lytteltons, and would rejoice at an opportunity of insulting them.' Johnson himself wrote of his visit: 'We made haste away from a place where all were offended'; but Mrs Thrale softens the grimness of this by suggesting that the causes of offence were no more than that Mrs Lyttelton made Johnson play whist against his will, and Mr Lyttelton may have further annoyed Johnson by declining to supply him with materials for the Life of his brother. This Life has that chilliness of tone which suggests that a writer is treating of a subject which does not much interest him, or a man whom he does not rate very high, but does not strike me as essentially unjust. No one could quarrel with Johnson for saying that Lyttelton's letters 'have something of that indistinct and headstrong ardour for liberty characteristic of the young', or that his poems 'have nothing to be despised and little to be admired—that the shorter ones are sometimes sprightly and sometimes insipid'. It is all perfectly true. There is one good example of that grave irony which gives so much enjoyment to readers of the *Lives of the Poets*, and, I suspect, to the writer. Lyttelton took immense care and a portentous time over his *History of Henry II*, and, says Johnson, 'one Andrew Reid had persuaded him, as he had persuaded himself, that he was master of the secret of punctuation, but before the third edition', Johnson goes on, 'Reid was either dead or discarded, and the superintendence of typography and punctuation was committed to a man, originally a comb-maker, but then known by the style of Doctor. Something uncommon was probably expected, and something uncommon was at last done; for to the Doctor's edition is appended what the world has hardly seen before, a list of errors in nineteen pages.' That is fair enough. But the same cannot be said of the statement, perilously like a sneer, that after his wife's death 'Lyttelton solaced himself by writing a long poem to her memory'. Probably grief that did not prevent the griever from marrying again two years after did not arouse much sympathy in the widower of Tetty.

And then, as always in any discussion about these two, arises the question 'Which was Chesterfield's "respectable Hottentot"?' The present company no doubt is solid in support of Doctor Birkbeck Hill's claim to have wiped this blot off the social and convivial reputation of Doctor Johnson. (The respectable Hottentot, you remember, threw his soup and wine anywhere but into his mouth, and mangled his meat.) You all probably know the pros and cons, with which I will not weary you. But there is one point which, as far as I know, has had no explanation, though some seems called for. In one of the four letters of Chesterfield's used by Doctor Hill to establish his proof, the man described—in almost identical terms with those in the other three letters—is called by Chesterfield 'a near relation of mine'. Well, if he was that he was certainly not Lyttelton—still less, of course, Johnson. But if the expression was what would now be called 'camouflage', what was the point of it in a letter to his son? I can throw no light on the small mystery. Still, though Boswell denies that Lyttelton was violent in argument (as the Hottentot was) just as strongly as he does that Johnson, though his table manners had their weak spots, was an untidy feeder, a collateral descendent must admit that the Hottentot was probably meant for Lyttelton, and must extract what comfort he can from the epithet which preceded it.

Of Lyttelton's politics Johnson says little, and I shall say less. Can the dry bones live of domestic politics two hundred years ago?

Certainly not to me. The dust lies thick upon Lyttelton's speeches, though some of them were praised at the time, even by Walpole. It still remains a nearly insoluble mystery how an absent-minded scholar, particularly weak at arithmetic, and apparently never quite clear about the difference between prices and duties, between discounts and premiums, became Chancellor of the Exchequer. Must he not have felt, when about to introduce his budget, as George du Maurier did in his nightmare on finding himself billed to sing 'The Lost Chord' at the Albert Hall? There is no sign that he did, though something may lie behind Johnson's dry remark that 'the office required some qualifications which he soon perceived himself to want'.

Lyttelton's literary remains consist of both prose and poetry. The two chief prose works, the *Persian Letters* and the *Dialogues of the Dead*, are both derivative, Lucian, Montesquieu, Fénelon and Fontenelle having already blazed the trail. The *Persian Letters* are still readable enough, though they suffer from comparison with the grace and humour of Goldsmith's very similar *Citizen of the World*, written some years later. In places they are surprisingly indelicate, almost Decameronian, to come from the pen of one whom Thomson called the true son of virtue; Lyttelton is said to have expressed regret for this in later life, but there is no extant evidence of his doing so, and it may be an invention of his biographer, who admits, with a frankness that somehow does not disarm, that his main object in writing the life was to please the Lyttelton family. The *Dialogues of the Dead* had many admirers, among whom were *not* Johnson and Walpole, who decry them for exactly opposite reasons. Johnson calls them nugatory and says that the names of his persons too often enable the reader to anticipate their conversation, while Walpole, who amiably changes the title to *Dead Dialogues*, says that the persons all talk out of character. Both are really right. The sentiments of, for instance, the goddess Circe are exactly what one would expect, but certainly not the polished and balanced phrases in which she clothes them. I am afraid Walpole's amended title is pretty near the truth.

What of Lyttelton's poetry? One is tempted to summarise it, as one might so much eighteenth-century poetry, in the form of a prescription or a recipe. Take a taste for romantic scenery, a decorous affection for a young lady, a profound admiration of Milton and Pope, a pinch—not more—of irony and demure playfulness, several slabs of moral sentiment, and serve cold with a rich sauce of poetic diction. There is, I think, the savour of genuine feeling in some lines of his Monody on his dead wife, but the Miltonic echoes are too blatant. 'Where were ye Muses . . . ?' 'Nor where Clitumnus rolls his gentle stream', 'the light fantastic toys', and so on. The worst of these is in the poem 'Blenheim' when he takes Eve's unsurpassable tribute to Adam—'With thee conversing I forget all time', and applies it, almost unaltered, to the Duke of Marlborough talking to his Duchess. How right Johnson was about pastoral trappings when employed by almost anyone except Milton: and how hard it is today to recapture the thrill which presumably our ancestors felt when Philomel was urged to resume her song or pour her plaint—or to sympathise when a man claims, as Lyttelton did, that his grief for his lost wife *must* be far greater than Petrarch's for Laura, because Petrarch was not married to Laura, or to realise the charm of that wife when she is summed up as 'though meek, magnanimous, though witty, wise,' which all may read today who leave Hagley Church by the west door.

It is when Lyttelton is considered not as a statesman or poet, but as a patron of literature, or more simply and broadly, as a friend, that his special virtues really do begin to emerge. As a patron he would of course not be likely to get a very warm word from Johnson, but his relations with authors, and indeed with men in general, do reveal a character of outstanding generosity and good nature. A man who could remain unruffled under the savage contempt of Pitt and restore him to amiability before the end of the sitting, who bore no long resentment against a cousin who referred to him in Parliament as 'hominem detestabilem atque imbecillum', who could keep without a break the friendship of Pope and Garrick and Bolingbroke and Shenstone, and ask and return a favour from Swift, who never ceased to defend and help Archibald Bower, regarded by everyone else as a detected impostor, whose letters contain hardly a hint of a grudge cherished or a slight resented—such a man must surely be credited with far more than ordinary magnanimity.

His kindnesses to authors were very numerous. The best known of his beneficiaries were Thomson and Fielding, both of whom wrote of him with especial warmth. The placid and indolent Thomson was, through Lyttelton's good offices, appointed surveyor-general of the Leeward Islands, a post which brought him, after paying a deputy to do the work, about £300 a year. He was often at Hagley, where a little shelter called Thomson's seat still marks his favourite spot in the park, 'the British Tempe' as he called it, whence he surveyed, not the Leeward Islands, but what he called 'the bursting prospect', or, more prosaically, a view over some ten midland counties.

Lastly there is Lyttelton's old schoolfellow Fielding, who, in dedicating *Tom Jones* to him, declares that it owed its inception to Lyttelton's suggestion, and its completion to his assistance. The characters of Lyttelton and another friend and patron, Ralph Allen, are blended to produce the flawless but unexciting Squire Allworthy, and in a breathtaking sentence in the dedication Fielding says that to associate his book with Lyttelton is a guarantee that there will be in it 'nothing inconsistent with the stricter rules of decency, nor which can offend the chastest eye'. I wonder how the good lord swallowed that. In fact one is left wondering about him. To have gained—leaving out smaller fry—the friendship of Pope and the enmity of Johnson surely argues a character of some force, substance and quality, but I confess, it eludes me. I have read the eight hundred prosy pages of his idle, unrevealing, inaccurate and immensely dull biography; I have read pretty well all that he wrote—except the *History of Henry II*—and much of what others said and wrote of him. But it is no good. His public and poetic life and words are there for all to note; so are the gaunt visage, the ill-compacted frame, the unlovely voice, the jerky movement. But what manner of man was behind this façade, I have still no clear idea. Horace Walpole was right. There *is* something spectral, something puppet-like about him. And yet this spectre has achieved one solid, splendid and indeed all but unique distinction. He and Fulke Greville are the only Chancellors of the Exchequer who are represented in *The Oxford Book of English Verse*; and surely the shared distinction is likely to remain for ever unique. It is of course possible that the song which, a few years ago, Doctor Dalton told us he had in his heart may yet emerge in words. But even if it does, I feel fairly confident that the anthology (if any) into which it finds its way will be more akin to *The Stuffed Owl* than to one which skims the cream of English poetry of the last six hundred and fifty years.

INDEX

Bradley, A.C., 93
Brain, Russell, 170n
Brecht, Bertolt, 3
Bridges, Robert, 193
Broadbent, H., 45, 48
Brogan, Denis, 85
Brontë, Charlotte, 62, 192
Brontë, Emily, 189
Brook, Sir Norman, 64
Brown, Ivor, 59, 65, 83, 94
Browning, Robert, 61, 105, 136, 166, 179
Brunner, Felix and Elizabeth, 208, 209
Bryant, Arthur, 202
Bullock, Alan, 88
Burke, Edmund, 212
Butler, Samuel, 7
Butterwick, Cyril, 37, 132
Byrne, L.S.R. (Fuggy), 94
Byron, 7, 50, 52, 61, 62, 65, 67, 68, 150, 179, 180

Caccia, Harold, 68, 70, 129, 167
Calvert, Phyllis, 103
Cameron, Julia Margaret, 179
Campbell, Mrs Patrick, 43
Campbell, Thomas, 23
Cansdale, George, 107
Cardus, Neville, 43, 126, 170, 185, 187
Carlyle, Thomas, 27, 28, 49, 86, 118, 125, 140, 159, 186
Carr, A.W., 94
Carroll, Lewis, 179
Carter, John, 23, 27, 34, 37, 39, 42, 45, 51, 53, 207
Causley, Charles, 89, 90, 91, 92, 94, 96
Cavendish, Lady Moyra, 44, 45
Cavendish, Lord Richard, 40, 44, 45
Cecil, Lord David, 62, 104, 111, 134, 136, 144, 152, 204
Cecil, Lord Robert, 40
Chapman, Guy, 2, 3, 6
Charles, see Cobham
Charteris, Martin, 14
Chatham, Lord, 186
Chesterfield, Lord, 211, 214
Chesterton, G.K., 79, 80, 193
Chesterton, Mrs G.K., 43
Chitty, C.J., 48
Christie, Agatha, 12, 197, 198, 199
Churchill, E.L. (Jelly), 16
Churchill, Randolph, 17
Churchill, Winston, 1, 17, 18, 22, 24, 35, 37, 43, 70, 118, 136, 160, 161

Clough, A.H., 172
Cobbett, William, 125
Cobham, Viscount (Charles), 36, 38, 54, 112, 118, 122, 128
Coburn, Alvin Langdon, 177, 179
Cockerell, Sydney, 42, 46
Coleridge, F.J.R. (Fred), 47, 56, 191
Coleridge, S.T., 36, 63, 74, 126, 136
Collins, William, 59, 61
Colman, George, 66, 67, 69
Colvin, Sidney, 99
Connell, John, 51
Connolly, Cyril, 10, 18, 85
Conrad, Joseph, 1, 3
Cooper, Diana, 26, 95, 124, 131, 134, 142, 154, 162, 204
Cooper, Duff, 16, 17, 18, 22, 46, 48, 49, 52, 63, 64, 77, 91, 93, 95, 134, 135, 136, 165, 182, 199, 204, 205
Corbett, Jim, 42, 52
Cornish, Mrs Warre, 37
Corvo, Baron, 94
Cory, William, 11, 12, 19, 20, 23
Cowdrey, Colin, 113, 120
Crabbe, George, 65, 66
Crace, Jan, 206
Craig, Gordon, 77, 81, 84, 88, 90, 92, 165, 170, 198
Craigie, Mrs, 102
Creighton, Bishop, 135
Croker, J.W., 213
Cronin, Vincent, 50
Crum, Walter, 181
Crutchley, Brooke, 195
Cummings, E.E., 197
Cunard, Lady, 4, 54, 67, 159
Cunard, Nancy, 170, 195
Cuthbert, see Headlam

Dalton, Dr, 217
Daman, Hoppy, 82
Darling, Mr Justice, 125
Darwin, Bernard, 193
David, R.W., 33
Davies, Nico Llewelyn, 21
Davin, Dan, 130
Day Lewis, Cecil, 85, 88, 130, 147
De Beer, Esmond, 168
De Kock, Paul, 180
De la Mare, Walter, 170
Dell, Ethel M., 109
Dent, Jock, 77, 203
Depew, Chauncey, 72

Devlin, Patrick, 189
Devonshire, Dowager Duchess of (Mowcher), 136
Devonshire, Duke of, 1, 25
Dickens, 2, 10, 36, 39, 41, 44, 132, 193, 194
Dilke, Sir Charles, 25
Dinesen, Isak, see Blixen
Dobson, Austin, 6, 8
Donne, John, 78, 113, 137, 140
Douglas, Lord Alfred, 8, 10, 11, 86, 92, 94, 139, 157
Drew, Mary, 25, 132, 163
Drinkwater, John, 131, 134
Druon, Maurice, 162
Dulles, J.W., 68, 78, 156
Dumas, 54
Du Maurier, George, 215
Dunsany, Lord, 16, 61, 70, 169, 174, 180, 182, 186, 188
Durrell, Lawrence, 91, 199, 201, 204
Duveen, Lord, 111, 112

Earlham, 79, 91, 94, 200, 202, 204, 206
Eccleshare, Colin, 33
Edel, Leon, 177
Eden, Anthony, 16, 20, 22, 37, 41, 42, 45
Edward VII, King, 206
Edward VIII, King, 163
Eisenhower, President, 68, 70, 173
Eliot, George, 87
Eliot, T.S., 7, 111, 135
Elliott, Claud, 19
Elliston, R.W., 31
Elton, Oliver, 178
Emerson, R.W., 21, 26, 27, 208, 210
Ervine, St John, 38, 40, 43, 78
Everard, John, 179
Evy, see Jones, Lady Evelyn

Fenton, Colin, 17
Fergusson, Bernard, 57, 61, 62, 65, 169, 170
Feuillère, Edwige, 71
Fielding, Henry, 216, 217
Finnegans Wake, 112, 115, 118
Fisher, Charles, 184
Fisher, H.A.L., 202
Fison, Sir C., 175
FitzGerald, Edward, 126, 189
Fleming, Ian, 58, 59, 61, 78, 80, 81, 84, 89, 92, 94, 116, 129
Fleming, Mrs Ian, 195
Fleming, Peter, 30, 41, 46, 48, 50, 58, 59, 64, 68, 85, 86, 88, 89, 92, 94, 100,

104, 116, 119, 121, 124, 128, 139, 142, 144, 145, 157, 161, 165, 169, 170, 182, 186, 189, 200, 209
Fleming, Mrs Valentine, 186, 189
Flower, Newman, 176
Forster, E.M., 71, 72
Fraser, Lionel, 195
Fred, see Coleridge, F.J.R.
Freyberg, Lord, 128
Frost, Robert, 89, 110, 112
Fulford, Roger, 5, 6, 7, 8, 10, 13, 15, 16, 24, 26, 51, 61, 63, 83, 88, 89, 109, 115, 157, 161, 180
Fulford, Sibell, 51, 53

Galsworthy, John, 21, 109, 151, 179
Gardner, Helen, 13
Garnett, Edward, 208
Garrick, David, 212, 216
Garrod, H.W., 196
Gautier, Théophile, 8
Genet, Jean, 107
George III, King, 52
George V, King, 9
George VI, King, 205
Gibbon, Edward, 94, 95, 97, 98, 99, 100, 103, 108, 126
Gide, André, 116
Gielgud, John, 199, 201
Gladstone, Mrs, 49, 163
Gladstone, W.E., 25, 40, 42, 44, 54, 186, 193, 194, 195
Godwin, E.W., 165
Goethe, 49, 200
Goldsmith, Oliver, 61, 215
Gollancz, Ruth and Victor, 14
Goodall, Miss, 137, 141, 144
Goodford, Miss, 141
Gore, Bishop, 136
Gore, Muriel, 134
Gosse, Edmund, 41
Gow, A.S.F., 9, 69, 94, 105, 109, 210
Graves, Robert, 111
Grenfell, Joyce and Reggie, 78, 80
Greville, Fulke, 217

Hailsham, Lord, 175
Haldane, J.B.S., 18
Haley, Sir William, 142, 145, 188, 191
Halifax, Lord, 82, 93
Hamilton, G. Rostrevor, 84
Hamilton, Hamish and Yvonne, 14, 17, 84, 134

Hammond, W.R., 126
Hansom, Joseph Aloysius, 36, 38
Hanway, Jonas, 155, 160, 163
Harcourt, 'Lulu', 194
Hardy, Thomas, 26, 27, 82
Harington, Sir John, 160
Harlech, Lady, 134, 136
Harris, Frank, 8, 10, 92, 94, 194, 196
Harris, Lord, 185
Harsch, Joseph, 188
Hart-Davis, Adam, 29, 36, 47, 56, 71, 73,
    81, 92, 96, 101, 127, 137, 138, 142,
    164, 167, 188, 208
Hart-Davis, Bridget, 29, 49, 60, 78, 137,
    142, 167
Hart-Davis, Comfort, 29, 31, 49, 138,
    156, 164, 183, 187, 191, 203, 208
Hart-Davis, Duff, 3, 29, 36, 46, 56, 60,
    62, 71, 74, 101, 115, 119, 121, 130,
    132, 137, 142, 145, 156, 160, 161, 163,
    164, 166, 167, 182, 188, 191, 199, 202
Harte, Bret, 196
Hartley, Grizel, 58, 105
Haydn, Franz Joseph, 68, 186, 187, 198
Haydon, Benjamin, 117
Haynes, E.S.P., 101, 102
Hayward, John, 85
Headlam, Cuthbert, 13, 16, 25, 57, 59,
    61, 70, 90, 115, 116, 129, 188, 190
Headlam, G.W. (Tuppy), 18, 21, 25,
    108, 153, 202
Headlam, Maurice, 25, 57
Helen of Troy, 7
Hemingway, Ernest, 153
Henson, Bishop, 197, 202
Herbert, A.P., 14, 15, 59, 60, 63, 134
Herford, C.H., 193, 196
Hesketh, Phoebe, 106, 110
Hill, G. Birkbeck, 214
Hill, M.D. (Piggy), 53, 56, 58
Hindenburg, Marshal, 6
Hirst, George, 98
Hogben, Lancelot, 202
Holland, H. Scott, 18
Holland, Vyvyan, 178
Hollis, Christopher, 18, 21, 75
Holmes, Mr Justice, 69, 101, 102, 125
Homer, 140
Hone, Joseph, 161
Hood, Alexander, 54, 183, 196, 198
Hood, Diana, 54, 55, 57, 93, 98, 183, 196,
    198
Hope, Anthony, 115, 117, 119

Hope, Lord John, 203
Hopkins, G.M., 175
Horder, Lord, 176
Hotson, Leslie, 67, 71, 81
House, Humphry, 94, 184, 194
House, Madeline, 67
Housman, A.E., 5–6, 7, 8, 10, 15, 32,
    46, 48, 49, 69, 80, 105, 109, 137, 150,
    159, 163, 171, 206, 210
Huddleston, Father Trevor, 118
Hulton, Edward and Nika, 207
Humphrey, see Lyttelton
Hurnard, James, 84, 86
Hutchinson, R.C., 192
Hutton, Leonard, 108, 118
Huxley, Julian, 85
Huysmans, J.K., 31

Ibsen, 115
Inge, Dean, 202
Ingram, Bishop, 136
Innes, Michael, 64, 78, 80
Irving, H.B., 90
Irving, Henry, 29, 30, 77, 90, 121, 126
Irving, Laurence, 29, 40, 47, 191

Jackson, Moses, 159, 163, 164
Jackson, R.L., 53, 56
James, Henry, 16, 25, 36, 44, 56, 58, 66,
    67, 69, 95, 96, 104, 105, 106, 140, 171,
    172, 174, 176, 177, 179, 189
James, M.R., 23, 31, 72, 76, 156, 169,
    175, 189, 202
Janek, Mr and Mrs, 196, 198
Jelly, see Churchill, E.L.
Jenkins, Roy, 59
Jepson, Selwyn and Tania, 50, 111, 135,
    146, 174, 207
Jerrold, Douglas, 179
Jessop, G.L, 126
Joad, C.E.M., 129
Johns, W.E., 107
Johnson, Dr, 9, 14, 33, 35, 54, 55, 57, 59,
    63, 73, 75, 83, 102, 129, 133, 136, 140,
    144, 150, 166, 210, 211, 212, 213, 214,
    215, 216, 217
Johnson, Lionel, 86
Jonah, see Jones, L.E.
Jones, Enid, see Bagnold
Jones, L.E. (Jonah), 8, 9, 10, 16, 25, 41,
    107, 115, 124, 125, 127, 134, 167, 170,
    171, 182, 186
Jones, Lady Evelyn (Evy), 41, 134

Moore, George, 4, 6, 8, 9, 12, 25, 27, 31, 40, 41, 42, 46, 54, 64, 66, 67, 71, 74, 82, 94, 95, 96, 99, 100, 102, 103, 106, 108, 127, 149, 159, 161, 162, 164, 166, 175, 193, 194, 197, 202, 207
Moorehead, Alan, 17, 22, 59
More, Sir Thomas, 14
Morgan, Charles, 63, 64, 103, 104
Morley, Edith J., 93, 108
Mortimer, Raymond, 16, 46, 48, 65, 205
Mottistone, Lord, 22, 134
Mottram, R.H., 109
Mount, Charles Merrill, 96
Mowcher, see Devonshire
Muggeridge, Malcolm, 75, 76
Muldoon, Guy, 39, 52
Munby, A.N.L. (Tim), 29
Munnings, Sir Alfred, 158, 161
Murdoch, Iris, 113, 153
Mure, Geoffrey, 104, 105
Mynors, Roger, 113

Napoleon, 175
Nelson, 135
Newman, Cardinal, 25, 34, 36, 42, 43, 46, 48, 49, 79
Nicholson, Jenny, 111
Nicolson, Harold, 16, 18, 21, 22, 24, 41, 46, 65, 82, 122, 135, 157, 161, 169, 170, 198, 207
Nijinsky, 77
Nixon, Sir Frank, 188
North, Lord, 42, 45
Nowell-Smith, Simon, 130
Nugent, Sir Terence (Tim), 57, 61, 115, 190

O'Casey, Sean, 81
Old English, see Stoic
Olivier, Laurence, 181
Oppenheim, E. Phillips, 18, 21, 203
Oppenheimer, Sir Ernest, 118
Orwell, George, 18, 21, 23
Osborne, John, 179, 181
Osbourne, Lloyd, 23, 101, 103
Owens, Jesse, 143

Paget, Paul, 22
Partridge, Eric, 125
Paul, St, 73, 122, 213
Pavlova, Anna, 75, 77
Pearson, Hesketh, 196
Perceval, Spencer, 42, 45

Peter, see Fleming
Petrarch, 216
Phillips, Sir Lionel, 167
Pinero, A.W., 95
Piper, John, 59
Pitt, William, 216
Playfair, Nigel, 3
Plomer, William, 13
Plum, see Warner
Pollock, Sir Frederick, 69
Pollock, Sir John, 69
Pope, Alexander, 61, 66, 153, 212, 215, 216, 217
Potter, Stephen, 188
Powell, Anthony, 198
Powell, Dilys, 51
Powell, L.F., 39
Power, the Rev. Manley, 109
Priestley, J.B., 11, 12, 13, 17, 22, 24, 84, 194, 196, 198
Pritchett, V.S., 85, 87
Pryce-Jones, Alan, 16
Pye, H.J., 60–1

Queen Mother, The, 199, 204, 205
Quennell, Peter, 85
Quickswood, Lord (Linky), 28, 29, 31, 93, 136
Quiller-Couch, Arthur, 93, 189

Racine, 74
Raleigh, Prof. Walter, 150
Ramadhin, Sonny, 108, 111, 113, 117, 120
Ramsay, A.B. (Ram), 48, 73
Ramsey, Archbishop, 191
Ransome, Arthur, 74, 131, 174, 204
Rattigan, Terence, 85
Raymond, John, 144
Reade, Charles, 23
Repington, Colonel, 94
Rhodes, Wilfred, 141
Richardson, Ralph, 124
Richardson, Tom, 185
Ritchie, Lady, 115
Roberts, S.C., 75, 77, 127
Robertson, Field-Marshal, 183
Robins, Elizabeth, 115
Roger, see Fulford
Rogers, Samuel, 94
Rosebery, Lord, 132
Ross, Alan, 127
Ross, Robbie, 167
Rossetti, D.G., 66, 67

Waley, Arthur, 71
Walkley, A.B., 62
Waller, Lewis, 52
Walpole, Horace, 121, 211, 215, 217
Walpole, Hugh, 39, 42, 61, 78, 111, 113, 117, 118, 176, 202
Walter, John, 191
Ward, A.W., 122
Ward, Mrs Humphry, 176
Warner, P.F. (Plum), 97, 196
Warre, Edmund, 201
Watson, G.L., 80, 96, 105, 151, 159
Waugh, Evelyn, 139
Webb, Mrs Sidney, 176
Wedgwood, Veronica, 104
Weekes, Everton, 117, 120
Welldon, Dean, 197
Wellington, First Duke of, 135, 140, 175, 211
Wellington, Seventh Duke of, 134
Wells, H.G., 43, 73, 86, 95, 172, 174, 175, 210
Wells, Mrs H.G., 43
Whalley, George, 63, 75, 76, 134
Whistler, J.M., 88, 89
Wilde, Oscar, 4, 7, 8, 12, 16, 29, 30, 32, 35, 36, 38, 41, 46, 47, 49, 56, 64, 68, 74, 77, 81, 85, 86, 94, 100, 103, 115, 119, 127, 130, 132, 135, 138, 142, 144, 145, 148, 151, 154, 157, 162, 165, 174, 182, 191, 198

Wilkes, John, 7
Wilkinson, C.H., 130, 132
Willey, Basil, 25
Williams, Francis, 75
Williams, Harold, 130
Williams, Tennessee, 110
Williamson, Hugh Ross, 51, 107
Wilson, Colin, 37, 158, 159, 161, 163, 164
Wilson, E.R., 98
Wilson, Edmund, 122
Winchester, Marquess of, 186, 189
Wise, T.J., 27
Wodehouse, P.G., 78
Woodruff, Douglas, 178
Woolf, Virginia, 28, 29, 31, 172
Woolley, F.E., 126
Woolton, Lord, 160
Wordsworth, William, 50, 52, 136, 171, 184, 187
Worrell, Frank, 108, 117
Worsley, T.C., 179
Wright, Almroth, 159
Wright, Hagberg, 159
Wright, W. Aldis, 99
Wrong Box, The, 18, 20, 23
Wyndham, George, 153, 157

Yeats, W.B., 107, 189, 191
Yeats, Mrs W.B., 131
Yee, Miss M., 62
Young, G.M., 63, 64, 186, 193, 195